CARMEN
in

Also by FRANK DIMATTEO

The President Street Boys:
Growing Up Mafia

CARMINE
the *Snake*

CARMINE PERSICO
and His Murderous
Mafia Family

FRANK DIMATTEO   MICHAEL BENSON

CITADEL PRESS
Kensington Publishing Corp.
www.kensingtonbooks

CITADEL PRESS BOOKS are published by

Kensington Publishing Corp.
119 West 40th Street
New York, NY 10018

All Kensington titles, imprints, and distributed lines are available at special quantity discounts for bulk purchases for sales promotions, premiums, fund-raising, educational, or institutional use.

Special book excerpts or customized printings can also be created to fit specific needs. For details, write or phone the office of the Kensington sales manager: Kensington Publishing Corp., 119 West 40th Street, New York, NY 10018, attn: Sales Department; phone 1-800-221-2647.

AUTHORS' NOTE

Although this is a true story, some names and locations have been changed to protect the privacy of the innocent. When possible, the spoken word has been quoted verbatim. However, when that is not possible, conversations have been reconstructed as closely as possible to reality based on the recollections of those who spoke and heard the words. In places there has been a slight editing of spoken words, but only to improve readability. The denotations and connotations of the words remain unaltered. In some cases, witnesses are credited with verbal quotes that in reality only occurred in written form. Some characters may be composites.

CITADEL PRESS and the Citadel logo are Reg. U.S. Pat. & TM Off.

ISBN-13: 978-0-8065-3882-2
ISBN-10: 0-8065-3882-1

First hardcover printing: September 2018
First trade paperback printing: August 2019

10 9 8 7 6 5 4 3 2 1

Printed in the United States of America

Library of Congress Cataloging-in-Publication data is available.

Electronic edition:

ISBN-13: 978-0-8065-3883-9 (e-book)
ISBN-10: 0-8065-3883-X (e-book)

To my mother,
Dee DiMatteo,
who brought me into this life
—not to mention This Life.

Every extreme attitude is a flight from the self—
the passionate state of mind is an expression of
inner dissatisfaction.

—ERIC HOFFER, moral and social philosopher,
1898–1983

CONTENTS

INTRODUCTION
The Body Count

Today, I sit down to write about a man that my dad on at least two occasions tried to kill. Other than that, no pressure.

FOR FORTY-FIVE YEARS I was in this life with blinders on. Once out, I looked back and reflected upon the only way of life I ever knew. It all seemed so normal to me—chicken wire on the windows, scores and swag, gunshots on the streets, suitcases full of cash, sudden violent death—but I realized that I only had the opportunity to walk away because I was lucky, and I had a dad who was unique and smart in a lot of ways.

I had the pleasure and opportunity to look back and dissect everything that happened to me, the things I'd done, witnessed, and believed in, and I came to the startling conclusion that I had lived a lie.

The world I lived in turned out to be smoke and mirrors. Every rule I learned had been broken many times before I showed up, but I couldn't see that at the time—forest for the trees.

Now, I see.

My father was with the Gallo brothers from the time I was a baby, and I was raised to believe that the Gallo crew was my family. I called many of those guys "uncle." They molded me into an up-and-coming hood, led me to believe that we were family—that we had to stick together. They taught me that everyone outside the family was wrong, bad, the enemy. I was taught to listen to Larry Gallo because he was the boss and we didn't question him.

So, when I was told that Carmine Persico had been like a brother to Larry, but turned on him and tried to kill him and that Carmine was a snake, I believed it and didn't ask questions. Mention his name on President Street, people hissed.

Now, reflecting over my own experiences and doing my homework, I realize that he was no more a snake than Joe "The Boss" Masseria was for murdering Salvatore D'Aguila, or Salvatore Maranzano for killing Alfred "Al Mineo" Manfredi, or Albert Anastasia for the Vincent Mangano killing, or Carlo Gambino for the Albert Anastasia killing, or John Gotti for the Paul Castellano killing. In that crowd, Lucky Luciano won the humanitarian award—he only made Frank Scalice step down.

Carmine Persico had no obligation to Larry Gallo. Carmine was always for Carmine, an old-school gangster. He did what he had to do to climb the ladder. He has been in jail most of his life and his men have been loyal. He remains respected and feared the way a real tough guy should be.

I know firsthand how to be loyal around tough guys and saw firsthand how you get stabbed in the back when you're not needed anymore.

Trust me, Carmine Persico is for real. Behind the myth is a man. If there were more like him, this thing of ours, right or wrong, would be in a lot better shape. This is his story.

Some men's lives are measured by wealth and power. By that standard, Carmine John Persico Jr. is a very successful man. His blood family is estimated to be worth upward of $1 billion. Even allowing for inflation, he became one of the richest gangsters ever. His superpower was instilling fear. He made many thousands afraid, and they paid him to stay safe.

From a warm-blooded human perspective, however, Carmine

Persico's life is best measured by what he destroyed, the pain and death and suffering he left in his wake. This book will detail only a fraction of the lives cut short, either by Carmine on his own or through his orders. He destroyed his own blood family. His older brother died in prison, his younger brother spent twenty-two years behind bars, both he and his eldest son will likely die in prison. Another of his sons was recently sentenced to five years. Family members that remain free are stigmatized by their name, a name that now wears a reptilian connotation because of Carmine's reputed chilly manner of doing dark business.

He inadvertently helped to destroy his crime family, by insisting that the Persicos stay in charge across generations despite lengthy prison sentences, like kings (or the Corleone sons in *The Godfather*), rather than sticking to Mafia tradition and the meritorious method of succession, like popes.

Indeed, Carmine Persico will be remembered for the swath of destruction he left behind, a street kid who started out threatening, and sometimes beating children for their lunch money, one that carried that same "born to extort" manner into adulthood.

Using a combination of brashness, cunning, and an appetite for extreme violence, Carmine Persico rocketed from gangbanger on a Park Slope, Brooklyn, street corner to boss of the Colombo crime family, where he reputedly became the longest-reigning godfather in modern Mafia history—mostly from behind the bars of a federal penitentiary.

One of the first stories I ever heard about Carmine "The Snake" Persico was that, as a kid, he beat a guy to death with his bare hands in a gang fight. It was a story befitting a legendary hood. Unfortunately, it appears that it's also untrue. True, there was a gang fight. True, Carmine was there. True, a guy died, and Carmine was arrested. But the victim was shot. Carmine was arrested again the following year in connection with another murder, a murder that involved many bullets and spraying brain matter, but again his fists had nothing to do with it.

I don't know where the misunderstanding began, but it was formalized in Selwyn Raab's fantastic book *Five Families*. When he cites the date of Carmine's arrest, it is March 2, 1951, the day Carmine was nabbed for the shooting murder of Stephen Bove alongside the putrid Gowanus Canal.

I had to admit, I was disappointed that, as far as we can document, Carmine never beat a guy to death Boom Boom Mancini-style. For the first time, in this book, you'll get the whole true story.

Don't worry, there are plenty of other ultraviolent Carmine Persico stories that you couldn't make up—Albert Anastasia, Joe Jelly, Frankie Shots, Larry Gallo, etc. Other things could never be pinned on him. Best we can say is that he was *frequently in the vicinity of murder*, that he left choppy waves of death, pain, and suffering in his wake.

Carmine understands that there's no benefit in publicity, and he has managed remarkably well to keep his brand name off nefarious activities. We see him best when he is captured or wounded, twice by multiple gunshots, and once almost blown to smithereens by a car bomb, incidents that would have killed lesser men, murder attempts into which I have inside info.

Whenever possible, Carmine was the guy whose name wasn't in the paper, the guy that eyewitnesses forgot to mention. He was the guy nearby. And so there are times in telling his story, when we must see all around him without seeing him at all, lucky if we catch a glimpse of shadow, as Carmine Persico quietly accrued power the way other men breathe.

ACT I

CHAPTER ONE
Red Hook

The first thing you need to know about gangsters back then is they were cowboys—and the streets of South Brooklyn was the Old West. Gangs ruled. The street corner Garfield Boys of Carmine's youth were a starter program, a farm system, feeding the behemoth of Joseph Profaci's South Brooklyn "brugad"—i.e., the borgata.

SICILY IS A TOUGH ISLAND off the toe of Italy. The poor soil refuses to grow food, and the weather is so harsh it'll make a young person old. Throughout Sicily's history, it has been overrun by the conquering armies of other nations. The Greeks, Romans, Byzantines, Muslims, Normans, French, Spanish, Austrians, and Nazis all took turns being in charge. The natives, almost universally poor, acquired a feeling of helplessness. Out of this atmosphere was born *la Mafia*, a fraternal order, a secret society, which offered a structure of power and protection for the natives outside the usually corrupt government.

Today the term mafia is used generically for ethnic organized crime. We refer to "the Irish mafia," "the Russian mafia," etc., but the Mafia we're talking about in this book is the original, the *comarada*, *la Mafia*, accent on the *fi*, with a capital M—the organization that initially formed in Sicily as a band of "Robin Hoods" to defend the peasants against the tyranny of the feudal lords by stealing from the rich and giving to the poor. (This is an idealistic view of what was actually going on, of course, as mob bosses from the start tended to be ruthless bullies and very rich, so at least some of the robbing was from the poor and to the rich.)

La Mafia came to the U.S. during the wave of immigrants from Italy and Sicily between 1880 and 1914. The American version developed both imported and homegrown. Some Sicilian Mafia leaders came over and continued their racketeering operations. Most Italian immigrants settled in American big cities where only the hardest work for the smallest pay was made available to them, so the industrious among them formed organizations along the lines of the Sicilian brotherhood.

Mafia members lived by the code of *omerta*, which said those who call the police are fools or cowards. Those who need police protection are both. If you are attacked, do not give the name of your attacker. Once you recover, you will want to avenge the attack yourself. A wounded man will pledge a *vendetta* upon his enemy, and say to his assailant, "If I live, I will kill you. If I die, you are forgotten."

In the early days of the American mob, the top moneymaker was "The Black Hand." The name came from the black handprint that would be left on the door of a family member who had violated the rules and was slated for death. In exchange for money, a person's business would be "protected." If the money wasn't paid, bad things happened, often involving incendiary and explosive devices—or black handprints. The government called it ex-*tortion*.

Prostitution was a big earner for the Mafia. Mobsters didn't actually run the brothels, of course. That would be demeaning. Instead, they took a cut in exchange for protection.

The American families—called families because the men in their ranks were considered brothers—maintained the same military-like structure as the original in Sicily. You had your boss, underboss, the *caporegima* or captains (in Brooklyn, captains were sometimes called "Skipper," like the captain of a ship or the manager of a baseball club; each captain ran his own crew), and the soldiers, a.k.a. button men or good fellows (spelled *goodfellas* today because of the movie). To become a member, you had to be recommended by a member, at which time a thorough vetting occurred to make sure there was no loose talk in the candidate's past.

For years it was necessary for a prospective new member to "make his bones." That meant participating in a murder. New members had to have Italian fathers (although the ethnicity of mothers and wives was open). New members were inducted only when membership was open and the commission said it was okay. There were very few new members brought into the fold during the late 1950s and early 1960s, which is why so many crews—like the one I knew on President Street, was comprised mostly of non-made guys (and in our case non-Italians). The last step before induction was an in-person interview with the boss, at which time the candidate's willingness to kill, and to obey all orders without hesitation, was determined.

Before the days of Vegas and legal casinos, gambling parlors were a product of organized crime, back-room affairs—quieter, smokier, and more private than the huge, brightly lit, and oxygen-rich casinos that grew with legality. Before OTB, mob betting-parlors took action from an assortment of tracks. In Brooklyn the man at the end of certain bars took bets, daily double, trifecta, whatever you wanted. If you ran out of cash, money would be lent with a two-point weekly vig. Before Lotto, the mob ran numbers out of a policy bank.

Prohibition proved that alcohol was America's favorite medicine, that boozers were many and the abstemious few. The Mafia went wholly into bootlegging and thrived, a welcomed alternative government in an era when the actual government was helpless to deaden pain or relieve despair. It was during the Depression that New York City mob organized into *families*.

Mobsters, being hotheaded and ambitious, sometimes did not get along with one another. Inter- and intra-family disputes erupted. Some battles were over turf. Others, internal battles over matters of leadership. There was always trouble if tribute payments failed to reach the top.

The bloody Sicilian tradition of the *vendetta* continued. Mobsters were the heroes of the day. They were brave, facing imminent death at all times. They flipped off a corrupt system that kept the Italians in their slums. By the mid-twentieth century, the mob's skim was so ubiquitous that it raked in upward of $50 billion a year. And nowhere in America was the Mafia as in control and as influential in all elements of life as in Brooklyn, New York, particularly Red Hook, where Italian men had two choices: be a longshoreman and break your back on the piers or be a hood with a chance of rolling in dough.

In the mid-nineteenth century, the topography at Red Hook was altered as businessmen rendered it more suitable to commerce. In its natural state, the Gowanus Creek flowed through abundant marshland into the Gowanus Bay portion of New York harbor. As the farmland around the creek urbanized, Brooklyn's officials converted the creek into a canal. It took from 1849 to 1869. By that time, the land around the canal, through Red Hook and ending in the area known as Gowanus, had been filled in, fully inhabited, and industrialized. Almost immediately the water went bad as industries, in particular gas refiners dumped their waste into it, creating a gurgling stew thick with heavy metals and coal tar. In 1911, an attempt was made to improve the quality of the canal's water, which had grown so sludgy in spots that it ceased to be technically liquid. They built a one-and-a-half-mile tunnel—called the Flushing Tunnel—that used the tides to provide a flushing system into Buttermilk Channel, the narrow waterway separating Brooklyn from Governor's Island. The system was only marginally successful, and by 1930, as our story begins, the low-rent Red Hook section of Brooklyn was known first and foremost for its stink.

Red Hook was a grimy neighborhood of narrow cobblestone streets built upon a hook-shaped piece of land that protruded into New York Bay, forming a perfect place for cargo boats to pick up and drop off.

At the turn of the twentieth century, the area around the piers and the Gowanus was Irish. In the mid-1920s the Red Hook waterfront was run by a gang called the White Hand. They were ruthless bootleggers. They whacked guys—and shook down the unions, wharf owners, and barge owners alike. Peg Leg Lonergan, Aaron Heins, and Needles Ferry were rubbed out on January 9, 1926, in the Adonis Social Club speakeasy/brothel in Red Hook. The Italians and Irish fought sometimes, got along sometimes. Things never had a chance to get out of hand because they went together to Mass on Sunday at St. Stephens on Hicks Street between Carroll and Summit. The Italians gradually took over. Or maybe they just stayed behind after the Irish moved. By the time of the stock market crash in 1929, Red Hook was known to outsiders as Brooklyn's Little Italy.

By 1930, the Great Depression had already begun to blanket Brooklyn with despair. To tour the streets along the Gowanus during the 1930s would be an assault to modern sensibilities. People were living in shacks, sagging wooden-frame houses, moldy cold-water flats. Men lived in a shantytown at the current site of the Red Hook Housing Projects.

The Hook's main drag was Columbia Street—crowded, boisterous, packed with street vendors and saloons where they'd fill your bucket with tap beer. If you were lucky enough to have coins in your pocket, you could buy ice, coal, fresh fruit, and vegetables, or drop a penny in the tin cup of an organ grinder's monkey.

There were still more horses than cars, and kids with shovels ran into the street to gather up fertilizer for their home vegetable garden. As in Sicily, the actual red soil of the Hook did not yield good vegetables without a boost.

And so it was when a white-collar worker in a blue-collar neighborhood named Carmine John Persico Sr., who lived only a block from the Gowanus Canal, socked his very pregnant wife right in the eye.

Carmine Persico Sr. and the strong-willed Assunta—American name Susan, maiden name Plantamura—were kids when they got married and lived at the bottom of the hill on Eighth Street. The couple, by neighborhood standards, were doing okay. They lived in a brick structure—over a garage, okay, but it wasn't going to blow away in a nor'easter. Neighbors got used to hearing shouts mixed with the thumping and crashing of violence in the Persicos' place. He was twenty, she eighteen and ready to pop. On the night Carmine gave Susan the shiner she waited till he was asleep and went outside, flagged down a beat cop, and had him arrested.

In the Fifth Avenue Court, on the same docket as a clash over cab fare and a case involving a lost dog, Carmine heard the charges read against him and was asked for his plea by Magistrate Sabbatino.

"Guilty, your honor," Carmine replied.

"Before I sentence you," Sabbatino said. "Tell me why? Why did you hit your wife that is so clearly with child?"

Carmine believed an explanation neither necessary nor anyone's goddamn business. It was part of the code. A man disciplines his wife. Still, he chose to answer: "I believe in curfews for wives, Your Honor," Carmine said. "Ten-thirty. On the dot. She got home late so I hit her."

We don't know what punishment Carmine received, although it's likely he was sent home after promising not to do it again. (Susan was probably given a lecture as well about the benefits of being home on time.) Soon thereafter Susan gave birth to her first child, a son Alphonse—called Allie Boy—and then, three years later, Carmine Jr., followed by Theodore (1937), and sister Delores.

Nature isolated Red Hook from its surrounding neighborhoods by bordering it with Gowanus Creek and its surrounding marshland. After World War II, that isolation became manmade as the construction of the Brooklyn-Queens Expressway and then the entrance to the Brooklyn-Battery Tunnel made it difficult entering and exiting Red Hook. Considering the isolation, it's no wonder that Red Hook developed a culture all its own, populated as it was by tough men walking to and from work on the piers with their longshoreman's hooks over their shoulders.

Along Red Hook's waterfront there were no beaches, no fishing—just piers. The water was for work, not play. In the mid-nineteenth century the Erie Basin was built in Red Hook, a system of protected piers and the State Barge Canal Terminal making it one of the busiest U.S. shipping centers, with ocean-going cargo vessels and canal barges lined up for loading and unloading, serving the entire northeast, South America, and Asia. For many years, the neighborhood was a storage and transshipment center for grain. The hustle and bustle lasted until after World War II when New York City ceased to be an industrial leader, taking Red Hook down with it. Once the neighborhood started to slip, poverty and despair again flourished. An epidemic of disinvestment and abandonment overwhelmed all efforts at revitalization.

Carmine John Persico, Jr. was born in a modern facility, but into a very old-fashioned world. In a time when most babies were born at home, Carmine entered the world in the Long Island College Hospital in the Cobble Hill section of Brooklyn, not far from

Gowanus, on a hot summer night, August 8, 1933. The hospital had existed at the location, on Henry Street just south of Atlantic Avenue, since 1858, but was in 1933 still state-of-the-art.

Today, the Italians of Brooklyn, though we still enjoy our traditions, are modern twenty-first century people. But back in the days of Carmine Sr. and Susan and their babies, Italian women were expected to stick with their own. It was not uncommon for women who spoke only Italian to arrive in Brooklyn as little girls and die seventy years later still only knowing a word or two of English. They simply didn't deal with the English-speaking world.

Most men who took up the life in mid-twentieth century Brooklyn did so because of their limited options. But that wasn't true of young Carmine, known as Junior right from the start. He could've done anything. He was smart. His dad had a white-collar job, legal stenographer, a regular job with a Wall Street corporation and steady freelance work from a coven of law firms—so the Persicos were much better off than most. Not long after Carmine Jr.'s birth, the Persicos were able to afford to move out of Gowanus and into the more affluent Park Slope section of Brooklyn, about eight avenue blocks uphill and to the east, where the air was comparatively fresh.

Almost all of Carmine's plentiful opportunities in life involved staying in school, but Carmine was nocturnal, not interested in the benefits of a classroom education, and he didn't care about the legitimate world, which was clearly rigged against Italians. An education on the night streets would suffice.

And on those shadowy streets, Junior thrived. There was something obstinate about him. He wasn't big, and yet he was the immovable object. Even as a child, no one convinced him to change his mind if he had it set. And nothing frightened him. He was the danger.

The term didn't yet exist, but the Persicos were middle class.

Still, Junior hung with poor malcontents often older than he. He was so smart. He had a chance to be a powerful man in the legit world. Instead, he chose to enter the life, just as did the sons of longshoremen. Older brother Alphonse demonstrated the same organized-crime proclivities, but somehow that was different. Less was expected of Alphonse. Carmine was the special one.

My mom, Dee DiMatteo, the former Dolly "Chubby" Fiore (although she'd stopped being chubby when still a baby), re-members Carmine from those teenage days. She grew up on Baltic Street, between Henry and Hicks, but moved to First Place when she was thirteen. She had a girlfriend that dated Joey Gallo and lived in the same building as Punchy Illiano. And they were tight with Carmine.

Her first memory of Carmine Persico was hanging out on Third Avenue and Carroll Street. They were all maybe fourteen years old. He didn't seem tough as much as confident. He wasn't big, but he was cute and smart, she recalled, a big mop of hair and big eyes, and he made it clear with the expression on his face that he could outthink you when he was asleep.

She says some of the guys that would be at Carmine's side when he became boss were already there. Cousin Andrew "Mush" Russo was on that street corner. So was a young kid, still little, named Gennaro "Gerry Lang" Langella. Lang's parents were from the Campania region of Italy. He looked up to Junior as a big brother, and he grew up to be his lifelong friend.

Anthony "Scappi" Scarpati was there from the start. He was a Garfield Boy. Other Garfields included nineteen-year-old Frank Brandofino of Fifth Avenue, Vince Caruso, and Anthony and Do-minic LaBua.

Mush Russo acted like a bully sometimes but he didn't think of himself that way. He had a protective side when he was around those clearly less fortunate than he. He couldn't stand it when guys picked on the handicapped kid, called him Gimp (polio was still a thing), and was quick to feed such bullies a knuckle sandwich.

Mush was different in another way. He was an artist, always drawing, painting, creative in little ways that seemed weird, but very smart, to the other kids. Carmine recognized Mush's artistic bent as part of a keen mind. He loved and trusted no one like his cousin Mushie.

(Frank Brandofino was executed in June 1970, when a man stepped out of a car and shot him five times in the head and body as he was leaving his home in the Flatlands section of Brooklyn. Frank's brother Anthony, a reputed "intimate of Joe Colombo" was shot six times in 1959 but survived.)

My mom had a crush on Gerry Lang, who grew up before her eyes. "He was such a sweetheart," she exclaims, seventy years later.

Hugh McIntosh, she recalls, wasn't around yet. The guy they called "Apples" or "Hughie Mac" later on became part of Carmine's crew.

So Chubby Fiore and her girlfriend Chickie hung out on the corner for a while with Mush, Lang, and Carmine. They went riding around together in cars the way teenagers do. Sometimes the car belonged to someone they knew, sometimes it was borrowed from a stranger.

At that time Chubby's other girlfriend Nancy went out with Junior, but that was long before he was married. (Nancy later dated Louie "Cadillac" Mariani, one of the Gallo crew's best, and an ill-fated gunman.)

My mom remembered it like yesterday. Carmine was behind the wheel, Nancy next to him, and he said he needed to stop and get gas. Chickie was quite the booster and while Carmine was getting gas Chickie left the car and came back walking funny.

"Chickie, why you walkin' that way?" Chubby asked in her normal tone of voice, which is loud.

"Shush," Chickie said.

Turned out, Chickie had stolen a car battery and was holding it between her legs. Carmine and Mush laughed until there were tears in their eyes. (Chubby could be a booster, too. She robbed a place without anyone noticing during John Glenn's three orbits because she knew everyone was watching TV.)

She remembered Junior as being wiry, fun—and, yeah, nice sometimes. He didn't have a dirty mouth. He wasn't nasty. She didn't know he'd be a crime boss, of course, but she knew he was going to be *somebody*. He would pull guys aside and whisper to them, and they would snap to, more subtle but like a soldier coming to attention. He gave off strong vibes of dominance. He was never abrupt. Him and Mush, too. Always calm and cool. Of course, she didn't know what they were like when they were doing business.

Carmine and Mush, my mom recalled, did have a mean streak, even when they were just having fun. Mom remembered she was going to a formal affair with her father and was wearing a new dress. The boys pulled up in a car.

"Hey Chubby, come here," Carmine said. She stood on the running board and Junior hit the gas, just a little, but enough to send my high-heeled mom tumbling. She wasn't hurt but ruined her dress.

"I'm never gonna forgive you. You're paying for this dress," she said, but they laughed.

So, if I get a chance, I should relay a message to Junior. You owe Dee DiMatteo, your old pal Chubby Fiore, for a dress.

Of course, mom was a good-looking girl. In other company, Carmine wasn't playful, but rather ruthless and moody. As a youth he could be soft-spoken, and speak grammatically correct English if he put his mind to it—grading on a curve to account for Brooklynese. He could be charming or as cold as ice. Everybody who encountered him understood, immediately and silently, it was much better to be on his side than against him. He didn't hide it. His dream was to one day be a top gangster, a man of great power, wielding his mighty sword while sipping espresso in a store-front social club.

CHAPTER TWO

Street Tough

Carmine was first arrested for murder at sixteen, brawling in a gang fight straight out of West Side Story, a rumble that left one youth still and cold on the dark side of Prospect Park and another screaming in agony with a stab wound to the guts.

CARMINE JOINED A GANG when he was still in grammar school, Garfield Boys midgets division, and quickly became its precocious leader. His gang grew up into being one of the toughest in the City of Churches, in fact *the* prototype of 1950s Brooklyn street gangs, the Carmine Persico edition of the Garfield Boys, so named because they hung out on Garfield Place's street corners in Park Slope, just around the corner from Carmine's house.

The age range of the senior gangs was from about fifteen to twenty-one. If a guy was in his twenties and still hanging with the gang of his youth, he was probably dim, destined to bag groceries and guard the front door. In order to discipline the "children," police sent a man from the Juvenile Aid Bureau to sit down with school principals. Police were alerted when a mom complained that her kid was every day losing his lunch money to a bunch of little thugs. Police prognosticated that the bad boys would graduate to shaking down store-owners and committing burglaries.

Carmine didn't go back to school in the fall of 1949, despite the fact that he was quicker than the others, with a gift for gab. He took those qualities, plus his strength of commitment, to the street corner. Because of his middle-class status, he ate three squares a day, and had a more aggressive and worldly view of his surroundings. Most of the kids in the Garfields, if they had dads around at all, were the sons of the unemployed, or the sons of longshore-men, sometimes disabled by the job. Dads filled their bellies with booze every night to ease the ache. In home after home, the neighbors could tell time by the state of dad's nightly rant. It was comedy if it was someone else's dad, tragedy if it was your own. As Carmine and his Garfield Boys grew, they became widely feared. If you see 'em coming, cross to the other side of the street. Like their competitors such as the Tigers, Devils, Wanderers, Gowanus Boys, Savages, DeGraw Boys, Socialistic Gents, Far-ragut Street Boys, Presidents, Nits, Tiny Tims, Jolly Stompers, Black Angels, Breakers, Brewery Rats, Shamrocks, Beavers, etc. Each had their own territory—turf—carved out on the map.

Not every gang was at war with every other gang. Some had things in common, cousins or something like that. They became *affiliated*, so things stayed friendly. Trouble came when there was a beef. Sometimes guys fought in reform school and sought to finish the score on the streets.

The thing post-WWII adults didn't get at first was that these gang members weren't just acting tough, they were actually af-flicted with a cultural malaise—jaded to the bone, cold-blooded, suffering from an existential despair and anger beyond their years. In other words, they were seriously fucked up.

Some said maybe it was World War II's fault. The war had such a profound effect on America that young people *saw* the world in terms of war, building small armies, with the front lines and battles taking place right there in the streets where they lived. Others said nonsense. Gangs went back to the days of the fucking caveman.

Gangs like the Garfields got into fights, and ran small-time money-making schemes. As they reached mid-teens they no longer lowered themselves to scamming kids' lunch money, but extortion remained the idea.

Not all of the gangs were criminal. Some just liked to fight. Some formed singing groups—the birth of doo-wop. But every neighborhood had them. That was the way it was in the late 1940s, every corner from the Hook to Downtown Brooklyn and over to Prospect Park had a gang of kids on the corner combing their Vitalis hair as they plotted schemes to press their advantage.

There was a (very brief) time in 1950 when zoot suits were the rage. A truck of them was found empty, and the Garfields all had one. On nights when they were pretty sure they weren't fighting, they wore them, heavily padded and draped coats, tapered pants with tiny cuffs, "pistol pocket pants" they were called, extra-large front pockets for the .22 if they had one. For a stretch there, they were almost comically sharp, shades, coiffed, and violent. They smoked Luckies and drank Rheingold.

Some combed their hair in an elaborate way, with elaborate curls spilling onto their foreheads and a duck's ass in the back. Carmine was different. He had a lot of hair, big mop on top, but it was dry and unruly. He could comb it all day and night and it would still do whatever it wanted. During the brief zoot suit fad, Carmine seemed lost in his, he was so small.

It's not the part people want to remember, but there was already a lot of heroin. In 1950 you could only get horse in two places in New York—Harlem and Red Hook. A lot of guys got ruined. A lot of guys like Carmine hated drugs as much as polio because they'd seen street brothers turn gray and die under the influence of the *babonya*.

They didn't know certain mob bosses were behind the drug trade, two-faced guys preaching an anti-drug policy one minute and importing ships loaded up with heroin the next. Kids were the victims, loaded up and criminal when they should've been playing football in Carroll Park.

There were two types of leaders on the street. There was Carmine's type, the brainy little bastards, who led because they could think things through, and the other type, the kid who was the toughest fighter. Some gangs had two leaders, the brainy one for strategy and the tough one for tactics.

During the fistfight era, rumbles were scheduled like baseball games, in series. There were even home-and-home double-headers where two gangs would fight at one's home base on Tuesday night and then at the other's on Wednesday. Guys were bruised and battered, but serious injuries were rare and combatants could fight every night.

The fights escalated over the years, going from fistfights, to sticks and bats, knives and guns. And the weapons were in the hands of younger and younger gangsters.

The weapons era, the dawn of which coincided with Carmine dropping out of school, spring 1949, lessened the frequency of rumbles because the potential consequences were increased so dramatically.

When a rumble was called now, the first thing Carmine's Garfields did was pick up the heavier weapons: baseball bats, chains, lead pipes, packaged in a beat-up old golf bag and hidden atop a movie-theater marquee. Two would climb up and then hand the stuff down to two guys on the sidewalk.

Not all gang members dropped out on their sixteenth birthday. Some remained in school, not for reading, writing, and 'rithmatic, but rather for access to the metal and automotive shops, where weapons could be made behind the teacher's back, including zip guns modified from cap guns with enough power to imbed a projectile two-inches deep in a plaster wall. Another ingenious form of zip gun was a .22 made of wood and part of a screen door, held together with adhesive tape and powerful enough to kill. One kid converted a gun used at a Coney Island arcade into a deadly weapon and used it to shoot up the house of a math teacher he hated.

Little wonder that the ranks of mob hitmen in the 1950s were bursting with former juvenile delinquents. Early on, they were desensitized to violence and indoctrinated into functioning within a criminal organization.

While the gangs waged their mini-wars, mob crews used gang members for cheap labor. It was common for a gang member to also have a side job working for the policy bank, off-track betting, or the sports book, mostly football parlays.

Unlike a lot of young punks, Carmine wasn't afraid of adults. He spoke well and appeared relaxed as he shook them down: "Hey Mister, you don't want to park there. Probably something could happen to your beautiful automobile if you park there. The kids these days. Of course, my friends and I could keep an eye on it for you until you get back—for a price."

Sometimes the Garfields raided a rival's turf and kicked ass. One autumn night, Carmine and his gang hopped turnstiles and rode the BMT to the end of the line. The rumbled with the Hamiltons at the corner of 92nd Street and Third Avenue. The fight was broken up by Patrolman Joseph Ragusa of the Fort Hamilton Precinct. The combatants dispersed on slapping sneakers. Three Garfields were arrested. Cops confiscated a few sawed-off billiard cues, weighted with lead.

Summers were when the kids in Brooklyn got in the most trouble. No air-conditioning back then except in the movies. You had to use God's A.C., and that meant the cool ocean breezes of Coney Island. If you were a tough kid, you paraded the boardwalk in a sleeveless T-shirt and got into a fight, which is what Alphonse and Carmine Persico did on the evening of July 24, 1949.

Visually, Alphonse was clearly the big brother, the older one—the protector. He stood six-foot and weighed two-hundred pounds. He had a tattoo, a scar on his left cheek, and a scowl of world-weariness. He looked dangerous. It was all in sharp contrast to the precociously jaded but fresh smirk on little Carmine's face.

Versus them was a guy from around the corner on Third Avenue, an older guy in his twenties, named Steve Bove. When cops tried to squelch the melee, the young men threw punches in the wrong directions and everyone got popped for assaulting police officers.

The Persico brothers and Jove bargained down to simple assault and received suspended sentences.

You'd think an event like that would bind guys together for life, but the beef between Bove and the Persico brothers festered.

The Garfield Boys' fights became legendary on Friday night, May 12, 1950. The rumble in the park was a tragic scene that contained several aspects later found in the climactic scenes of the movie *West Side Story*. It was a real-life incident that, because of the location and political climate had a disproportionate effect on 1950s life in America. One fight in one park on one night influenced public opinion nationally. It got to the point where the average American thought juvenile delinquents were a bigger threat to a foundering America than Communism. Back then, that was saying something.

The Tigers hung out at the corner of Seventh Avenue and 14th Street in the South Slope. They had a rep as a gang that drank a lot, but laid off dope. One of them admitted to having marijuana cigarettes smuggled in to him at reform school in a peanut butter jar, but that was it for drugs. Tigers drank booze. Come fight time, that meant they'd all be into it.

At 8:30 P.M. more than forty gang members met in Prospect Park near the Swan Lake Boathouse.

Under clear skies and a waning crescent moon, it was an elegant scene for a gathering tempest of street toughs. They would wage war not under a rusty basketball rim, on broken glass and cracked pavement, but rather at a breathtaking natural and man-made setting, a Beaux Arts structure built in 1905 overlooking the Lullwater Bridge, a colorful flotilla of tied-together rowboats, and a lake that had actual swans; not in an ambiance of crumbled

brick and peeling fire escapes, but rather in what was in the sun-
shine certainly one of the most beautiful settings in all of Brooklyn. At night though it was very dark, and the majesty of the
boathouse blackened into a shadowy monolithic menace.

According to the Garfields, trouble started when one of their
guys, Dominick LaBua, traveled into Tigers' territory to visit a
girl, an invasion of turf to which the Tigers took exception. Most
agreed the fight was over a girl. That was often the case. Sometimes it was because one guy hit on (or insulted) another guy's
girl, and that was legit. Sometimes it was bogus: just *deb* shit.
Debs were the loud-mouthed girls who hung out and were into
drama and instigating. The papers sometimes called them molls,
which made them sound as if they looked like Bonnie Parker,
which they did not. The debs had their own gangs—the Shangri-
Las (thus, the biker-chick singing group of the 1960s), the Chan-
deliers, the Robinettes. When it was convenient, guys used the
debs to hide their weapons. Cops were very slow to search debs
as they would scream they were being touched in the wrong way
and get the flatfoot in trouble. You needed a police matron to do
a search, and there usually wasn't one handy. The debs were also
useful as alibi-givers. A guy in trouble could *always* get a deb to
vouch for him, that he was with her at a dance or a movie.

The rumble had main-event style preparation, a formal sit-
down, Carmine doing the talking for the Garfields. Ground rules
were agreed upon—rules designed to prevent all-out war. One
fighter and two seconds from each side would meet at the spot.
No one else allowed close.

Carmine ended the meeting with a stern warning: "No double-
crosses."

One of the advantages of the boathouse turned out to be that it
was like a stage, and the action could be watched from a variety
of vantage points, from the grassy slope just north of the building, to the picturesque arched bridge that crossed the pond.

Why fight all the way over on the east side of the park? The

site, best guess, was the idea of one of the neighborhood hoodlums. Teen gang fights bring cops into the neighborhood—not a
good thing for a grown-up guy playing an angle on that same
block. Don't draw heat. The Ocean Avenue side of the park, not
far from Ebbets Field, couldn't have seemed farther from Red
Hook.

The rules prohibited the two fighters and their seconds to bear
arms, but there was no controlling the Garfields and Tigers who
were supposed to watch from afar. Some of them were armed to
the teeth "just in case." Guys were itchy to "ruin somebody."

At the boathouse, the fair fight broke down right away when
the seconds went at it. Then, boom, all hands on deck. Kids came
running from all directions, down the hills, around the pond. It
became a pitched battle, weapons came out. Bats. Tire chains. A
brandished knife, a scream of pain, and then two .22 pistol shots.

In the movie version, a rumble may protract with choreogra-
phy and eloquent verbiage. In reality, gang fights were short and
sweet, and almost always a draw. Often the ending note was a
paranoid shout—"cheese it!"—(or a distant siren) that caused
everyone to disperse.

On the night of Garfields vs. Tigers at the boathouse, it was the
gunshots that caused everyone to run. Not the flat crack of a zip
gun, either—sharp reports, real gun.

The Garfields—including Carmine, Mush, Gerry Lang, and
Anthony "Scappi" Scarpati—ran westward through the park, taking surreptitious paths over Breeze Hill, the Terrace Bridge, and
Lookout Hill, where George Washington fought during the Rev-
olution, toward Prospect Park West and the streets of the Slope.
They slowed to a fast walk all the way down to the canal, to the
Carroll Street bridge where one of them tossed a gun into the
"water" of the Gowanus. They half expected it to bounce, but
there was a thick splash and the gun was gone.

*   *   *

Back at the park, the gunshots caught the attention of Patrolman Frank Mantegari of the Park Slope Station, who came running toward the boathouse and found two boys down. Left behind were two Park Slope kids, eighteen-year-old James "Jamesie" Fortunato, a Tiger who was shot twice in the belly, and was lying up the grassy incline north of the boathouse, and Alfred Vento, who was knifed in the abdomen, down and bleeding directly in front of the boathouse, center stage.

By the time Officer Mantegari got to Fortunato, he was almost gone. The kid was rushed by ambulance to Jewish Hospital where he died a short time later. An ambulance also came for Vento and rushed him to Methodist Hospital where he made a complete recovery.

The day after the rumble, the *Brooklyn Eagle* ran a banner headline, "BOY SLAIN IN PARK GANG WAR," in a size type usually reserved for things like V-J Day or FDR's death. That got the publicity ball rolling.

In the papers, Jamesie came off as a great kid, the youngest of eight children, the baby, clean cut and hard-working, only weeks from graduating from vocational school and beginning his first job. Fortunato's older brother Nick, thirty-three years old and the father of three at the time of his brother's death, told the *Brooklyn Eagle,* "I tried to form a club with the co-operation of storekeepers in the neighborhood. I thought a couple of able-bodied men could get together and do something for these boys. Jamesie and his pals were chased all the time by the Garfield Boys who outnumbered them twenty to one. At least I tried, but it takes cooperation. Most of all, it takes money."

Jamesie, he added, joined the Tigers to play football. They were going to rumble only on the gridiron. But the organized sports thing fell through, and the gang regressed to its old ways.

Emotion overcame ballistics as Nick added, "He was going to

work as a packer at Bush Terminal. Instead of that he got a bullet
in the back. I kissed him as he lay on his slab in the morgue and
held him in my arms. I don't think he had a chance."

The cop said that Carmine and his Garfields were the terror of
Brooklyn, that they would surround isolated boys and beat them,
even in schoolyards and classrooms. The average Tiger was only
sixteen or so years old, and they lived in fear of the Garfields,
some of whom had already done prison time. Tigers couldn't
even walk to and from school.

Alfred Vento was in the prison ward at Kings County Hospital
with his gut bandaged up. His mom, a widow, had seven kids to
support. She'd just gotten home from a double shift when one of
Al's friends knocked on her door and told her about the Prospect
Park bloodbath. She said the rumble had been misreported in the
papers and was eager to tell the *Eagle* the real story: "This boy
LaBua had challenged my Al to a fist fight. Al refused and LaBua
called him chicken. So they agreed to a fair fight and then they
were to shake hands and be friends. That's all there was to it."
Jamesie, she said, had been Alfred's friend since they were little
and went along to second. She said the Tigers was a football
team, not a gang, and that Jamesie and her Al had won two cham-
pionships, back to back, in games played at Park Circle.

Following the Prospect Park rumble, the police youth squad
rounded up all of the gang members they could find, more than
fifty of them, including Carmine Persico. Police hauled their bel-
ligerent asses down to the Fifth Avenue station.

At the police station, cops told Carmine that, because he was
the leader of the Garfields, he was being arrested as a material
witness to murder, a legal process that allowed police to hold
someone who has info about a crime. If he didn't give it up, he
was going down, taking the rap for everyone. Carmine smirked
and said nothing. Carmine did not talk, but others did, and a story
emerged.

At dawn of May 13, police arrested sixteen-year-old Anthony "Scappi" Scarpati, a Garfield and one of fifteen kids in his family that lived on Third Street. He'd confessed to the shooting. Said he fired two shots, one in the air and one wild. Just to break it up after he saw the knife. The gun was a .22 caliber revolver. Gone. Long gone, he said. He threw it into the Gowanus off the Carroll Street Bridge. (Police went as far as to drag the Gowanus in search of the weapon. No luck. Perhaps the gun dissolved.) He told the police Vento and LaBua—a baby-faced kid with a protruding upper lip, they called him LaBoo—were scheduled to have a fistfight over a girl. But LaBoo pulled a knife and chaos erupted. The rumble was the culmination of a long-standing feud between the two gangs, which until then had been limited to skirmishes.

Carmine's murder charges were dropped, but he and six others were charged with lesser crimes such as disorderly conduct and unlawful assembly.

The story was big and went a long way toward creating the "juvenile delinquent" gestalt that overwhelmed America in the 1950s, evident in the media of the time in everything from bad B-style drive-in movies to classics like *Rebel Without a Cause*, *Blackboard Jungle*, and the previously mentioned *West Side Story*.

The piece of show biz that struck closest to home was a 1956 picture that was set in Red Hook and called *Rumble on the Docks*. It was cheaply made and cornier than hell—actor James Darren's first picture, also starring Robert Blake, Diggers versus Stompers, Freddie Bell and His Bell Boys rocking the gymnasium dance with "Giddy Up A Ding Dong"—but it dignified the idea that teenaged gang members might be *stars,* that the gangs were a path to being somebody. *Rumble on the Docks* was based on the 1953 paperback bestseller of the same name by Brooklyn's Frank Palescandolo (writing as Frank Paley).

* * *

Scarpati's murder trial began in November 1950. Carmine Persico had never been to a Broadway show, so this was as close to theater as he was going to get. And, in a weird way, it was love at first sight. Perhaps the part of Carmine that should have gone to law school was bubbling to the surface, but he was a human sponge, learning, absorbing, whenever in a courtroom. He observed the players, the formality of the ceremony, the oratory—some of it powerful, even magnificent. Some of the language might take some time getting used to—sidebar, objection, voir dire—but he was pretty sure he could be a great lawyer if he put his mind to it. And Scappi's trial, Carmine's first show, had moments of amazing drama worthy of the Great White Way.

The hard-nosed and merciless Judge Samuel S. Leibowitz was presiding. As a young man Judge Leibowitz defended Al Capone and Capone walked. He'd defended 140 murderers and only one was executed. After a while though he declined requests to defend hoods. Lucky Luciano, and several of the Murder Inc. guys wanted Leibowitz defending them but the future judge declined. Now, in his eleventh year as a Kings County court judge, he had no patience for killers. He said they were all scum—the organized guys, the lone wolves, all of them. Asked how he could defend gangsters and then sit in harsh judgment over them, Judge Leibowitz would say that he might've *defended* them but he never *consorted* with them. Capone did not slap his back and call him Sam. It wasn't like that. He was a lawyer, doing his job. This junior version of gangland he was looking at in the Prospect Park murder needed to be treated harshly as well. It was clearly the farm system, to use a baseball term, for organized crime.

Everyone, including Carmine Persico, looked up at the judge. The judge was in charge, like a god, literally above everyone else up on his bench. This was *his* court, he *was* the court, and everything that occurred there was done only with his permission.

A panel was drawn from 150 blue-ribbon jurors. It was unusually tense in the courtroom. Members of both the Garfields and
Tigers were in the gallery, having been subjected to a patting
down in the hallway before being allowed inside, and the guards,
usually charged only with preventing escape attempts by the defendant, had additional worries with the warring factions in the
room.

But there was no trouble. The boys sat politely, in awe. Tigers
behind the prosecution, Garfields behind the defense. Carmine
sat in the front row, so he could watch the mouthpieces work, and
lend Scappi maximum support.

The highlight of the trial came at the end, when while giving
Scarpati a verbal dressing down, the judge said, "There isn't a
kid in this court today who would get up and say anything nice
about you. You're a big wheel. Nobody will say anything on your
behalf."

At that moment, the stony silence that the judge had been hoping for was broken by a voice from the Garfield side in the back:
"I'm a friend of his and I have something to say for him."

You could have heard a pin drop into a cotton ball. Mouths
agape, the gallery gasped in unison as it turned to look at the
painfully thin young man who had risen from his seat in the back.

The voice continued: "You think he's bad? Well, all the people—teachers, police—who helped make him bad are bad, too."

The speaker was a Garfield, an underfed twenty-year-old
meatpacker named Joseph Senatore, who ignored the judge's disciplinary gavel.

"Look, judge, you're not going to reform him by sending him
to jail for a long time. You're just going to make him bitter. Just
as bitter as I am. I was in jail. I know what they did to me there.
You can't stop this trouble. It's the neighborhood, the environ-
ment. We've got no place to go, nothing to do. If the cops had

more understanding, maybe this wouldn't have happened. They come out of their cars swinging their sticks, instead of asking us to move. What can we do? We can't stay home seven days a week. Look, we go into a poolroom or someplace and the cops break in on us. Judge, we've got no place to go."

Finally Judge Leibowitz decided to engage the man who was already in contempt of court: "Young man, you mentioned the police, what have you to say about them?"

Senatore accused the cops for all to hear of taking a cut of corner crap games and beating kids when they didn't like the way they were dressed. He admitted that he'd been in trouble, did three years for burglary, and since then his luck was all bad.

"Nobody trusts an ex-jailbird," he said, and sat down a little embarrassed, but jazzed by the moment. He'd been a true Garfield, a true brother to the accused. That was all that really mattered.

And his message, perhaps surprisingly, came through loud and clear. His conclusion was that crooked cops and lack of understanding by law enforcement was responsible for the dilemma of youth in his neighborhood.

Interestingly, Judge Leibowitz would in the next couple of years supervise a grand jury that returned indictments against eighteen NYPD officers that took bribes from pro gamblers.

A photographer captured Scappi moments after Senatore's speech, overcome with emotion, holding a handkerchief over his eyes as he held hands with his sobbing, bespectacled mother.

Of course, for Senatore, there was hell to pay. He was subjected by police to an ordeal, hounded by men in blue overheard saying they were looking for an opportunity to "kill that bastard." The cops sent mixed messages when they offered him an opportunity to look at a line-up of cops so he could pick out the ones who were cutting into the dice games. Senatore took a pass.

The trial was never completed as the sides dealt and seventeen-year-old Scarpati pleaded guilty to manslaughter. Soon thereafter, Senatore became the successful pet project of the Rev. Edward O'Connor from Aquinas who, trusting a jailbird, offered Senatore a position as an offertory collector at mass and usher at a church dance.

On December 8, 1950, Scarpati was sentenced to fifteen to thirty years in prison. Hearing the judge, his mother collapsed into her daughter's arms in a dead faint. Police had to restrain the crowd. There was a "near-riot." (By the time Scappi got out, Carmine was in a position to give him a key place in his crew shylocking and running numbers.)

With Scappi's time in court wrapping up, police received an anonymous tip. The Tigers were out to avenge Fortunato, and had even picked which Garfield they were going to hit. (We have to guess.) Police and the Brooklyn Youth Board tried to get between the gangs and get them to make nice. The Brooklyn Youth Board was financed by the State and was hired to teach kids how to have fun in wholesome ways, like boxing, basketball, and dancing with girls. One official said that he was hesitant to organize a dance for these guys. The Tigers in particular were a problem. They showed up to dances drunk and once, when they had no one to fight, they "tore the dance hall apart." He added, "They are going to have to learn to act like gentlemen."

The Youth Board had a lot of takers, but not always the gang members. They saw such efforts as strictly squaresville, man.

Each gang sent representatives to a two-and-a-half-hour meeting at the precinct headquarters with the police and a couple of priests, members of the decent element who were there to dish the guilt onto the Catholic boys. It worked to a point. Carmine and Mush were on their best behavior in front of the "fadduh." During the meeting, outside the spell of the Lord, close to a hundred gang members filled the room like a French watercolor. It was the peak of the relatively short zoot suit fad, and they were a sea of purple trousers and sharply cut green jackets, and they roamed the halls putting their cigarettes out on the floor. Knowledge of the police station's layout might come in handy some day, in case you needed to bust a guy out, so they wandered. If a cop called to them, they said they were just looking for the john.

The meeting broke up, and the parties had come up with an agreement to disarm. Further disputes, if absolutely necessary, were to be settled with the fists. Like men. Gang members were to turn in their weapons, switchblades, zip guns, no-questions-asked. Weekly meetings between gang reps and cops were scheduled.

The numbers of weapons turned in voluntarily was a disappointment—a slingshot that looked like it might've come out of Dennis the Menace's back pocket, a sawed-off pool cue handle, and a bent carpenter's level—and by the following spring the whole peace talks thing was a distant memory.

By that time, Carmine Persico would have outgrown his rumbling days. He'd be nursing bullet wounds and plotting to whack guys.

CHAPTER THREE

The Murder of Stephen Bove

On February 23, 1951, gunshots echoed along the bricked
streets of Gowanus. A body, its head ruined by an up-close and
personal pumping of lead, was rolled like a sack of garbage into
a frozen gutter near the Carroll Street Bridge.

ON JANUARY 9, 1951, Carmine Persico, now seventeen years old, was returning on foot from the movies to his home on Carroll Street, walking with his twenty-year-old brother Alphonse. They walked on icy sidewalks, and later said they had just seen a double feature on Court Street—*Where Danger Lives* with Robert Mitchum, and *Mr. Lucky* with Cary Grant.

The brothers had almost made it home when three young men sprang from a nearby parked car.

One said, "There they are."

Another pulled a gun and fired twice, striking Carmine once in each leg.

The hit team scrambled back into the car and laid rubber out of there—but they didn't get far. The driver careened wildly down the street, and crashed into a parked car less than a block away. With the getaway car disabled, the shooter and his pals ran for it and disappeared into the night. The entire incident had been well-contained in a small area. The attackers stole the car from a woman who lived just a few blocks up, also on Carroll Street.

An ambulance was called, and Carmine went to the hospital. Alphonse was questioned by police. He explained that he was just trying to be a good older brother. He knew that Carmine—

just a kid really, look at him—was in that bad, bad gang. Garfield Boys. And he needed to stay on the straight and narrow if he was ever going to make something of himself. There'd already been trouble that led to tragedy. Alphonse said he was trying to talk Carmine into quitting the street life and spending more time on his studies. That was why they went to the movies. It was all part of Carmine's "rehabilitation program." He said it with a straight face, too. Cops had to admire him for that.

No worries. Carmine saw who shot him. It was Steve Bove, the guy from the 1949 Coney Island arrest, already in his mid-twenties but still hanging out. He lived over on Third Avenue, worked for the Maritime Commission as a dock sweeper, currently assigned to a Staten Island pier. He also had a record of three arrests and had twice been sent up by the state, once to Sing Sing, once Elmira.

Cops went to the hospital to talk to the victim. They recognized the kid with the mug on him from the Prospect Park thing. You couldn't forget the face or the attitude. And Carmine never said a word to the police. He merely gazed upon his interrogators with an expression of mild distaste.

Carmine's silence didn't completely stifle the investigation, however. The beef between the Persico brothers and Stephen Bove was well known. As doctors were still yanking lead from Carmine's lower extremities, cops brought Bove in, questioned him, and let him go. Not enough evidence, blah blah, blah—but it made no difference. Steve Bove didn't have long to live.

Carmine had been in the papers before, of course, but with a bullet in each leg, Carmine made the *headlines* for the first time, his shooting sharing the banner of the *Eagle* with news of the Korean War battle at Wonju Gates, a plan to draft eighteen-year-old boys into the military, and the death of novelist Sinclair Lewis.

On February 22, 1951, as Brooklyn buzzed over the L.I.U. basketball point-shaving scandal, only a few feet from the scene of the previous year's rumble, winter maintenance guys in Prospect Park were in front of the boathouse draining Swan Lake to repair a faulty valve. As the noisy machinery cranked away, sucking the water from the lake, it became apparent that there was something in there that didn't belong. The thing turned out to be the body of seventeen-year-old Thomas Mongiove, who had lived at Fifth Avenue and 30th Street next to Green-Wood Cemetery—all the way on the other side of Prospect Park and then some—and had been missing for about one month. The body had managed to avoid discovery because it had been trapped beneath the ice. The kid delivered telegrams for Western Union, had disappeared on Sunday morning on his way to mass at St. Xavier, and had no known gang affiliation—but still, police didn't like the proximity.

The story of the body in the lake made the papers in the New York area, of course, but it also went national because—coincidentally, we are told—the boy's kid sister was "picnicking at the lake" with relatives (in the mud and blustery February wind) when the body was discovered. She reportedly screamed, "That's my brother!" It was the boathouse's second death in less than a year. Post-mortem said death was by drowning, no evidence of foul play, the kid probably fell through the ice. Cops closed the case.

The family screamed. Tommy was an excellent swimmer. "How can we be sure Tom wasn't slugged?" his older brother Frank said. Frank looked it up, the lake hadn't even been frozen when Tom disappeared. He'd seen the body. The face was all bruised. Significantly, he said, Tommy always carried money and none was found on his body.

The night after Mongiove's body was discovered, February 23, 1951, Carmine and Alphonse Persico were riding in a car with Steve Bove, who was very inebriated following copious drinks in a Red Hook saloon. Driving the car was a well-known thoroughbred-racehorse jockey named Albert "The Blue Beetle" Grillo.

We don't know how the evening got started, or at what stage in the drinking the Persico brothers showed up. It's hard to imagine Bove agreeing to sit down with Alphonse and Carmine for a cocktail or twelve. He must've known they were not his friends. Perhaps Bove had been drinking with Grillo and the Persicos' arrived at the last moment, just in time for the car ride. Maybe Bove had been drinking with others and his state of extreme inebriation struck the Persicos as an excellent opportunity to get the job done without much fuss.

The jockey at the wheel, Grillo, worked at all of the top tracks, including Belmont Park and Aqueduct Racecourse in New York City, and Monmouth Park in New Jersey. Who sat where in the car is a matter of speculation, as there have been intimations that the *official* version of the night's events were altered. According to the official story, Carmine sat shotgun and kept a close eye on the diminutive driver. Allie Boy was in the backseat with Bove. There was one other passenger, presumably also in the back, who has never been publicly identified. The car worked its way through the sooty dark streets near the Gowanus Canal. They drove slowly through the industrial lowlands, deserted at that hour, the only sound was the car's tires singing over the bricked street. At one point, Alphonse calmly pulled a snub-nosed police special from his pocket, pointed it at Bove's head and shot him five times.

Grillo jumped so high his head almost hit the roof. Allie Boy ordered the terrified jockey to pull to the curb and stop the car. Carmine gave the Beetle a look that said everything: Do as you're told or you're next.

The jockey did as he was told, and Alphonse rolled Bove's body into the gutter only yards from the Carroll Street Bridge, crossing the fetid canal. Bove's gruesome remains were found later that morning by an unfortunate pedestrian.

Cops tried to reconstruct the victim's last hours. As far as they could tell, Bove had last been seen in a neighborhood "ginmill" engaging in a "drinking bout" with some friends. It was unclear who the friends were, but the guy Bove left with was on the puny side.

The body was autopsied by Dr. George W. Ruger, Assistant Kings County Medical Examiner, in the county morgue. The bullets that killed Bove came from a .38. Four shots had entered the back of Bove's head and a fifth bullet struck Bove a glancing blow in the back. All five slugs were recovered, four still inside the body, and a fifth in the gutter under his body where it was found. Toxicology tests confirmed that the deceased had been drinking heavily at the time of his death.

Of special interest to investigators was the twenty-eight-year-old jockey, Anthony "Blue Beetle" Grillo, who was suspected of being the small fellow seen exiting the bar with Bove.

Investigators struck paydirt when they took a quick look at Grillo's car—which was a mess. A search warrant was quickly obtained, and the evidence, much of it once part of Bove's head, was confiscated, bagged and sealed. They had Grillo red-handed.

Cops made like they would pin the murder on Grillo if he didn't spill, and eventually the jockey gave up the Persicos. Police went in search of Alphonse and Carmine, only to discover that all of their friends and loved ones shrugged their shoulders and said they had no idea where they were. Everyone was deaf and dumb.

But the Law had its ways. People close to the brothers were tailed. Places they frequented were staked out. During the early hours of March 2, 1951, Carmine was found, arrested, and charged with Bove's murder—his second arrest in connection with a murder.

Carmine clamped his lips together and asked for a lawyer.

The lawyer subsequently explained to prosecutors that there was an outside chance that Carmine might have *seen* a murder, but no one—not even the investigation's key witness—said that Carmine hurt anybody that night.

The murder charge against Carmine was dismissed by Magistrate James A. Blanchfield in Felony Court on March 9, but Carmine continued to be held as a material witness in County Court, bail set at $50,000—a big number for a seventeen-year-old. As of March 10, Alphonse was still missing.

The police went to the public. It was announced in the papers that they were on the lookout for Alphonse Persico, suspected of being the gunman in the death of Steve Bove. Alphonse, they explained, had "disappeared."

Carmine kept mum. Cops poured over Alphonse's car, which they found in a Carroll Street parking lot. Alphonse, investigators said, was the killer. Carmine, as far as they knew, was just "tagging along."

Details of Alphonse Persico's arrest are lost in the mists of time. When we next see Allie Boy he has been captured, charged with Bove's murder, and thrown into a septic tank called the Raymond Street Jail. Carmine, in turn, was released.

As was true during the Prospect Park murder trial, Carmine haunted the Kings County courtroom during his brother's trial—and again paid rapt attention to the figures that made the theater of so-called justice so compelling.

His attention was even more focused than it had been at the Prospect Park trial. His active mind dug past the showmanship to the inner workings behind the scenes. It seemed to Carmine like the fate of the defendant hinged largely on the tenacity of his defense attorney. Allie Boy's guy was good, fought hard, but came off as tepid. Defenders should fight for their clients' lives as if they were their own, but that wasn't how it was. Carmine had seen the prosecutor and defense attorney standing in the hall, on the stairs, smoking together, complaining about the goddamned heat, talking about what they were going to have for lunch. It was just a job to them. Carmine felt that, should he ever get the opportunity, he could outduel any lawyer—not with smarts but with heart.

The Prospect Park trial had been intensely dramatic. Carmine would never forget the way the room felt when Senatore began to drill into the causes of juvenile delinquency. But there was something small about that trial when compared to Allie Boy's. Now, up on that lofty bench was the Honorable Nathan R. Sobel, a forty-five-year-old legal scholar. Judge Sobel was born on the Lower East Side of Manhattan, but grew up in the Borough Park and Brownsville sections of Brooklyn, went to Boys High School, boxed for a while in the 1920s, and put himself through Brooklyn Law School by working as a telephone operator at a Wall Street firm for four bucks an hour. Before WWII, he counseled New York's Governor Herbert H. Lehman regarding a new workman's compensation bill, and at the time of Alphonse's trial, had been a Kings County Court Judge for seven and a half years. But all of that understates his public persona. He was *society*, the equivalent of a rock star, and had many show-biz friends like actor Edward G. Robinson and the song-writing team of Rodgers & Hart. In his robe he radiated pure Brooklyn.

Sitting beside Alphonse was fifty-seven-year-old Leo H. Healy, who in 1911 had held the title of World Champion Intercollegiate Orator, defeating the German Carl Guggenheim in the finals. It's hard to gauge the size of the talent pool for a competition like that, but it's safe to say that Healy could speak with great articulation. He was the valedictorian of his class at Fordham Law in the Bronx. Healy, back when he was a young man in the early 1920s, earned fame for combatting the Black-Star Line, African-American leader Marcus Garvey's attempt to set up a pan-African economy. Healy started out as a kid from Boston but married a Brooklyn girl and had lived there for decades. It was a bit of a fall for him that he now defended gangsters for a living, but his career had not been without hiccups. In 1930, when he was a judge, he was charged with a "job buying" scheme. He was cleared of the charges, but resigned for "health reasons." Despite the scandal that seemed to have derailed him as a judge, the fact that Sobel was presiding—and that Healy was defending—indicated to the press that this murder-one case was special.

The people were represented by Assistant District Attorney John E. Cone, chief of the homicide division and in charge of the county court division of the Brooklyn D.A.'s office. He was born in Brooklyn and received his law degree at St. John's.

As with Anthony Scarpati's trial, a blue-ribbon jury was to be selected, a jury consisting of "highly-qualified persons." It was code for "no women." Bored reporters doodled in their note pads during several days of voir dire. There was no air-conditioning in the county courtroom, and the air was close with the sour scent of men in soggy suits. Out of an initial panel of seventy-five veniremen summoned on Monday, July 16, many felt Red Hook hoods deserved what they got. Others had misgivings about standing in judgment of someone who might have connections. Only a few felt they could be impartial. As fans blew the steamy air around, eight men were empaneled in the first week. A fresh batch of seventy-five were brought in on July 23, and jury selection was completed.

The hellish heat was tough on everyone in the courtroom except Alphonse, who found it far more comfortable than his nighttime accommodations. Since his arrest and during the trial, Alphonse made his home in a poorly-lit dungeon that reeked of an unholy combo of urine, shit, puke, B.O., and mildew. There had been a jail, always a hellhole, on that spot on Raymond Street since 1836, although the current building was constructed in 1909. It was designed like a West Point fortress, the emphasis so security-conscious that the builders finished construction and realized they forgot to put in the front door. It had to be cut in later. There were maybe places in America where jail time was preferable to prison time—cleaner, safer, more humane, where Aunt Bee brought over a hot supper—but not in Brooklyn in 1951. (The Raymond Street Jail remained in operation until 1963. Don't try to find Raymond Street on a map. It has long-since had its name changed to Ashland Place. The location is at the current corner of Ashland Place and Willoughby Street. A medical building stands there, and the current jail, called the Brooklyn House of Detention for Men, is on Atlantic Avenue.)

Alphonse's trial was scheduled to start in the furnace, but to almost everyone's relief was delayed a month because the medical examiner left on vacation. By the time opening statements were made and the people began calling witnesses to the stand, the heat had broken. That was the summer that the Dodgers seemed assured of winning the National League pennant. During jury selection, the team was cruising toward a championship. By the time the trial began, those dreams were shattered. The New York Giants of Manhattan stole the pennant on the last day of the season in the Polo Grounds behind Bobby Thomson's "shot heard 'round the world" home run off our beloved pitcher Ralph Branca.

The highlight of Alphonse Persico's trial was the testimony of the Blue Beetle himself. A courtroom journalist wrote that Alphonse "swallowed hard" when hearing Grillo's damning testimony. Grillo said the party had started at a tavern, and then into the car.

"Your car?"

"Yes, sir."

"Who was driving?"

"I was."

"How many were in the car all together?"

"Five. Alphonse Persico and Bove were in the backseat." Grillo was not asked and did not name the other people in the car.

"And why were you together?"

"We'd been out drinking, at a joint at Eighth Street and Third Avenue."

"And you left together?"

"Yes."

"At what point did you look back into the backseat?"

"After the first shot."

"And you saw Mr. Persico shooting Mr. Bove?"

"I saw Bove slumped over and Persico pointing a gun at him. Then I saw him shoot him."

"How many times?"

"Four more times. He emptied his revolver into him."

"Why didn't you stop the car?"

"Persico threatened me. He told me I drove where he told me to drive or he'd kill me too."

"Where did he tell you to drive?"

"To Carroll Street."

"What if anything happened on Carroll Street?"

"He told me to stop the car so he could throw out the body."

"And that was what happened?"

"Yes. When the body was out, he closed the door and told me to drive him home." They were already on the Persicos' street. He only had to drive a few blocks up the slope to drop them off.

That sort of testimony was difficult to impeach. Alphonse and his counsel Leo Healy could read the writing on the wall. The jury would never deliberate as, on Tuesday, August 7, Allie Boy and Healy took a deal, pleading guilty to second-degree murder.

Judge Sobel asked Alphonse, "You admit firing the shots that killed Bove?"

"Yes."

"You understand that that calls for a mandatory sentence of twenty years to life?"

Alphonse nodded.

The judge said, "Let the record show Mr. Persico answered in the affirmative."

Healy addressed the judge briefly, "I would request, your honor, that the sentencing be delayed a month as Mrs. Persico is due to have a child in that time."

Many in the courtroom were struck by this news. It was one thing to be reckless with your life and play shoot-'em-up cowboys in the streets, but to do it while your wife was pregnant? And it wasn't even for a piece of the pie. What did Alphonse get out of the killing? Revenge. That was it.

The judge pondered the request for a delay.

"It will take that long to make a probation report anyway," Judge Sobel replied.

The official sentencing was delayed and Alphonse was led away, the delay buying him an extra thirty days at the Raymond Street Jail—where rats both human and rodent skittered during the inky night.

From there, he'd move to prison. By the time he was released, his kid brother would be a very big man in Brooklyn, and Allie Boy—like Anthony Scarpati before him—had a job waiting for him.

Some may wonder how the Blue Beetle managed to survive after testifying for Alphonse's prosecution—and he did, for quite a while. He put Alphonse behind bars. And yet he lived—and not on the downlow either.

Guys that worked in or around horse racing had to fuck-up repeatedly to get whacked. Simple fact: they were worth far more alive than dead. The Beetle was a jockey and in a position to be a fantastic earner.

(Years later, we knew the Beetle. He was partners with our pal Tarzan in a joint on Ninth Street and Third Avenue called The Blue Beetle, the same Tarzan that did the cooking for my pal Mondo and his mom in their club on President Street. Tarzan was Johnny Lusterino, a kid from Hull Street in Bed-Stuy. He'd come up through the gangs as had Carmine and knew the inside of police stations and courtrooms before he turned seventeen. He once did a lengthy prison stint for stealing furs. When I was a kid, the President Street Boys went to Tarzan's place often. When war broke out, it was Tarzan who came to President Street and cooked while the crew hit the mattresses. He was there to do more than cook though, and always let it be known that he and his gun were available for assignment. In 1972, Tarzan was kidnapped after visiting his mother and never seen again.)

The Beetle was well-liked. He may have testified, but most people understood the tough position he was in. He wasn't in on the hit on Bove at all. He was an innocent. Why should he do time for that?

Then again, the Beetle's style irked some guys. He should at least be grateful he was alive and show a little humility. Sometimes, it almost seemed like he was exploiting the fact that he hadn't been whacked in retaliation. He was always doing something to draw attention to himself, asking for it.

No bullets came—yet—but Grillo ran into a streak of bad luck. In the spring of 1953 he was playing dice on the corner of Garfield and Fifth, home of the Garfield Boys. There was a pile of money right on the sidewalk. A group of grown men gathered tightly around the cutter, who apparently hadn't greased the flatfoots the way he was supposed to. While one threw dice, another laid odds, faded bettors, and raked in cash. Some of the shooters may have been kneeling but you could tell it wasn't a prayer meeting. There was tension. The guy who hadn't paid the Law must've known there was the risk of an interruption. Sure enough, two cop cars arrived simultaneously, one on Fifth, one on Garfield, and cops came from all sides. Some ran, some fought. In the resulting melee, Grillo—who, though not large, was a professional athlete—grabbed an officer's nightstick and broke it over the cop's head.

In 1955, years after Bove's murder, the New York Racing

Commission banned Grillo from racing in New York State, not because he'd assaulted a police officer, but because he had admitted to driving a car in which one guy shot another. So Grillo went west and rode at Santa Anita in California, where according to historian William J. Mahoney races were fixed so that track regular J. Edgar Hoover could win. Grillo thrived in Southern California.

It took a long time, but Grillo eventually crossed life's finish line in a violent manner. He'd been living in California for years but returned east to see his brother Frank. His little jockey body was found dead on December 29, 1968, on the floor of the Oceanside Boys Club on Long Island, with four bullet holes in him. Police said it looked like there might have been a card game involved.

On President Street word was that Allie Boy had ordered the hit. The Beetle's earning days were through, so it was time to pull the plug.

CHAPTER FOUR
Frankie Shots

*Some kids graduated from high school and moved into
the workplace. Some kids went into the army and were
promoted to corporal or sergeant. Carmine Persico
graduated from the Garfield Boys into the dangerous
but lucrative world of big-boy crime.*

FRANKIE "SHOTS" ABBATEMARCO was born on the Fourth of July
in 1899 and grew up in Red Hook, where as a kid he was finger-
printed so often there should've been permanent ink stains on his
fingertips. Frankie Shots was first arrested as an adult in 1921,
when he faced narcotics, grand larceny, and gambling charges.
He skated on most of it, did two years for the drugs. Now he was
a fifty-year-old man and ran rackets for the Profaci family, the
guy in charge on President Street, the boss of the bank, where the
Gallo brothers—Larry, Albert (a.k.a. Kid Blast), and Crazy
Joey—were the big up and comers. Frankie Shots knew who
Carmine Persico was, of course. Everyone did—and Frankie
Shots was always on the lookout for new blood to join his crew,
kids who could be trusted with good heads on their shoulders.
Leader of the Garfield Boys, pretty good resumé. Frankie Shots
had Carmine called in for a job interview.

Abbatemarco took bets and had the skills that made for a good
bookie. He could add and subtract large numbers in his head. He
had an excellent memory, and calculating odds and payoffs came
easy to him. It was what he did. During his first interview with

the kid, he saw some of these same skills in Carmine—and knew the teenager was destined for greatness. Frankie appreciated both Carmine's smarts and his balls. Carmine was cool under pressure, and had no time for remorse.

Frankie Shots almost immediately put Carmine in charge of important operations—robberies, running numbers, and collecting debts (which sometimes included sending brutal messages). In addition to having a quick head for calculating, Carmine also demonstrated a certain zeal when it came to violence that turned him into Frankie Shots' go-to for dishing out hurt. Most goons were huge and physically intimidating. Carmine intimidated with that smirk, which he wore invariably even as he used a loaded-up nightstick to break kneecaps, ankles, and the occasional head.

It was while working on Frankie Shots' crew that Carmine became close with the Gallos—not Albert so much, but Joey and Larry and Carmine were blood-brothers, running numbers, collecting debts, hurting people, and going out together on scores.

During this time Carmine was arrested more than a dozen times—numbers, craps, loans, burglary, assault—but had the full backing of the Profaci family legal team. He spent a night on Raymond Street every now and again, but the bail money was always there and the charges, whatever they were, eventually dropped.

There were a couple of factors in play here. For one thing, it seems clear that Carmine had a "get out of jail free card," like in Monopoly, most likely indicating that Joseph Profaci had Law and Order in his hip pocket. But there was something else going on. Carmine had a reputation despite his tender years of being a very dangerous fellow, Brooklyn's own Babyface Nelson. People were reluctant to testify against him. He came to court with well-connected lawyers, guys who had an in with the legal rigmarole, a system that generally had a great respect for Mr. Profaci and therefore his associates. Despite his many arrests, two of them associated with murder, in the 1950s, Carmine never spent more than fourteen days in a row in jail, that for the Bove murder as cops searched for Allie Boy.

During Carmine's early years with Frankie Shots, their arch-enemy was not someone from a different gang, but Kings County District Attorney Miles F. McDonald. With a degree from Ford-ham Law in the Bronx, McDonald had been with the D.A.'s of-fice since 1940, and the boss since 1945. McDonald fought corruption wherever he saw it—and understood that there was funny business on both sides of the street. His racket-busters not only went after hoodlums, they went after crooked cops and politicians as well. McDonald's investigations had led to the res-ignations of a New York City mayor and police chief.

In March 1952, the D.A.'s attentions turned to South Brooklyn and raided Frankie Shots' $2.5 million policy ring, his numbers racket. Carmine, now eighteen, was hauled in along with nine others, including Frankie himself and his son Abby. The arrests were based on wiretap recordings and "some sheets" that indi-cated numbers were being run.

The men were arraigned before Judge Samuel S. Leibowitz, the same judge who had presided over the Prospect Park murder case. The ring operated in Bed-Stuy, East Flatbush, and South Brooklyn. It was, the D.A. bragged, the largest such ring ever busted.

And so again Carmine found himself in a courtroom. This time though he didn't have to sit in the gallery and crane his neck to see what the lawyers were doing. This time there was a seat re-served for him right up front.

Frankie Shots' son, Anthony Abbatemarco, thirty years old, was called in the indictment the ring's number-two man. The D.A. told reporters that Anthony—called Abby by his friends in-cluding my dad—was arrested with $2,500 on him. Judge Lei-bowitz described the roll as "big enough to choke an elephant."

Abby had recently purchased a new Lincoln although he lacked a visible means of support.

"Where'd you get all the money, Anthony?" the D.A. asked.

"I get a monthly pension check from the government," Abby replied.

"That it?"

"Uh, I shoot crap once in a while."

Anthony's dad had a similar method of explaining his income. He said he had no business, and made a living just "maneuvering around, making bets, winning and losing."

Frankie and some of the older members of the crew were held on upward of $100,000 bail. When it was Carmine Persico's turn to be arraigned, Judge Liebowicz softened as he looked down upon what appeared to be a harmless rapscallion.

The judge remarked, "Why, he's just a kid."

But Assistant District Attorney Julius Helfand advised Judge Liebowicz not to take Carmine lightly, that despite his tender years he had many arrests under his belt, twice in connection with homicides. Authorities had never been able to place Carmine's finger on the trigger, so to speak, but bad things tended to happen in Carmine's vicinity.

Taking that into consideration, the judge ordered Carmine held on $10,000 bail.

Also arrested in the raid were Joey and Larry Gallo, twenty-three and twenty-four years old at the time. Indictments described them as "collectors" for the ring. They lived on East Fourth St. in the Kensington section of Brooklyn, but they had their headquarters on President Street in Red Hook. Larry was found to be in possession of two port patrol badges entitling him to admission to the piers, and twenty brand new suits of clothes estimated to be worth $75 apiece. The suits were established to have been the proceeds of a recent warehouse burglary in Manhattan.

Carmine walked on the deal, as usual, but during the summer

of 1952 the Abbatemarcos, father and son, pleaded guilty to the policy charges. Frank got a year at Riker's, Anthony nine months.

As the tumultuous Junior worked his way through young adulthood, his life expectancy seemed pretty short. Nonetheless, Carmine was becoming a young family man. He met a gorgeous brunette named Joyce Smaldone, married her in a church wedding, and in 1954 they had their first child, named Alphonse Theodore in honor of Carmine's brothers. A daughter, and two more sons followed. The boys were Lawrence (born 1955) and Michael (1957).

Carmine was now fully into adulthood, yet the world of teen violence he left behind continued to make headlines in Brooklyn. Within days of Carmine and Joyce's wedding, two Park Slope teenagers shocked the borough by kicking to death a man who had criticized their manners.

When the Gallos went on TV in 1958 to testify before a Senate rackets committee they earned instant fame. Joey in particular gained superstar status, wearing sunglasses and chewing gum as he was questioned by camera-hog politicians. The committee said the Gallos were "heirs to Murder, Inc." Every time you put a coin in a machine in NYC—jukebox, cigarettes, Laundromat—the Gallos got a piece. Kings of the hill in Red Hook on President Street, last block before you hit the piers. That was where my dad was, and that's where I grew up.

It seems like a cliché now, describing the way things were in Red Hook when I was a kid. There were no more organ-grinder monkeys, but it remained a unique universe.

The neighborhood was *a living thing* back then. There were multiple pool halls where a kid could hang out and learn the ropes from the older hoods as they shot eight ball, bakeries that gave the entire neighborhood a heavenly smell, pizza joints, and fancier restaurants where they put a tablecloth on the tables and every meal started with bread and oil. There were bars for the young hoods and bars for the old men with the busted blood vessels in their noses, and everyone in between. Jimmy Rosseli or Frank Sinatra was always on the jukebox or someone's record player. And everyone yelled. We didn't need cell phones—or even telephones of any kind. If a mom wanted her kid she threw open the window and called out for him. If he wasn't within earshot, the chances were good that the message would be relayed.

One of the social clubs on the President Street block was run by Armando "Mondo" Illiano and his mom. Mondo was a dwarf, a little man with a great big heart. When Joey Gallo decided to use a real mountain lion to terrify gentlemen who were tardy in their loan payments or otherwise in need of disciplinary action, he kept the big cat in a cage in the basement of Mondo's social club. He would take the already scared shitless men down the rickety steps and show them the lion. It always worked.

The Gallo crew and their environs were bigger than life itself, the future subject of a brilliant Bob Dylan song "Joey," and my dad was one of them, hired because of his boxing skills—he once decked middleweight champ Emile Griffith while working as a bar bouncer—to be Larry Gallo's bodyguard. (My mom says my dad also beat the shit out of Henry Hill one night in the Golden Door out near the airport. I asked her why. She said it was because Hill was an asshole.)

Point is, my dad Ricky was hired as Larry Gallo's bodyguard, but became a trusted member of the crew, good on any kind of job—*any* kind of job. If the Gallos had been able to give buttons, my dad would have been a made-man like *that*.

But the buttons were in Joseph Profaci's control, and membership was sealed because some of the bosses were selling buttons, which was not the Sicilian thing to do.

Everything that happened back in those days, Ricky DiMatteo was there, and he knew Carmine Persico as a friend, a brother— and eventually as a snake. I've read—albeit in a Chicago daily— that Carmine was called Snake because he slithered out of tough spots. Bullshit. His moniker referred to the snake in the Garden of Eden. Cross Carmine Persico and he was quick to strike. Hell, life was war and he was quick to strike even those that hadn't crossed him, those that were simply in his way.

CHAPTER FIVE
Making His Bones

*October 25, 1957, Carmine pulled on the black glove and
entered a Park Avenue barbershop, more front-page violence
that put him on the gangster fast track . . .*

AT 10:18 A.M. ON THAT DAY, a fifty-three-year-old man reclined in
a Manhattan barber chair, his face obscured by a hot towel. He
was Albert Anastasia—controller of the waterfront, founder and,
with Louis "Lepke" Buchalter, Lord High Executioner of Murder, Inc. Statistics were unofficial, of course, but sixty-three murders were attributed to Murder, Inc. between 1931 and 1940. Of
those, Anastasia was said to be responsible for thirty-six of them.
Now, he relaxed, maybe even dozed a little, in barber chair number-
four with his back to the door off the lobby of the Park Sheraton
Hotel on Seventh Avenue and West 55th.

At that moment, four men—the "barbershop quartet," as they
would become known—approached the Sheraton. One, Larry
Gallo, took up a post on the sidewalk, just outside the hotel's 55th
Street entrance. The other three went in. Joe Jelly stood guard at
the barbershop entrance, as Carmine Persico and Joey Gallo entered the barbershop.

Carmine and Joey were in business suits. Each wore one black
glove on his right hand, a bandana over the lower half of his face
like an Old West outlaw, a fedora like the gangsters in Hollywood
movies, and aviator sunglasses.

They didn't start firing right away. They were too cool for that.

They circled a bit. Carmine used his gun to gently push the barber out of the way. The shooters positioned themselves so that one was on either side of Anastasia's chair.

Anastasia was one of the original guys, a kid whose first smuggling job was getting himself ashore in New York in 1917. He was born in 1902 as Umberto Anastasio in the fishing village of Tropea in Calabria, Italy. He and his brother were working the crew of a ship crossing the Atlantic, jumped ship in New York and went to work on the Brooklyn piers, where over time the man now known as Albert came to control Brooklyn Local 1814, which repped longshoremen employed by stevedore companies. Ostensibly a dressmaker and milliner, the papers called him "The Mad Hatter," after the *Alice in Wonderland* character. He was convicted of murder in 1921. It looked like his Mafia career would be a short one until he avoided the electric chair when a key witness abruptly returned to Italy. Anastasia was acquitted at the retrial. He was in the army during World War II, and after the war, rose up the ranks of the Vincent Mangano crime family, assuming the boss position after Vincent disappeared and his brother Philip Mangano was found shot to death in a Sheepshead Bay marsh.

On the morning of October 25, Anastasia had been driven to the barbershop by his chauffeur-bodyguard Anthony Coppola, who stayed outside to "park the car" and never returned.

Anastasia now sensed the interruption, pulled the towel off his face, and had time to look around. He started to get up. He raised his left hand to protect himself and two slugs tore through it, one gun so close that it left powder burns.

Ten shots were fired. Three struck him in the head, one in the hip, two in the hands. Four caught nothing but barbershop. Anastasia swung his arms like a boxer on his last legs before collapsing at the barber chair's pedestal. He ended up dead on the floor on his back between chairs two and three.

The shooters—one described as five-foot-five, the other five-eight—retreated to the street, climbed into an American-made car the size of a boat, and fled with a squeal of tires down West 55th Street.

The manager of the next-door flower shop, Constantine Alexis, said he was returning from the nearby Mermaid Room when he heard six or more shots in three flurries. One shot, pause, two or three shots, another pause and then two or three more shots. He saw "five or six" men run out of the hotel. Some went out the Seventh Avenue exit, and others ran out the 55th Street exit. Alexis said that not all of the fleeing men were shooters. A few were frightened barbershop customers running for their lives.

Arthur Grasso owned the shop and was head barber. When Anastasia came in for his regular trim, Grasso himself made sure to take care of him. (In 1997, the barber chair in which Anastasia sat was curated! It was a primary display in New York's Gershwin Gallery, surrounded by classic photographs of mob hits. In 2011, it went on display at the Mob Museum in Las Vegas.)

Alexis ran into the shop, and recognized the body on the floor as that of Anastasia. He knew him because he used to buy flowers. Things were so still. The customers had fled. The barbers stood frozen. The only sound and movement came from the manicurist who let out one short conclusive scream before slumping over in her chair.

Along the same corridor that led to the barbershop was a luggage shop owned by Joseph March, who was entering the hotel and ran into several men running out. One still had a little shaving cream on his face.

One running man stumbled and fell to the floor on his back. While he was down he screamed, "They're going crazy in there! They're shooting!"

Virginia Nelson—the red-headed owner of The Red Headed
Woman, a hotel dress shop—was first to call police.

This was not the first time the Sheraton hotel had been the
scene of mob violence. Twenty-nine years earlier, on November
4, 1928, Arnold Rothstein, the gambler who fixed the 1919 World
Series (Black Sox scandal), was severely wounded by gunfire
during a poker game at the hotel, then known as the Park Central.
Rothstein lived for two more days in a Manhattan hospital but
never gave up the guys he saw shoot him.

It also wasn't the first time someone had tried to kill Anastasia.
The previous attempt was in 1951 when he defied an order to get
out of town or die. He didn't die, escaping when he was tipped
off. Fifty-seven-year-old racketeer Willie Moretti was sitting
down for lunch at a Cliffside Park, New Jersey, restaurant called
Joe's Elbow Room. He was with a handful of other men joking
loudly in Italian. At 11:28 A.M., shots were fired, and when the
smoke cleared Moretti was on his back on the restaurant floor
with bullet holes in his head and face. The story is that Anastastia
would have been dead also if he'd been at the lunch, but there
was plenty of reason for mob bigs to want Moretti out of the way.

Anastasia was a lucky man. He evaded every hit attempt and
beat five different murder raps. But his luck ran out with Carmine
Persico and the barbershop quartet.

The hit was big because Anastasia was big. Some speculated
that the killers were paying homage to assassins of old, their
black gloves being symbolic of the ancient Black Hand murders.

The Anastasia hit stemmed from events in the spring of 1957
when, in an attempt to expand his gambling turf, Anastasia sent a
gunman to bump off Frank Costello in the foyer of his apartment
house at tony 115 Central Park West, but managed to give him
only a new permanent part in his hair.

Talk about punishing the victim: Costello had a neat groove

through his scalp, yet was later jailed for contempt when he refused to testify regarding the meaning of a gambling slip with
numbers on it found on him when he was shot.

When Anastasia heard the hit on Costello had failed, he knew
his own life expectancy was not good. He only hoped that they'd
hit him, and not members of his family. He prayed the target
wouldn't be his son, Albert Jr., who was only twenty-two.

Albert Sr. pumped up security after Costello was shot. Three
men now guarded him, and his wife and son had full-time guards
as well. The pressure was getting to him. The Saturday before his
death he'd been spotted at Jamaica Racetrack tearing up a handful of $100 losing tickets. He looked old. Asked what was wrong,
he said he was worried about his family.

His Fort Lee, New Jersey, home was built like a fort, a palatial
structure with a ten-foot fence around it, and two killer Dober-
man Pinscher dogs roaming the grounds. Inside on the evening of
his assassination, Mrs. Anastasia was sedated.

Reporters hung out at the police station and watched the pa-
rade of underworld characters coming in for questioning. Little
Augie Pisano was questioned. Little Augie was one of the usual
suspects. A dapper dresser, he was known for his white felt fedora with black silk band, his finely tailored suits, and his shiny
shoes. He was a Genovese capo, ran nightclubs, and was a man
with a history and many real enemies. He would kill for Genovese, of course, but he freelanced as well. For a price he sometimes shot people for Lucky Luciano and Frank Costello. Before
he was through, Augie would be arrested for murder six times,
but each time they had to cut him loose. Augie was in charge of
collecting the Genovese cut from New York's garment district.
Because of his garment-district status, Augie also controlled
labor unions there, and may have used his muscle to rig a few
city elections. He told cops he knew nothing about a hit on the
Mad Hatter.

Harry Stasser, Anastasia's garment partner, came in for questioning, as did Anniello Ercole, who brought his lawyer with him. Others being grilled before dawn were a friend named Mike Mirant, and the victim's chauffer Anthony Copolla.

Investigators got nowhere. Nobody saw the shooters' faces, and like Little Augie no one knew anything.

Anastasia made his bones popping Joe "The Boss" Masseria, a hit that proved to be a pivotal moment in mob history, one that established the mob leadership for a long time to come. Here was a guy who himself made his bones in spectacular fashion. Now graphic photographs of his body splashed across the front pages of the tabloids.

Masseria had battled Sal Maranzano, in what became known as the Castellammarese War. Both men wanted to be *capo di tutti capo*. Sal was a visionary of sorts. He saw a world in which the families worked together rather than warring amongst themselves, thus increasing La Cosa Nostra power ten-fold. Masseria could have cared less about Maranzano's Big Picture. Masseria had a Big Picture of his own, one in which New York City was all his, and he shared it with no one. The war went on for two years, lots of guys dead on both sides. Bugsy Siegel, Meyer Lansky, and Lucky Luciano had a clandestine meeting with Sal in the Bronx Zoo. There, while feeding peanuts to the elephants, they came up with a way to end the war: ice Joe the Boss. It was Luciano who asked Joe to join him for dinner at Scarpato's in Coney Island on April 15, 1931. The men ate and ate. The feast lasted for three hours. Luciano patted himself on his belly, belched and left the table to go to the can. As soon as Masseria was alone at the table, four gunmen—Albert Anastasia, Bugsy Siegel, Vito Genovese, and Joe Adonis—burst into the restaurant and aerated Joe the Boss. Joe tried to hide but couldn't avoid the path of six bullets, at least one of which was fatal. Fourteen more slugs tore up the restaurant wall behind Masseria. Luciano came out of the rest room and left the restaurant before the police arrived. For the four gunmen, it wasn't a silky-smooth getaway. When the get-away driver stalled the car, Bugsy slugged him. But Anastasia and the others escaped anyway. Killing without remorse.

The hit on Anastasia, the world later learned, was Carlo Gambino's idea. He'd gone to Joe Profaci and asked him to supply the hit team. Profaci figured Anastasia's demise was to their mutual benefit and said OK. Now Anastasia was dead on a barbershop floor. It was Carmine Persico making his bones and doing it sensationally.

As Carmine fled the murder scene, he had to have seen the pattern. He knew he was a potential target. He had a bullet hole in each leg to prove it. One day he might be the one getting whacked. Such was the Life.

Within minutes of the shooting—Carmine probably hadn't even crossed the bridge yet—photographers from the major news outlets, and there were many back then in New York, began barging into the shop to photograph the body.

Someone covered Anastasia's ghastly head with a towel, but his still form remained a vivid sight. Even after police managed to keep members of the press outside the shop, spectators could still look in the window and see the belly-up body on the floor.

It was the biggest mob hit in New York in thirty years, and you could watch the crime scene and initial investigation from the sidewalk along one of Manhattan's most fancy stretches. Every few minutes another official vehicle would scream to a halt outside, and detectives, assistant D.A.s, and the boys from the press converged.

While patrol cars searched for the gunmen's vehicle, beat cops near the hotel interviewed those who didn't run away, including lightweight boxer Johnny Busso who was staying with his manager Andrew Alberti in a room at the hotel because Busso had a fight at the Garden that night. Minutes before the shooting, Busso and Anastasia ran into each other by coincidence and had a conversation in the hotel lobby during which the upcoming fight was discussed. The happenstance of the meeting was thrown into doubt by Alberti's long association with Anastasia, which earned the boxer Busso a grilling in the immediate aftermath of the hit. Despite the distraction, Busso won his fight that night.

Initial information gathered by the FBI indicated that the .38 and .32 caliber guns used in the Anastasia hit were being stored for pick-up in the hotel room occupied by Busso and Alberti.

Two guns were found, a .38-caliber Colt recovered from the corridor outside the barbershop, and a .32-caliber Smith & Wesson located at the 57th Street BMT (subway) station.

That early report of guns in the boxer's room wasn't good enough to cause Busso legal troubles, but the subsequent guilt-by-association investigation cost Alberti his boxing manager license and in 1962 he blew his brains out with a shotgun rather than give grand jury testimony against a compadre.

The first doctor on the scene was Dr. Robert Cestari of St. Clair's Hospital who pronounced Anastasia dead. Dr. Cestari got on the horn with Chief Medical Examiner Milton Helpern. An officer was assigned to contact next of kin, who was Albert's brother Tony, leader of Brooklyn's longshoremen. This was accomplished, and Tony said he was on his way to the hotel. Additional barber sheets were eventually used so the body was covered completely.

Police asked folks from the hotel if they had folding screens, and someone ran over to the redhead's dress shop and returned with temporary walls that were placed around Anastasia's body. This helped to disperse the crowd on the sidewalk outside the barbershop window.

Tony Anastasio arrived on the scene at 11:17 A.M. He threw himself on the barbershop floor, his arms around the body. He yanked away the sheet so he could kiss his brother's face.

Strong men had to look away.

The union leader began to weep uncontrollably. He had to be pulled out so Dr. Helpern could have the body transported to Bellevue Hospital morgue for autopsy. Later in the day Tony officially identified the body at the morgue. In the paperwork, he listed his brother's occupation as "dress maker." He was later seen stoically entering the West 54th Street police station to answer questions.

At Bellevue, Dr. Helpern determined that either one of two bullets, one in the back, one in the back of the head, could have been responsible for death.

Anastasia's body was buried in a $900 casket in Brooklyn's Green-Wood Cemetery. Spectators were few and for the most part silent, with the exception of widow Elsa, who sobbed uncontrollably.

The FBI dug into the Anastasia hit and learned that the barbershop ambush had not been a spur-of-the-moment thing. Indeed, Anastasia had been under constant surveillance for months, and during that time it was determined that you could time Anastasia's haircuts like clockwork—twice a month.

Doing a favor for Don Carlo could give the ol' career a boost, and that was how it worked for Carmine Persico. Six months after the Anastasia hit, Carmine stood in a candlelit cellar beneath a Bensonhurst social club, surrounded by a half-circle of men with their heads bowed. He declared his presence in the holy night, the silent night, under the light of fire. The ceremony would seem familiar to anyone who'd observed the rites of freemasonry. Carmine proclaimed his allegiance to the holy society, took the pledge of *omertà*, and swore that he would also keep one bullet for himself—in other words, that he would rather blow his own brains out than dishonor his new family. He would be faithful to the family and understood the family in return would be faithful to him. He understood that he would burn in hell if he betrayed his friends. Carmine took his pledge with his left hand on a knife, while the celebrant, most likely Joe Profaci himself, pricked his finger to draw blood, and placed an image of the archangel Michael in Carmine's upraised palm and set it afire (to demonstrate that Carmine, like the archangel's image, would burn if he didn't keep his solemn oath). When the ceremony was over, there was much joy. All of the men kissed Carmine on both cheeks, and shook the scorched hand of the youngest made man in family history. Carmine precociously received his button at the tender age of twenty-four. Fuckin' kid. The *amigos nostri* retired to the upstairs bar where solemnity dissipated into a boozy cloud.

ACT II

CHAPTER SIX

Winds of War

*They say that all true businessmen are sociopaths, that you
can't maximize profits with a conscience—and there was no
better example of that than Joe Profaci, a guy who milked the
poor and invested those pennies into his own opulence.*

GIUSEPPE "JOE" PROFACI was born in 1897 in Villabate, Sicily,
and came over on the boat. His crime family, which would evolve
into the Colombos, was the youngest of the five, formed as a legitimate business by Profaci, *Carmela Mia*, largest distributor of
olive oil and tomato sauce in the U.S. He was already a very rich
man when he branched out into organized crime, gathering up
wealth and power as a bootlegger, bringing in whiskey by the
boatload through Jamaica Bay on the southern shore of Long
Island, and driving truckloads of the stuff in through Canada. His
operations diversified into gambling, extortion, hijacking, prostitution, and extorting entire unions, a form of shakedown that he
might have invented. He'd been boss since 1928 when he was appointed at a national commission meeting in Cleveland. By 1931,
Profaci had a seat at that commission. He lived on a sprawling
compound in the Bensonhurst section of Brooklyn.

For decades, authorities thought Profaci was legit—but there
were clues as to his secret identity. His name and address were
found in the little black book of a mobster named Giroloma
Adamo when he was arrested in L.A. Profaci himself was busted
in 1938 when a commission meeting was raided in a Cleveland
hotel room. Cops had no idea who they had, just that they also

found thirteen guns. Still, up until the Kefauver hearings, when Profaci's secrets were bared, he was mostly known as a good guy, a man who was involved in church activities and multiple charities. By the time he was arrested by New York State troopers at the Apalachin Conference in 1957, his secret might've been out but he never went to jail.

In time-honored mob tradition, Profaci became boss of one of the Five Families by bumping off the previous boss, Salvatore D'Aquila. Weak men were befuddled by obstacles. Strong men removed them. And Salvatore D'Aquila was in Joe Profaci's way in 1928. Profaci was now boss of the smallest of the Five Families.

Joey and Larry were also made in the aftermath of the Anastasia hit, but Joe Jelly was not. Mr. Profaci apparently didn't feel Joe Jelly had done enough to warrant a button.

Now a made man, Carmine entered a chilly world, even tougher than the one he'd known on street corners. Carmine took over his own crew, and for the first couple of years, operations ran smoothly. Every once in a while, a little muscle was called for but there were no logjams in the money flow. Scores went off without a hitch, not always like clockwork, but usually without injury or incarceration. Many of the scores were hijacks, considered good jobs for young hoods because they were relatively easy to pull off. It took balls to do it, of course, but it wasn't complicated, not a lot of thinking involved.

None of which took Murphy's Law into account.

On July 28, 1959, Carmine's crew hijacked a truck with $50,000 worth of piece goods in it from the Akers Motor Lines Terminal in Brooklyn, built right along the Gowanus Canal in between Nevins and Union Streets.

At the time it seemed like just another score, but in April 1960, an indictment was filed by a U.S. Court in Kings County charging Carmine and his crew—close friend and man-mountain bodyguard Hugh "Apples" McIntosh, plus Salvatore Albanese, Ralph Spero, Joseph "Joey Mags" Magnasco, all from the neighborhood, and George Lanfante who was originally from South Ozone Park, Queens—with hijacking and conspiracy to hijack.

Thus, began one of the longest and most complicated cases in the history of American justice. So allow us to step out of chronology for a moment. Five times Carmine and his co-defendants would go to trial over this crime. Joey Mags was only around for two of those trials. After the second trial, after a conviction but before sentencing, Magnasco was shot dead. Much more about that, later.

At all five of Carmine Persico's hijacking trials, the prosecution's case hinged on the testimony of two men, Gasper Vaccaro, a co-conspirator who'd taken a deal and turned against the others, and Edward Kennedy, an employee of Akers Motor Lines and the driver of the hijacked truck. He could testify that the truck had been hijacked all right, but not to the identity of any of the hijackers as he'd been forced to wear taped-over sunglasses.

Vaccaro testified that on July 27 or 28, 1959, he was in a Brooklyn bar with Carmine Persico and the other defendants and that they planned to hold up a truck carrying piece goods and take it to a garage they knew. It was a plan that turned out to be only almost perfect: Vaccaro spotted the truck at Akers Terminal as it loaded. Albanese fetched a previously stolen Buick. Vaccaro, with Spero and Albanese, followed the truck and when the opportunity arose, kidnapped the driver, and drove the truck themselves to the garage. Albanese and Vaccaro drove the kidnapped truckdriver around in the Buick until they were notified that the robbery was complete. McIntosh rented a truck, and loaded the dry goods onto it. Carmine, author of the plan, was at the garage to help make the transfer onto the new truck. Vaccaro and Albanese called Joey Mags, and said it was cool to release the truckdriver. Everything went off without a hitch. The stolen goods were sold to a fence, and, minus the almost two grand in tribute, the seven conspirators split the money. Then Vaccaro got popped and turned on his co-conspirators because he had priors and was threatened with a life sentence unless he blabbed.

It was Vaccaro's testimony that troubled the defense lawyers. If the jury believed Vaccaro, checkmate. So, they went all out to make Vaccaro seem bad and untruthful.

The first trial lasted twelve days during the spring of 1961, and resulted in a hung jury.

The second trial lasted nine days that summer, and ended with a conviction. Persico and McIntosh received sentences of fourteen and nine years respectively on each count, the sentences to run concurrently. Albanese and Spero received suspended sentences and were placed on probation. Mags was convicted on both counts, but never had the opportunity to be sentenced.

No one actually went to prison, however. There was a successful appeal. The second-trial conviction was reversed because of "errors at trial," those being both judicial and prosecutorial misconduct.

The third trial was held in May 1963 and ended in a mistrial after the eighth day because, one, there was a hung jury, and two, Carmine Persico was hospitalized with gunshot wounds.

Carmine got into minor trouble in December 1963, between the third and fourth hijacking trials. A cop tried to pull him over for a traffic violation. Carmine hit the accelerator and allegedly ditched a gun. He was caught and booked at the Bergen Street Precinct station.

The fourth trial was the longest, lasting from January to April 1964, approximately sixteen weeks. Carmine and four remaining co-defendants were convicted and sentenced by U.S. District Judge George Rosling in Brooklyn to fourteen years and nine months in prison. During the trial, the prosecution called Persico, "one of the most dangerous criminals in the east."

Those verdicts were also overturned in appellate court because of errors in the trial judge's jury charge, as well as yet more of the dreaded prosecutorial misconduct. Albanese's defense witness, a guy named Eppilitto, died between the fourth and fifth trials.

Eppilitto's testimony was part of yet another attempt by Albanese's defense to make Gasper Vaccaro look like a bad guy. The other part came when Mrs. Albanese took the stand and testified that Vaccaro had tried to rape her. Vaccaro was even impeached by defense witnesses for getting things wrong. He testified that when the truck was hijacked it was parked on the Nevins side of the terminal, so the defense put on a witness who said, no, the truck was on the Union Street side.

The fifth trial took place in Courtroom 8C in Brooklyn Federal Court during April and May 1968, with U.S. District Judge John F. Dooling Jr. presiding. Carmine was defended by Maurice Edelbaum, a Fordham Law grad considered to be a bit of a miracle worker. He had in 1962 worked tirelessly, and pro bono, for the freedom of one Isidore Zimmerman, a New York City doorman who spent a quarter century behind bars for a crime he didn't commit. In 1967, Edelbaum successfully got a medical student off for the murder of his mother-in-law with an insanity plea, the story being that his client dropped LSD before the murder and wasn't responsible for his actions.

But there were indications that luck was not running Edelbaum's way as he prepared to defend Carmine. He tripped on a rubber mat in the courthouse's entrance hall while leaving for lunch and fell heavily, breaking his arm. He was rushed to the Long Island College Hospital emergency room. The trial was delayed a week, and he spent the rest of the trial in a sling.

Special prosecutor Victor Woerheide tried the case for the Department of Justice in Brooklyn federal court. Woerheide would go on to gain fame as the prosecutor of Dr. Jeffrey MacDonald, who was supposed to have murdered his family, a case that spawned two bestselling true-crime books, *Fatal Vision* and *Fatal Justice*.

The fifth trial looked to spectators familiar with the first four, to be a ho-hum affair. Then came the morning when there was extra security in the courtroom. The doors were double-guarded by armed deputy marshals. There were ten marshals in all displaying sidearms. In addition, FBI agents and city detectives were sprinkled into the gallery. Spectators were searched before entering the courtroom, a commonplace practice now but an indication of particular security concerns in 1968.

Edelbaum complained about the show of force: "Your honor, it looks like an armed camp in here."

Judge Dooling all but ignored the comment and said, "Will the prosecution call its first witness?"

"Prosecution calls Joseph Valachi."

That got everyone's attention. Valachi was already famous as the mob's first nationally famous rat. He'd been delivered to the courthouse by helicopter. His notoriety stemmed from his nationally televised gravel-voiced testimony before the Senate Investigation Committee in 1963. He introduced America to the term *La Cosa Nostra,* our thing, which he may have been using generically, but it stuck. Valachi told the world he'd been a made man since 1930 when he was twenty-seven and he'd been inducted in the back room of a New York City restaurant. A gun and knife were on the table. Blood was drawn from his finger as he told his inductors, "If I talk, I die." His sponsor was Vito Genovese. For thirty-two years he kept his lip buttoned. He spent eighteen of those years in prison—for burglary, robbery, assault, gambling, and dope.

Carmine shot Valachi a nasty glance as the surprise witness took the oath, but Valachi made no eye contact. As history would have it, this was the only time Valachi ever testified for any prosecution.

Carmine's defense immediately objected. Valachi couldn't testify because it was a well-known fact that he was nuts. Judge

Dooling agreed to a brief competence hearing with the jury out of the room.

"Who is President of the United States?" Judge Dooling asked Valachi.

"Still LBJ, right?"

"What is today's date?"

"It's about April 20," Valachi replied. "I'm guessing, I've lost track. I haven't been paying too much attention to that." He'd been in solitary confinement in Milan, Michigan, for the past twenty-five months.

He was asked about a suicide attempt he'd made when he was first thrown into solitary. Was it because of disappointment that he hadn't been rewarded following his Senate testimony?

"It was a little of this and a little of that. There was a thirty-year draft in my cell. I was cold and upset."

Judge Dooling proclaimed Valachi competent and ordered that the jury be brought back in.

Valachi's testimony revolved around statements he had heard by and about the defendants in April 1959 and June 1961. Valachi said Albanese told him that "Chink" (Vaccaro) and "Junior" (Persico) went out with him on hijackings, including the Akers Motor Lines Terminal job. Valachi said Junior was a street guy. Always on the streets. He fought on the streets at a very early age, and he was always at his best outside. If there was business on the streets, Carmine was there. A tremendous earner, a guy with range: labor, extortion, loansharking, gambling, hijacking, hitman. Of course, hitman, yes. Once, Valachi testified, Carmine "wanted some advice. He knew I'd been around. I knew who he was, he knew who I was, through friends. He wanted to know—first he told me that he'd been paying taxes on all the hijackings that he'd been pulling especially the one he was on trial for, Akers truck. He paid Joe Profaci $1,800. He wanted to know if he was in his rights having trouble with Joe Profaci."

"And what did you say to him?"

"I told him it was not taxes at all. It was an out and out shake-down and he was one-hundred percent right in having trouble with Joe Profaci."

"Did Mr. Persico say anything to Mr. Albanese or to Mr. McIn-tosh in your presence?"

"He told them in the future to pay attention to Joe. Listen to him. You want any advice, ask him. That's all."

"When he said Joe, to whom was he referring?"

"Me."

Mrs. Albanese did not testify at the fifth trial regarding Vac-caro's attempted rape because Valachi had already testified that Albanese admitted the rape story involving his wife had been fabricated.

As Valachi testified, he was serving a life sentence for the mur-der of a cellmate he believed had been assigned to kill him. The underworld had a 100K price tag on Valachi's head, but Valachi got the assassin before he could get him. The victim could run but not hide as the men shared a prison cell.

The court was trying to keep the jury in the dark regarding "possible organized crime connections." Best guess is that the ju-rors figured that part out on their own. That task became more difficult after Valachi testified. The press was out to sell news-papers and didn't care what the jurors knew and didn't know. Newspapers said the defendants were mob, that the case had been tried four times previously, and that the people at this trial were represented by a special prosecutor.

Judge Dooling refused to call a mistrial because of the public-ity, after individually interviewing each juror regarding what he'd seen and heard, and if it affected his ability to make a fair determination of innocence or guilt. The defense, of course, ar-gued that the very calling of Valachi as a witness told the jury that this was a mob trial.

The jury convicted across the board on May 9, 1968. It seemed to legal experts as if the fifth trial did the trick, but not so fast. The appeals of the conviction would take Carmine Persico's name all the way to the Supreme Court of the United States.

The sixties as we'll see might've been Carmine's best decade, but it was spent with the constant threat of imprisonment hanging over his head, and it seemed like no more than a week or two went by between court appearances. The appeals following the fifth trial were considered by the Supreme Court during its October 1970 term. The convictions of Persico, Albanese, and Spero were under scrutiny. Longtime friend and bodyguard Hugh McIntosh was also appealing but under separate petition.

The case had set records for longevity, longest in New York Eastern District history. Surely there had to be a point where the gnaw-on-your-ankle-till-you-fall methods used by federal investigators and prosecutors came to a halt, a time for the U.S. Government to say uncle.

So among the questions the SCOTUS agreed to look at were the many trials (all five of them) the defendants were forced to endure. True, it was up to the prosecutor's discretion whether or not to re-try a case if it ended in a mistrial, but after four attempts and no clear-cut decision, a fifth trial could be construed as piling on. Shouldn't there be a point when it becomes a legal necessity for a prosecutor to concede defeat? Shouldn't something approaching double jeopardy apply? The appeal referred to the way the defendants were treated, now more than a decade past the crime, as "overall unconstitutional aggressiveness."

SCOTUS not only had to determine if the overall oppressiveness of the five trials was constitutional but also if the fifth trial in particular met with the minimum standards of fairness, in that the springing of surprise witnesses such as Joseph Valachi with a lot of *La Cosa Nostra* talk had to have influenced the jury. The Valachi surprise was a prosecutorial ambush. The petitioner wondered if this didn't infer judicial misconduct as well, as it would have been impossible for the ambush to have been pulled behind the judge's back, and it certainly shouldn't have been pulled behind the defense's back. Didn't the eight years between the indictment and the conviction in itself demonstrate that the defendants had been denied their right to a speedy trial?

The answers to these questions were no. And Carmine eventually did a long stretch for hijacking.

And now back to our chronology . . .

There can be argument as to what gunshot or garrote started the Profaci-Gallo war, but the seeds were planted in 1959 when troublemakers Joey and Larry Gallo convinced Frankie Shots that all of this tribute money going to Profaci was madness. Frankie Shots said, yeah, he'd had it with Profaci, and he wasn't paying the tithe anymore. The Gallos said they would go to Profaci and get Frankie a better deal. That never happened.

Frankie's numbers game, the same game that Carmine worked on when he joined Frankie Shots' crew, earned $7,000 a day, almost all in one-dollar bills. The numbers' popularity was the reason the government took it over, called it Lotto, and turned it into a "voluntary tax." The numbers were making millions of dollars for Profaci, even as Profaci was alienating the Gallo crew with increasing tribute demands.

When Profaci learned that Frankie Shots had stopped paying tribute, he was a dead man. Profaci could be every bit as deadly as he was avaricious. Mutinous behavior needed nipping in the bud. A message needed to be sent: Tribute was to be paid promptly and in full—or else. Just to be cruel, and to test loyalty, Profaci wanted a member of Frankie's own crew do the dirty work.

The Frankie Shots hit was initially given to Joey Gallo who turned it down, which sent a message to Profaci that Profaci didn't like. Joey said he couldn't do it. He was bloodbrothers with Frankie's kid Anthony.

So Profaci went to Carmine who said, sure, he'd do it.

On November 4, 1959, eight P.M., Carmine was one of two shooters in the hit on Frankie Shots. Twin gunmen plugged holes in Shots as he exited his cousin's saloon, Cardiello's Tavern at Carroll Street and Fourth Avenue. His cousin was Anthony Cardiello, who was tending bar. The shooters—in topcoats, fedoras, and masks—coolly followed the wounded Frankie as he retreated back inside, and filled him with lead on the saloon floor. The shooters ran out, one of them dropping a .32 caliber revolver on the sidewalk, climbed into a car, and sped away. Anthony and the tavern's only other customer dove behind the bar when the shooting started, and stayed there until they were sure the shooters were gone.

When cops arrived they found Frankie Shots prone in the sawdust, the barroom door splintered apart by gunfire. The medical examiner counted the holes. Frankie Shots was shot eight times, all striking him either in the face or the stomach.

Since Frankie's rep with law enforcement was as a man of chance, the first thing the NYPD did was round up all professional gamblers in Red Hook, guys who might've wanted to erase a debt or otherwise had a beef with Frankie. Had to be a local thing, a neighborhood thing, investigators figured. Frankie was a neighborhood guy.

Looking back, maybe police were trying too hard to make it look like they were doing something/anything, when in reality the killers had nothing to worry about. Six down-and-out, sleeping-on-the-sidewalk men were arrested in connection with the murder and eventually were charged only with vagrancy. Joseph and Anthony Cardiello were brought in and held for a while as material witnesses. But they remained silent.

Frankie Shots was buried in Holy Cross Cemetery in Brooklyn. His grave read, "Blessed are the dead who die in the Lord." The site features a statue reminiscent of Michelangelo's *Pieta* depicting Mary holding Jesus's post-crucifixion body.

* * *

Whenever management becomes wealthy while labor suffers, there's bound to be trouble. Profaci lived in luxury, an empyrean mansion in Florida, another in Holmdel, New Jersey. The Gallos were hanging out in the downstairs club of a President Street tenement. It wasn't the cut of the rackets that got under the Gallo crew's skin so much as the personal tithe they were all supposed to come up with. It cost $25 a week to be in the Profaci family no matter how low you were in the pecking order, no matter what struggles for survival your family might be enduring.

Profaci wasn't a lovable father figure the way some bosses were. He was more like Ebeneezer Scrooge sneering "Bah! Humbug!" to the folks of Red Hook.

After Frankie Shots' death, the Gallo crew naturally figured they would get a chunk of the old man's rackets—but that didn't happen, widening the chasm between the factions. Control of Frankie's numbers game went to Profaci's relatives, and the Gallo crew was out of work. The poor neighborhood got poorer, while Profaci got to build an extension on his Florida mansion.

CHAPTER SEVEN
Snake Eyes

August 1961, Profaci ordered the killings of Larry, Joey, and the
rest of the Gallo crew. And it was then that the President Street
Boys realized that they had been betrayed by one of their own.
There was a turncoat among them.

WE DON'T KNOW THE DATE, but the story goes that Frank Costello
took one look at Carmine Persico and saw the future. The kid was
going places. Costello called Carmine in.

Carmine was fairly certain that he was going to be scolded
about something. He didn't know what he'd done to piss off
Costello, but whatever it was, it couldn't be fatal, right?

Persico knew enough about Costello to know he had some serious balls. This was the guy who from 1950 to 1952 testified
several times on TV before a Special Committee of the U.S. Senate investigating organized crime in interstate commerce. This
was back in the early days of television when the screens were
round and everything was black and white. Costello was the only
don to testify, all the others took the Fifth, and he came out of the
hearings with a national reputation as America's number-one
gangster. His testimony earned an element of mystery when cameras were ordered to show only Costello's hands and not his face.
They asked him a lot of questions about his finances, how he
lived such an extravagant lifestyle when he was making beans in
the legit world. Costello danced as much as spoke, eventually becoming so evasive that he served eleven months in prison for

Contempt of Congress. Now, Costello had a vision and it concerned Carmine, and Carmine liked the way it sounded a lot.

Costello said that he was speaking as a true friend of Joe Profaci, and he was aware of the bullshit that was going on over on President Street. This Joey Gallo was nuts and would start a war, and when he did the Gallo crew was going to lose. When that happened, Carmine wanted to be certain to be on Profaci's side, as his future was a bright one, and being true to Profaci was the most direct and certainly the healthiest path to take.

Carmine no doubt didn't need to have any of this spelled out for him. He was adept at the chess game of life as well, and capable of thinking several moves ahead.

According to legend, Costello went on to say that, if he really wanted to serve Profaci in the most efficient way, he would not make the move off of President Street just yet, that he should work as an intelligence agent, letting Profaci know what moves the Gallos were planning.

Carmine said he understood.

Sick of paying Joe Profaci, Joey Gallo came up in February 1961 with a bold plan. Frankie Shots' problem with the boss was that he hadn't been dealing from a position of strength and it cost him his life. Joey and his crew would kidnap the top Profaci guys: Joe and Frank Profaci, Joe Colombo, John Scimone, Joseph Magliocco, and Sally "The Sheik" Musacchio. The Gallos would negotiate new and more favorable terms for themselves in return for the safe release of the detained mobsters. The plan, as it turned out, was overly complicated and had way too many moving parts. Not surprisingly, things didn't go well.

On February 27, 1961, Joey and Carmine sent out a crew in a phalanx of limousines to make the pick-ups. This part went pretty smoothly. They kidnapped everyone on the list except for Joe

Profaci. A little bird told him what was up, and Profaci fled to Florida.

Joseph Magliocco pissed his pants while in captivity, a humiliation that left him with a lifelong hatred for the Gallos.

After a few weeks of his captains being held hostage, Profaci made a peace agreement just to get them back. What Profaci didn't know was that Joey and Larry were at odds over what to do with the hostages, so much so that they came to blows. Joey didn't trust Profaci and wanted to kill the captives one by one, starting with Magliocco. Larry talked him out of it.

Joey had been right not to be trustful. Joe Profaci had no intention of keeping his word. It took Profaci a few months to get around to it, but he eventually reneged on every promise he made to get his men released.

In retrospect, the kidnapping scheme had been a devastating failure. All the Gallos had managed was a few false promises, and some strong enemies. My dad Rick DiMatteo always said that he loved Larry Gallo like a brother, and Joey Gallo was a maniac, but in this case Joey had been right. Larry was naïve. As it turned out, money wins over morality every time.

And not just in organized crime. It was true in life in general. Larry's decision to be fair backfired. Profaci's capos returned to a crime family that felt humiliated, pissed off beyond belief.

"I want every one of them President Street fuckers dead," Profaci said. That cheered the boys up.

Like Carmine, the Gallos were fearless. On Sunday, August 20, 1961, Carmine Persico invited Larry Gallo to the Sahara Lounge, a bar on Utica Avenue in East Flatbush. Larry believed he was to discuss strategy regarding the upcoming struggles against Profaci. Larry had backup outside, but he wasn't expecting trouble and, disregarding advice to the contrary, went into the bar alone.

In the dim tavern Larry found Carmine Persico and two others—
Sally D'Ambrosio, and forty-nine-year-old John Scimone—there
to meet with him. No one else was around. Not even a bartender.

Larry didn't know Carmine was going to be there, but discov-
ering him there wasn't cause for alarm. He and Carmine were
cool. While Larry was sitting at the bar talking to Carmine and
Scimone, Sally came from behind, produced a two-foot piece of
rope with knots on either end, and wrapped it swiftly and sav-
agely around Larry's neck.

Larry turned purple and his eyes bugged. The audience made
noises of encouragement and Larry himself thrashed with taut
muscles and emitted all his crunched vocal cords could muster—
a high-pitch wheeze of distress. He looked to be a goner, until
two cops, Sergeant Edward Meagher and Patrolman Melvin Blei
in a police cruiser, happened by.

Back then bars weren't allowed to open until Sunday evening
because of blue laws, so seeing the bar's front door ajar prompted
them to investigate. Blei stayed in the car and Meagher went to
check and see what was up. As he approached the slightly opened
door he could hear the commotion inside, and when he walked
in, he couldn't tell right away what was going on because his
eyes were slow to adjust to the dimly lit bar.

"What's going on here?" Sgt. Meagher said. "You open or not?"

Larry moaned and slumped to the floor semi-conscious. Carmine and everyone else—except Larry, who was down for the
count—ran for the door with heads down, so all the cop could see
was their fedoras.

Patrolman Blei, watching from the police car, jumped out and
chased the three running men to a nearby parking lot where they
climbed into a Cadillac. As Blei approached on the run, a gun
emerged from an open window and shot Blei in the face. I heard
the shot was fired by Sally. Published sources have attributed it to
Carmine Persico. The Caddy roared off.

At that moment, Sgt. Meagher emerged from the darkened interior into the harsh mid-afternoon sunlight, saw his partner down, and fired two shots at the Cadillac as it sped away.

The car hauled ass for two blocks before the driver slammed on the brakes and Scimone either jumped out or was thrown out. The Caddy then drove away to freedom and Scimone, one eye swelling from the fall, was promptly scooped up by the law.

Larry lived, but he had to go to the hospital for treatment, the rope having burned the skin off. There was a mark around his neck for the rest of his life.

Police asked Larry who attacked him and he said, "What attack?"

"What happened to your neck?"

"Cut myself shaving," Larry said, his voice sounding like he'd gargled with rocks.

Back at the Sahara Lounge police found the two-foot piece of rope with the knots on either end that had been around Larry's neck. In better light it showed evidence of the ordeal, speckled with pieces of Larry's skin and stained by his blood.

Blei was rushed to Kings County Hospital and listed in critical condition. Because of the cop shooting, the incident even made the out-of-town papers, and in Philadelphia Larry was referred to as "jukebox kingpin" Lawrence Gallo, while Patrolman Blei, who recovered from his wounds, was said to have looked at a stack of photos and identified "underworld figure" Anthony Abbatemarco, thirty-nine years old—Abby of the President Street Boys—as the guy who shot him. (This was a clear clue that the cops didn't know who was on who's side. Not to mention an indication that Blei hadn't actually seen the shooter's face clearly.) The same article said that the Gallos had "fallen out of favor with the underworld" and were "marked for elimination." That part they got right.

Apparently, the cop really did I.D. Abby as his shooter. Abby and Scimone were held.

That slightly ventilated getaway car was abandoned and found to be registered to "underworld figure" Sonny Pepitone's twenty-something girlfriend Lila "Lips" LaPietra, who—with a cute shrug—said that she had no idea where the bullet holes came from.

Police arrested everyone they could get their mitts on and held them as material witnesses in the shooting of the cop. That meant that Larry was being held on $100,000 bail for the attack on himself. Also held was Sahara-owner Charles Clemenza. No one talked.

Obviously, among those who got away and whose names were never publicly associated with the attack on Larry was Carmine Persico. Say that name out loud and you were dead. But Larry remembered who was there, and when he finally returned to President Street, out of earshot of the law, he said Carmine Persico was a *dead man*. Frank "Punchy" Illiano called Carmine "the snake" that day, the first time anyone called him that, and the name stuck.

Judge Samuel S. Leibowitz, who had presided over the Prospect Park murder case, was as merciless as ever and in charge of the arraignment of the material witnesses in the cop shooting. He made the connection right away between this case and Prospect Park.

The judge however didn't mention names when he commented that the juvenile delinquents who had given the cops such a bad time at the beginning of the decade had grown up. "Now they're trying to murder policemen," Judge Leibowitz said solemnly.

On the last day of October, police arrested thirty-four-year-old Aurelius Cirallo and, claiming he was the getaway driver, held him as a material witness as well.

By November, it appeared, cops thought they had the incident sorted out a little bit better. They still didn't have Carmine's name in connection with the garroting of Larry, but they realized Blei's I.D. of Abby was off the mark and Sally not Abby was indicted for the officer's shooting.

During the twenty-four hours after the attempt on Larry Gallo's life, someone took a shot at Joey Gallo's car (Joey wasn't in it), and the finger of Joey's top enforcer, Joseph "Joe Jelly" Gioelli, was delivered to Jackie's Charcolette, a restaurant run by the Gallo brothers' parents.

Carmine had a new crew, and one of his boys was Freddie No Nose, an ex-boxer who'd taken one too many to the kisser, and had no remaining cartilage in what used to be his nose. According to Sal Polisi, No Nose—with Sally D'Ambrosio and Carmine Persico—was in on the Joe Jelly hit.

Sally had a boat he kept at the man-made bulkhead harbor at Sheepshead Bay. He asked Joe Jelly if he wanted to go fishing in the ocean for blues. Jelly said sure, and left his girlfriend's house that morning in a relaxed mood. Jelly liked to fish, he'd gone fishing with Sally before, so he had no reason to think anything was up. He didn't even get it when he learned Carmine Persico and No Nose were going out on the boat also.

They came back with fish but without Joe Jelly—well, all but his ring finger. They turned it into a messy business, removed Joe's clothes, dismembered him, put the pieces in a fifty-gallon drum and dropped the drum overboard into the Atlantic.

(Sally and No Nose disappeared in December 1969 and were never seen again. Legend has it they were garroted in a bar, with no sun-blind cop to come to their rescue.)

With the finger, they delivered the fish. Joe Jelly sleeps with the fishes. It was war with style, a riff copped by *The Godfather*.

The Profaci family declared war on the Gallos, and the boys on President Street hit the mattresses.

Carmine Persico was now officially "Snake" with the Gallos. Warring with the Profacis was courageous. The President Street Boys had balls of titanium, no doubt about it, but Carmine and Profaci badly outgunned them.

The Gallo crew slowly realized that Carmine Persico had betrayed them long before the attempt on Larry's life. He was a dirty double-crosser from way back. A spy. And probably the reason Profaci fled so he couldn't be kidnapped. The boys thought of the many times that Carmine had been there, an accepted and trusted friend, while everybody drank, and tactics and strategy were loudly discussed. And all the time the Snake was a human wire transmitting intelligence directly to Profaci.

How far back did it go? Was Carmine *ever* really their friend, or was he always a spy? There were many long-and-loud discussions on this subject in the social clubs of President Street, where chicken wire covered the windows so no one could toss through a bomb or Molatov cocktail.

Evidence showed that Profaci wanted Carmine on his side very badly. He paid Carmine well to spy on the President Street Boys while Profaci planned his war. Besides the obvious advantages of being on the side that would win, Profaci guaranteed Carmine several lucrative rackets.

Looking back at Carmine's behavior with the benefit of hindsight, it's easier to see that Carmine's allegiance was, as always, to Carmine. Sticking with Profaci was an excellent business move.

The Gallo-Profaci war was raging, a war in which Carmine Persico was active but, gauging by the public record, something next to invisible. It was a vicious business, gangland combat, but imperfect.

During the summer of 1961, Carmine found a bomb under his car that never detonated. He had his car customized in case a second bombing attempt produced a working bomb, which it did.

Near summer's end, a couple of guys tried to kidnap loanshark Ruby Stein, an associate of Nicholas "Jiggs" Forlano, but failed when Stein put up a noisy and attention-grabbing fuss.

On September 21, 1961, members of the Gallo crew beat the shit out of Aniello Dellacroce, who was a capo with the Gambinos at the time, while he ate at Luna, a tablecloth *ristorante* in Little Italy.

The next victim was Joseph Magnasco, a South Brooklyn product, and Carmine's hijacking co-defendant. He was a solid player for the Gallos with hands of steel and a "no holds barred" type of attitude. Mags developed a deep hatred for Profaci early on, and had joined the Gallos just as hostilities commenced. He bought it on a chilly evening in the autumn of 1961, only days before New York Yankees outfielder Roger Maris hit home run number sixty-one for the season, breaking the Babe's record, and the Yanks cruised to the American League pennant. The Dodgers had already been in California for four seasons, although New York was getting a new National League team, the Metropolitans, the following spring.

Joey Mags was shot to death outside the Union Street Diner. His death graced the cover of my book *The President Street Boys: Growing Up Mafia*. In fact, Joey Mags' death is one of my first memories. I was there, just five years old, with my mother, visiting my mother's girlfriends Chickie and Lillian in their apartment, and we were standing twenty feet away when Joey Mags was wasted.

An informant talking to the FBI said that he believed the hit on Mags had been intended for Joey Gallo. The gunmen were inside

the diner and Gallo and Mags got out of their car, Mags went into
the restaurant while Gallo crossed the street to say hello to someone he recognized. The same informant said that Profaci's man
Charles LoCicero had been opposed to Larry and Joey Gallo
being allowed in the family from the start, despite the Anastasia
hit, that he felt the Gallos and their crew—who were mixed ethnicity and religion with Irishmen, Syrians, and a dwarf—were
not "the right type of people." The informant said he'd been to
meetings between the sides held at the Golden Door Restaurant
at Idlewild Airport (now JFK), and that these meetings were
marked (really ruined) by the antisocial behavior of Crazy Joey
Gallo. Even before the meetings, he'd known that a civil war was
on the horizon because Carmine Persico and the Gallo brothers
had approached him about quitting Profaci and going on their own.

One of the best photos of all time was taken the night after
Joseph Magnasco's murder. A bunch of the Gallo crew were
picked up on President Street and run in and there's a photo of the
lineup, with the dwarf Mondo's head coming no higher than the
other guys' midsections.

Cops asked Mondo if he saw the killer.

"I saw his belt buckle," Mondo said. "Show me a line-up of
belts and I might be able to recognize it."

Because my mom and I were too-close-for-comfort when
Mags was whacked, it was often the talk at my house. I learned
that, with Magnasco that day were my dad's friends Punchy and
Chitoz. Punchy was Frank "Punchy" Illiano, Mondo's first cousin and coiner of the name "Snake." He was tough as nails,
fought in the Golden Gloves when he was a kid, and hung out on
President Street since Day One. Later, he used those hands to put
a hurt on the Gallos' enemies. A lot of guys are called Punchy because they've been on the receiving end of too many punches,
but this Punchy got the name for dishing them out, often in crisp
and destructive combinations. He ran all of the street fairs in

South Brooklyn and finally became a made man in the 1970s. Punchy was close to my father, and they stayed close their whole lives. Chitoz was Gennaro Basciano, a real South Brooklyn tough guy, born and raised in the heart of Red Hook. He was a stone-cold killer, but you would never know it by speaking to him. He was right-hand man to Joey and Larry Gallo for many years. Like my dad, he could've earned a living in the ring. He had one-punch knockout power. He was quiet but deadly—and loyal.

So those guys and Joey Mags were driving up Union Street looking for Harry Fontana. They were looking for him because he was supposed to be on the Gallos' side but hadn't been doing as much as he could. In fact, it seemed like he was avoiding the Gallo crew, as if he might have something to hide. They found him in front of the Union Diner at the corner of Union and Fourth Avenue. Mags jumped out of the car and started arguing with Fontana.

In the heat of the argument, Harry's bodyguard killed Mags on the spot. My mom, being an adult when it happened, remembers it clearly. She became aware that there was some running around, some commotion nearby, a scuffle, car horns blaring, and gunshots. She grabbed me and started heading away from the action. She saw a couple of guys running away, just a glimpse out of the corner of her eye, so she couldn't say for sure who they were. Not that she would have said anyway.

"I'm smart enough not to look," she says. "None of my business."

I was little but I remember seeing Mags yelling and then falling to the ground. I knew that these were friends of my father's, but I didn't realize until later that I had seen Mags die there on the street. Even when I did figure it out, which was pretty quick, I was young and it didn't bother me very much.

Later, while doing research for my first book, I found a photo that had been taken by a newspaper photographer of Joey still on the sidewalk, looking for all the world like he's taking a nap, a police chalk mark around him, and a priest, Father Benny Calleja, administering the last rites. That's how I know the date, October 4, 1961.

Later that month, the Gallos gained intelligence that the "olive oil king" was hiding out at his hunting lodge in the wilderness of New Jersey, so a crew went there to take care of business. They were met at the door by an aged caretaker who convinced them Joe Profaci wasn't there.

Still in October, errant shots were fired by two gunman, one of them being "Cadillac" Louie Mariani, at former Gallo business associate Jiggs Forlano outside Forlano's home in Astoria, Queens. The sound of bullets whizzing past his ears gave Jiggs pause, caused him to reconsider life's priorities. He left the Gallos and joined Profaci, eventually becoming a capo under Joe Colombo.

At just before 3:00 A.M. on November 11, 1961, in a smoke-filled Brooklyn nightspot called the Hi-Fi Lounge, gunfire erupted, sending an estimated one-hundred customers screaming into the street, while others cowered under tables. Police later had trouble finding two eyewitnesses who saw the same thing, but eventually concluded that two or three men had entered the joint and started firing guns. Forty-two-year-old ex-con John Guariglia and twenty-seven-year-old club-owner Paul Ricci, a.k.a. Paul Rich, were dead. Thirty-one-year-old Thomas Riccardi also needed an ambulance for a bullet to the knee. FBI documents suggested that WW II vet Sal Mangiameli and Michael Rizzitelli may have been the gunmen. Rizzitelli was originally a New York gun but had been living in California for years before returning east to help out the war-torn Gallo crew.

On November 22, cops raided two Sheepshead Bay apartments and confiscated an arsenal of weapons that, according to

NYPD Assistant Chief Inspector Raymond V. Martin, were to have been used to "finish off the Gallo gang." Martin said the war was being run on behalf of Joe Profaci, by Sally, who was connected to at least one of the apartments and was free on $40,000 bail in connection with the cop shooting outside the Sahara Lounge. (The other apartment, at 2701 Ocean Avenue, belonged to an "attractive divorcee" named Zoya Linova.) The weapons were six high-powered hunting rifles, two of them with telescopic sights, two shotguns, a sawed-off shotgun, a revolver, and ammunition for all of the guns. Also seized were $8,500 in clothes stolen from a freight warehouse in the city.

The Gallos were facing two sorts of attrition during the first weeks of the war: guys getting shot, and guys defecting to the other side because they could read the writing on the wall.

Maybe he'd just seen the Billy Wilder picture *Some Like It Hot,* which combines cross-dressing and gangsters, but on December 2 Carmine Persico decided that wearing drag would make a perfect disguise for a hit squad. And so it was that he and Sally D'Ambrosio, neither one of them very pretty, dressed up as women, climbed into a convertible sports car, and hunted down Larry Gallo. Sally drove, Carmine sat shotgun with an actual shotgun across the lap of his dress. They found Larry, and Carmine managed to get off a shot but missed. Maybe his earrings got in the way.

On December 11, three Gallo associates, including Larry "Big Lollipop" Carna, age thirty, were fired upon eight times from a drive-by car. Carna was wounded in the ankle, and a passer-by was slightly injured. Carna was stepping out of a paint store along a busy Red Hook street when he was shot. The two men with him, Angelo Pafumi and Sal Mangiameli, ran to their cars and fled.

Police asked Big Lollipop who shot him.

"I have nothing to say to you," Carna replied.

In mid-December, Profaci declared a ceasefire. Assigned hits were canceled. Peace talks broke out. Charles LoCicero approached Larry Gallo with an offer of peace and Larry told him he liked the idea of a ceasefire but thought the undisclosed terms ridiculous. Profaci wanted subservience. The Gallos wanted Profaci to step down.

On December 18, a pretty twenty-two-year-old brunette named Palma Vitale was in court facing criminal contempt charges before Kings County Judge Hyman Barshay based on her refusal to testify before a grand jury investigating gangland tumult. She was there because she was Sally's special friend, and her refusal to talk had Assistant D.A. Aaron Koota calling for her to be jailed, but the judge gave her a suspended sentence and warned her to stop consorting with "worthless characters." On her way out of the courtroom, Miss Vitale was handed a subpoena to testify before the next grand jury, a move that made her roll her eyes.

On January 5, 1962, Carmine Persico, along with turncoat Jiggs Forlano, and Dominick "Donnie Shacks" Montemarano, went to the Copacabana. (Donnie grew up less than a block from the Persicos on Carroll Street but was younger, born 1939, and didn't hang with the former Garfields until the President Street days.) There, they encountered a guy named Sidney Slater who was behind on his loan payments. So, taking care of business that had nothing to do with the Gallos, they beat the shit out of him, left him howling. Jiggs wore a newspaper hook on his ring finger and Slater almost lost an eye.

January 29, Michael and Philip Albergo, Gallo associates, came out of a restaurant and found their parked car with a flat. Upon closer inspection, they saw the tire had been ice-picked. So they were pretty pissed off as they started to put on the spare. As they squatted beside the car with jack and lugnut wrench in hand, a car drove by and shot them. The ceasefire was over.

March 5, bullets flew in Joe Profaci's general direction but he was unharmed.

March 11, Carmine, Jiggs, and a couple of other Profaci capos sent out word that the old man was sick, Profaci was very ill, and it was time for him to step down. This might have sounded ungracious on Carmine's part because the olive-oil king had given him the big break that would make him a very rich man. But he was forgiven when it became obvious that he was not being disrespectful but merely addressing an actual problem. Simultaneously, the Gallos—who were taking a licking in the ongoing war—went to the commission to ask that they handle the Gallo-Profaci dispute. Carlo Gambino advised Profaci of the Gallos' request, and meetings were held on the subject in Chicago and Detroit. Gambino and Tommy Lucchese asked Profaci nicely to step down.

By this time, the papers, citing anonymous sources, were referring to Carmine Persico as "Profaci's top gun," the man who "held the contract to liquidate the remaining members of the Gallo gang," a guy who cruised the streets of South Brooklyn in a car full of guns "hunting Gallos."

Profaci guns, under Carmine's command, tended to shoot straighter than Gallo guns. Anthony "Tony Fats" Regina in particular had skills. He was considered a "small arms expert" and had been decorated for sharpshooting in Korea (before he went AWOL)—interesting in that President Street would be plagued by sniper fire.

With the Profacis pre-occupied with civil war, the other four families were growing increasingly concerned. Publicity over the death count was bad for business.

All the squabbling over Profaci was moot as Profaci died before the month was out, on June 6, 1962, of liver cancer. He was buried five days later in St. John Cemetery in Queens, also the resting place of Lucky Luciano, and later of Joe Colombo and John Gotti.

It was custom for a family to take some time to mourn when a boss died before naming a new boss, but in this case, because of the war, Joseph Magliocco immediately and unofficially took over the family. He was never okayed by the commission, and his reign was brief.

The Gallos had no voice in the decision as they were not recognized as an entity by the commission. The Gallos were out, and if they wanted to get back in they were going to have to apologize to the commission for their upstart behavior and maybe, just maybe, they would be received back into the Profaci family.

Now, while Carmine Persico was rapidly rising up the ranks, a shooting star gaining influence and power with each shake-up at the top, Magliocco was a guy who had been stuck in place for a long time. He had been with Joe Profaci when Profaci was given the fifth New York family and had been Profaci's underboss for thirty-four long years. So, when he was elevated to the top spot after all that time, he was a frustrated man, an ambitious man who became suddenly power-hungry—not to mention the fact that he was still angry with the Gallos for kidnapping him and not allowing him to use a toilet when he needed to take a leak.

So it's no surprise that one of Magliocco's first moves as boss was to order a skim of all gambling operations to go into a war fund, money ear-marked solely for the destruction of the Gallos. In the meantime, no such fund existed on President Street, where morale was scraping bottom. Guys getting scared and bailing continued to be a problem. The first turncoats switched over to the Profaci side, but as that side lost some of its structural integrity during the exchange of power, others went to the Gambinos looking for a safe spot to work.

June 1962, the FBI filed a report saying the Gallo-Profaci war was hurting the numbers business.

October 1962, two low-level guys who were friends of the Gallos, Anthony DiCola and Marco Morelli, simply disappeared, poof, reportedly hit by Carmine Persico and Jiggs Forlano. Carmine wanted the Gallos to know he would hit big men and little men, that he knew no distinction.

There was a period of peace until Johnny "Bath Beach" Oddo had his car engine torn up by gunfire while he sat behind the wheel in 1963. And that brings us to the most famous of all attempts on Carmine Persico's life.

CHAPTER EIGHT

Indestructible Carmine

Carmine—shot in the cheek, hand, and shoulder—got out of the vehicle, took several sideways steps, lurched forward and collapsed to the sidewalk. There he spit out a bloody bullet. Loved dearly by his crime family, he was the Man Who Could Not Be Killed, and now had a new nickname: "The Immortal."

IN MAY 1963, Punchy shot and wounded Carmine Persico's bodyguard, the hard-to-miss Hugh McIntosh. Days later a hit team from President Street—my dad Rick DiMatteo, Punchy, and Chitoz—attempted to take out Carmine.

And they did it in a surprisingly high-tech way. Rick, Punchy, and Pete "The Greek" Diapoulis teamed up with Sal Mangiameli—a union president, and former explosive ordnance specialist during WW II—who knew how to make a bomb and gave them instructions. Knowing those guys, they probably had a few drinks to steady their hands as they built the bomb.

And it worked. My dad was among those who built the bomb, successfully placed it under Carmine's Cadillac, and detonated it with Carmine in the car. Just the fact that the bomb went off was considered a great success with a lot of backslapping—but they didn't kill Carmine.

Sure, the bomb exploded on cue under Carmine's Cadillac, and for that matter under Carmine as well. Fortunately for the intended victim, however, there was a steel plate under his seat, and he walked away with a concussion, permanent tinnitus, some cuts and bruises, and a sore ass.

Back on President Street:

"Next time let's just shoot him."

"Yeah, yeah, yeah, let's just fucking shoot him."

They weren't satisfied with going hunting with pocket guns. A job like this demanded superior weaponry so they brought with them an M-1 carbine. If it was good enough for American soldiers in WW II, it was good enough for President Street. It was light, easy to use, semi-automatic .30 caliber, and absolutely built to kill men.

So, on May 19, 1963, my dad, Pete the Greek, and Punchy tried to kill Carmine with bullets. Pete carried the rifle. The targets were Carmine and his longtime associate, thirty-eight-year-old Alphonse "Funzi" D'Ambosio. The men were in an AMC Rambler at Bond and DeGraw streets in Gowanus, after leaving the home of Carmine's girlfriend, and on their way to downtown Brooklyn for a court appearance, when they were ambushed by the gunmen in a panel truck.

The shots neatly pierced the car's windshield. Carmine took hot lead to his cheek, left hand, and shoulder. He stumbled over to the sidewalk and spit out a bloody bullet. I've read that Carmine got up and drove himself to the hospital, but that's bullshit. He was down. Both wounded men were taken by ambulance to Kings County Hospital. As Carmine was being wheeled into the emergency treatment center, his face a crimson mask, a hole in his hand large enough to put a pool cue through, he was pestered by cops.

"You got five bullets in you, Junior," an Irish plainclothes guy said, stride for stride with the guys pushing Carmine's gurney. "Look, you're going to die any minute now. Before you go, why don't you straighten this thing out and tell us who did it? You know who it was. What's the difference if you talk now? You're going to die."

He didn't talk. For one thing, he'd just been shot in the mouth. But he also refused to talk. He shook his head at the annoying cop, who thankfully was left behind as Carmine was transported into surgery. Even as his mouth healed, his lips remained sealed.

Carmine was reported in "poor" condition, while Funzi was in "good" condition. Along with "Junior" and "Snake," Carmine now picked up a new nickname, one he'd earned the hard way: The Immortal.

They say what doesn't kill you makes you stronger. Such bullshit. Sometimes what doesn't kill you leaves you a drooling vegetable. This shooting did permanent damage to Carmine Persico. He never regained full use of his now twisted left hand.

Of course, the cops knew who shot Carmine. They just wanted a witness to say it out loud, but they couldn't find one so they rounded up seventeen members of the Gallo crew—including Larry and Albert Gallo—and charged them all with illegal gun possession. Criminal Court Judge Louis Wallach set bail ranging from $1,000 to $15,000. The low price tag went to blond, twenty-four-year-old Mrs. Paula Levatino a crewmember's curvaceous and accommodating girlfriend. Top price went to the least active of the brothers, "Kid Blast" Albert Gallo. The judge originally said his bail would be $10,000, but Albert "talked back," saying like a smart aleck, "Thank you very much, Your Honor," at which point Wallach added 5K to his bail.

Deputy Chief Inspector James E. Knott led the investigation. He said he was fairly certain that those responsible for the shooting were among those he'd rounded up. Figuring out which ones, of course, was a different matter. The President Street crew was mum.

The day after the attempt on Carmine's life, it was announced that a special squad of veteran detectives had been assigned to keep their eyes on Red Hook gang activity around the clock, and they were known as PISA, the Police Investigating Suspected Assassins. The word *assassin* was esoteric at the time, but it went way mainstream that autumn in Dallas.

* * *

Desperate for money to keep up the battle, the Gallos took contributions. One of their benefactors was a local businessman named Emil Colantuono. Recruiting other contributors, however, became difficult when Colantuono was the victim of a homicide on June 6, 1963.

That same D-Day, they found the body of gun-dealer and Gallo-associate Alfred Mondello. Authorities suspected Mondello had been supplying arms to the Gallos.

June 12, someone shot at Punchy. In the return fire, Vincent DiTucci was killed by Chitoz, who was arrested in connection with DiTucci's death but later released for insufficient evidence.

Some Profaci guys defected to the Gallo side. We don't know why. Maybe they, like the Gallos, were disgruntled over the excessive tribute money. Maybe they wanted to side with the guys with the biggest onions. Maybe they just preferred the underdog role.

Such a man was fifty-nine-year-old Joseph "Bats" Cardiello, one of the brothers from the bar where Carmine whacked Frankie Shots. Bats was once Profaci, now pro-Gallo, and on August 9 was cut down in daylight by a volley of slugs in Brooklyn. Cardiello was shot four times from a high-powered black car as he sat in his own auto waiting for a light to change. He was a good guy from the neighborhood. We could compile a short list of probable shooters, and Carmine Persico would be at the top. For one thing, Carmine's top guns were at that very moment out on Long Island.

Only hours after Cardiello bought it, about 1:30 P.M., fifty miles to the east, Carmine's team—including forty-seven-year-old John J. "Moose" Battista, a longshoreman who lived on Coney Island Avenue in Brooklyn, and twenty-nine-year-old Tony Fats Regina, the Long Island sharpshooter—were out on a hunt, driving along the Nesconset Highway near Port Jefferson, Long Island, with their target in sight.

The subject of the hunt was Gallo crewmember "Cadillac" Louis Mariani, twenty-six, the boyfriend of my mom's friend Nancy.

The gunmen drove alongside Mariani's car and fired twelve shots. Also in the car was twenty-six-year-old Anthony Getch, and the thirty-three-year-old Mrs. Dotty "Vavavoom" Vivino.

Four bullets had plowed into Getch's body, and he was taken to a Port Jefferson hospital where he fully recovered. Mrs. Vivino, in the excitement, forgot to say she'd seen and heard nothing and instead blurted out to first responders that "Fats" was the one shooting, referring to Regina.

Suffolk County police subsequently put together a winning case against Regina and Battista. The trial was in Riverhead, Long Island, Suffolk County Judge George F.X. McInerny presiding. Cops kept Getch in hiding, and he became the star witness of the four-week trial.

From the witness stand, Getch said that Regina was driving the vehicle that pulled up alongside the victims' car. Tony Fats Regina was also the shooter. Battista was one of three others in the shooting car. Getch said he knew who Regina was because he'd seen him cruise by in a car a few times while Getch was standing on the sidewalk in Brooklyn. Getch said he knew Battista because he'd seen him ten to fifteen times over a two-year period. On cross-examination Getch admitted that he'd never spoken to either of the defendants.

The prosecution didn't call Mrs. Vivino to the stand, but the defense did. Under cross, she denied saying anything about Tony Fats after the shooting. She'd been hysterical.

During summary, the Suffolk County D.A. made it plain: these two guys were "assassins assigned to the Profaci top gun, Carmine Persico"—Carmine "The Snake" Persico, the guy who held the "contract to liquidate" the Gallo gang.

Following more than two days of deliberation, the jury convicted both defendants of murder one, and Carmine Persico's army suffered a different kind of attrition, losing two gunmen to the law.

Carmine's multiple legal troubles were put temporarily on hold each time he was wounded in an attack, but even when he was convalescing, the war went on without him.

On July 24, 1963, Gallo crewmember Ali "Baba" Hassan Waffa was shot to death in Hoboken, New Jersey. Waffa was forty-nine years old, a short and swarthy Egyptian, a guy that Joey Gallo met in prison, a seafaring cook, thief, and hashish smuggler. He'd been known to supply weapons to both grown-up and teenaged gang members. In 1955, he'd been prosecuted for "piracy on the high seas." Legend had it that Ali Baba was murdered by Joe Yack and Sonny Pinto.

That summer Joe Magliocco plotted with Joe Bonanno to kill rivals Tommy Lucchese and Carlo Gambino in an attempt to take over the commission. Magliocco made the mistake of ordering Joe Colombo to hit the two bosses, but instead Colombo told Gambino and Lucchese of Magliocco's plan. Magliocco somehow survived this sequence of events. On September 3, Magliocco was given an offer he couldn't refuse and "retired," that is, he stepped down as Profaci's replacement. Joe Colombo became boss and the war against the Gallos ended. The boss no longer held a grudge against the Gallos because of a kidnapping incident. The Gallos no longer hated the boss because of his excessive demands. It was time for peace.

Magliocco, as it turned out, had a startlingly short retirement. He almost immediately had a heart attack and was rushed to

Good Samaritan Hospital Medical Center in West Islip, Long Island, where he died on December 28, 1963.

Given that he was ousted after being caught scheming to kill other commission members, Magliocco's quick demise was considered highly suspicious—despite the fact that all outward appearances indicated natural causes. (In 1969, an FBI wiretap picked up a New Jersey mob boss, Sam DeCavalcante chitchatting about Magliocco's death, saying in his humble opinion, the commission had him hit with some sort of poison that wouldn't make itself obvious unless you went looking for it. The feds decided that they would go looking for it, exhumed Magliocco's body from its not-so-final resting spot in St. Charles Cemetery in Farmingdale, Long Island, and found no poison.)

In 1964, the name of the family was changed to the Colombo Family. The death toll in the civil war, according to FBI figures, which may be low, was nine dead, three missing and presumed dead, eleven injured and nine fired at but missed. The FBI didn't know all of it, though. Some wounds were treated by mob doctors—"bite the belt"—and never became public.

It was in 1964 that Carmine Persico and the work "kingpin" first appeared together in a daily newspaper. During the wee morning hours of October 27, 1964, squads of detectives rousted as many bookies as they could find from their beds and hauled them, thirty-five of them, to Brooklyn's antiracketeering headquarters. Twelve more were being sought. According to D.A. Aaron J. Koota, the prize among those captured was gambling "kingpin" Carmine Persico. Koota said Carmine was the "overlord of the operation," which brought in upward of $35,000 a day. Koota said that his investigation had bared a conspiracy between the hoods, the cops, and employees of the New York Telephone Co. One of the "prime movers" in the conspiracy was,

Koota said, William J. Hussey, a fifty-eight-year-old former chief of the security division of the phone company.

Despite Koota's proclamations, Carmine was back on the street without missing a shave.

With Colombo secure as boss, Carmine moved up yet another notch. One of Colombo's first executive orders was to promote Carmine to *caporegime*. Carmine and the boss could regularly be seen in conference, their heads together, no one else privy to the topic.

Colombo was respected but not popular. No one said anything nice about him. Carmine, on the other hand, was the popular choice, the competent, street-savvy leader they wanted to take orders from. Persico had that tough-guy reputation. He was the way they liked to envision themselves. He scared the shit out of people, a power that often benefitted those who worked under him. Guy gets behind in his payments, say, "You don't want I should tell Junior." Guy pays up like that. Worked just like Crazy Joey's lion. Carmine was the incredible earner, chilly cold killer, creator of plans that worked, former legendary teen phenom, and made-man at an age when others were still running errands. A fucking legend. Carmine was the real deal, a hood's hood.

One of Carmine's top hit men during the Gallo war was Dominic "Little Dom" Cataldo, whose chiseled features made the ladies swoon. He dressed as if valeted by Damon Runyon, straight out of *Guys and Dolls*. Cataldo eventually married Albert Anastasia's niece. A housewife from Kansas could've taken one look at him and ID'd him as a New York gangster. He made his bones taking contracts from Carmine Persico, at the expense of the President Street Boys. Still, Cataldo remained un-made because of the moratorium on new buttons. Cataldo had an uncle who ran casinos in Havana until Castro came, and a tough grandmother, former bootlegger Ervolino Cataldo, who by the 1960s was using her East New York house as a front for a horse and sports book. Little Dom used his well-dressed tough-guy image to loan-shark at the track. His image was such that violence was often not necessary, just an insincere smile and a poke in the chest did the trick. No one wanted he should tell Junior. Dominic finally got his button after Carlo Gambino's death in 1976 when the "books were opened." Technically, you weren't supposed to be bumping guys off without permission, and you weren't supposed to be dealing drugs, but Cataldo had been doing both for years and now he had a button himself. He was also in on the 1980 hit on Gerard Pappa, who had connections with both the Colombo and Genovese families. Cataldo had his own restaurant, place called Villagio Italia where he reputedly whacked guys in the back room, put them in the trunk of his car and, according to Sal Polisi, dumped them upstate off the Taconic Parkway. Like many hoods of the era, Cataldo worked himself into a nice coke habit in the 1980s, and his resulting paranoia led to ever-increasing amounts of bloodshed. Cataldo was convicted in the Pizza Connection case in 1987 of smuggling more than $1 billion in heroin over the previous decade. He died of natural causes in prison ten years later.

The government learned much about the commission's existence in 1962 through their ace informant. Only many years later would the source be revealed as Gregory Scarpa, a guy who ostensibly worked only for Carmine Persico. (It was not unheard of for the government to use hoodlums in unexpected ways. Mob guys came in very handy for U.S. intelligence services during World War II, offering up their knowledge of Sicilian and Italian geography before allied invasions there. There was cooperation between feds and hoods over Cuba after Castro took over and kicked the mob out. The mantra was "Just because I'm a hood don't mean I ain't a patriot!")

The source said that the commissioners were the heads of the families and considered of equal rank. There were five in New York, and one each in Florida, Arizona, Nevada, California, Pennsylvania, Detroit, Boston, and Chicago. When a problem arose that the commission needed to rule on, there was a team of two or three men who went around the country and contacted the commissioners with the where and when of the meeting. The commissioners—or, after Apalachin, a panel that they appointed— would listen to both sides of the beef, like the Supreme Court, and the ruling was binding throughout what was essentially a national crime organization. Scarpa said that the former Profaci family had about four hundred members, made guys. Of the five NYC families, he said, the Gambinos were the most populous, with a membership of about one thousand. He said that when the head of one of the families died or was imprisoned, the commission would "recommend" a replacement, who would serve as a member of the commission. If a commissioner got out of prison, they would resume their position on the commission and their replacement would step down.

Colombo thought all of this La Cosa Nostra business, everyone quoting Valachi, was out of control. Too many headlines. Too much star status. Business was best done without a light shining on it. Their cover story needed freshening and brightening, and this was the sort of thing he was good at. He formed the Italian-American Civil Rights League, a loudmouth group whose job was to convince the world that La Cosa Nostra was a figment of Valachi's imagination, that all of those Mafioso he described were actually legitimate businessmen trying to get their piece of the pie, trying to live the American Dream. The IACRL's chaplain was Father Louis Gigante, brother of Vincent the Chin.

*   *   *

During the summer of 1965, there came to light an audio tape of a police detective, James Daly, and Francis J. Farrell, an agent for the Federal Bureau of Narcotics, trying to force an ex-con to shake down Carmine Persico. The recording was made from a phone booth not far from the *Journal-American* newspaper office building in Manhattan.

The tape made headlines largely because it had ghoulish appeal. The ex-con, Joseph Kadlup, was already dead by the time the tape played. Papers got to talk about a "voice from the grave," through the miracle of Memorex.

On July 31, 1965, Kadlup was killed by a cop, after he killed a brother officer, in a wild shoot'em-up in a Bay Ridge, Brooklyn, tavern. The detective and agent were under investigation by a grand jury for the plot. The tape was made by Kadlup "for two newspapermen" from the *Journal-American*, it was reported.

The plot, it was explained, was to collect $2,000 a month from Carmine Persico. To earn this, they would threaten him with a false drug arrest. Carmine, the theory went, wouldn't fear being arrested—but being associated with drugs would be defaming. He'd pay, they figured.

Kadlup approached the reporters on July 27, 1965, a vulnerable three-time loser. One more conviction meant life. He told the reporters, "That's what the cops and the feds are holding over my head. I'm caught in the middle."

Kadlup told the newspaper that he'd gone as far as to make a date to meet Carmine, but was frightened off, suspecting he'd been double-crossed by Farrell and Daly. When Kadlup first spoke to the reporters he told them, "I'm going to be hit by a cop or a fed. Believe me, I know what I'm talking about."

To protect Kadlup, Dom Frasca, city editor at the paper, gave Kadlup a note addressed to the fed and the cop saying, "This is to let you know I have tapes which are going to be used if anything happens to Joseph Kadlup." The note was found in Kadlup's home after his death, reported D.A. Aaron E. Koota.

Koota later explained that there was no connection between the tapes and Kadlup's death. Despite the fact that the targets of the D.A.'s investigation were members of law enforcement, Koota said, "I concluded that the matter was of the greatest importance to law enforcement and required a thorough investigation before a grand jury where all the facts and circumstances could be fully and completely explored. As of now, I have formed no definite opinion as to whether the detective and the narcotics agent were engaged in some form of skullduggery or criminal conduct."

Both the fed and the cop denied the charges. Farrell told his supervisor, according to the *New York Times*, that he had just been "joking along" with the ex-con. Their defense was predictable:

Look at the accuser! He was diagnosed as a psychopath. He'd done a long stretch in that hellhole in Dannemora, and he died a cop-killer. Who are you going to believe?

The 1960s was Carmine Persico's best decade. He had dough, power, and a healthy sex drive. Just as in the 1950s, he went to jail periodically but was always granted quick release. He lived the life of a well-to-do hood: part most wanted, part celebrity.

On any given night Carmine and his friends could be seen sitting facing the door, in one of his three favorite Brooklyn restaurants, either New Corners or Romano's in Bensonhurst or the Ember Steakhouse at 100th Street and Third Avenue near Fort Hamilton.

Sometimes he hung out in the old neighborhood, at his cousin Mush's club, on Sackett Street between Third and Fourth avenues. Junior and Mush dated starlets. According to reports,

Carmine went out with Goldie Hawn on his arm, who at the time was a barely legal dancer looking for a break in show biz. Mush dated Lainie Kazan, a graduate of Hofstra University drama school and then veteran of one episode of the TV comedy, *Car 54, Where Are You?* In 1966, Goldie and Lainie were complete babes—Lainie was in *Penthouse*. Beautiful women of all occupations were drawn to top organized-crime figures. There was the money sure—but there was danger, too. It's been known to get women worked up. Hawn, of course, went on to bigger and better things, first as a break-out star of the revolutionary TV show *Rowan and Martin's Laugh-In*, parlaying that fame into a movie career that won her an Oscar for her role in *Cactus Flower*. She has never commented on her experiences with Carmine. That would be indiscreet as he was and is a married man. Lainie Kazan went on to have a successful singing and acting career and returned to the limelight in the more recent past as the mom in *My Big Fat Greek Wedding*.

Carmine was in with the in crowd. He hung out in hip nightspots, like the dark and narrow Bachelor's III, the super-swinging joint owned in part by New York Jets quarterback, and future Super Bowl hero, Joe Namath. Carmine wasn't the only mobster who held court at Bachelors III. Police surveillance, both human and electronic, had determined that hoods were both hanging out and doing business in Joe's place. There was evidence of one meeting in the back in the dark that included thirteen "undesirables," eleven of whom were involved in the rackets. The connection between Broadway Joe and mob stuff dated back to 1966, not long after the Pennsylvania-born Namath graduated from the University of Alabama and came to New York to play for the Jets. As a rookie still wet behind the ears, Joe was alleged to have had meetings with gangsters about co-owning nightclubs in Manhattan. By 1969, the situation became so notorious that Pete Rozelle, the long-time Commissioner of Football, ordered Namath to give up his fifty percent share in the nightclub or face suspension. Namath showed nads of steel and told the commissioner to go fuck himself, and announced his retirement from football. It was the NFL that backed down. Namath eventually sold the bar but only after Jets coach Weeb Ewbank asked him to.

In Carmine's crew during the late 1960s was Sammy "The Bull" Gravano, who later switched to the Gambinos and became a well-known hit man. One day Carmine summoned Gravano and told him to give a beating to a Long Island washing-machine distributor who was having an affair with the wife of one of his brothers.

Carmine's parting words were, "Bring me back his ear!"

Gravano later said he didn't intend to cut off the man's ear, but while he was administering the beating with a blackjack he accidentally severed the guy's pinky finger, so he brought that back with him. Carmine was pleased. It was a gruesome act that reportedly earned "The Bull" kudos from Joe Colombo himself.

One of the primary reasons for the 1960s being great was the cops, who were often dirty. It wasn't until Frank Serpico's undercover work that the extent of NYPD corruption became known. One plainclothes unit in Brooklyn had to be entirely revamped when it was revealed that it, as an entity, was on the take. In 1969, the Knapp Commission was formed. Of course, there would always be dirty cops, but throwing on a light made the roaches scatter.

In 1968, Larry Gallo, my dad's good friend, the guy who bore the Mark of the Snake on his neck, died of natural causes. With Larry gone, Kid Blast had to step up, while Crazy Joey tried to run things from prison.

In 1969, Carmine was out on $15,000 bail regarding the ever-ongoing hijacking charges, and burning the candle at both ends. (Despite Carmine's legal nightmare when it came to his hijacking bust, hijacking continued to be popular, often in mixed family crews. On April 10, 1967, when a team—including Henry Hill of *Goodfellas* fame—stole almost a half-million dollars in Air France cargo, Colombo capo Buster Aloi received $50,000 in tribute, which he distributed appropriately.)

By the time Carmine Persico was in his mid-thirties, he had moved his family out of Brooklyn and, like many thousands of other Brooklynite businessmen, to the suburbs of Long Island. He lived on Sunset Drive in Hempstead, just off the Hempstead Turnpike, only a few miles east of the Belmont Park racetrack. It was a beautiful two-story home, with a finished attic and basement, and a sweet screened-in porch on one side. Step out the front door and you were looking at the Hempstead Golf and Country Club. Built in 1930, it was not a show-off house by any means. Not like those fortresses along Shore Road in Bay Ridge. This was home sweet home. Two and a half bathrooms.

His home-life conditions improved, but the rest of his life kept the same ol' scenery. His headquarters were at the Diplomat Social Club at the dingy corner of Carroll and Third Avenue, only a couple of blocks from where Steve Bove was murdered, just around the corner from Mush's club.

And he hung out with the same guys all the time, the guys he trusted. His crew. Humongous Hugh "Apples" McIntosh was always at Carmine's side. Gerry Lang was always there. Sonny Franzese's brother Carmine, maniac Greg Scarpa, and, when he got out of prison for the Steve Bove murder, Carmine's brother Alphonse.

Also hanging around was a stone-faced kid named Tony Sirico. He was a half-generation younger, born in the forties, and could be very scary when he wanted to be. He was arrested twenty-eight times while working in Carmine's crew—but it all ended up looking surprisingly good on his resumé when he was cast as Tony Stacks in the movie *Goodfellas*, and went on to play Paulie Walnuts on *The Sopranos*.

In 1970, Joe Colombo's son was busted by the feds on a conspiracy charge. Former Profaci underboss Sal Musacchio, one of the guys kidnapped by the Gallos, and capo Sebastian "Buster" Aloi were busted in Nassau County on Long Island for gambling. In response, Joe transformed his activist Italian-American Civil Rights League into an anti-FBI group. The initial group consisted of the Colombo family and about thirty friends, but it grew. For two months during the spring, the organization picketed FBI headquarters in New York every night. The harassment of the FBI was steady but weak. Colombo wanted to up the ante, so he planned a major event—the sort of thing that would bring him national, perhaps even global publicity—maybe initiate a congressional investigation.

On June 29, 1970, there was to be a massive rally at Columbus Circle at the southwest corner of Central Park in Manhattan. The IACR and its supporters were scheduled to march on FBI headquarters. Some of Colombo's activists prepared signs to be handed out that read: "More Power to Italians."

To appreciate what Colombo was doing you had to know the climate of the country, which was very protest oriented. Students were protesting the Vietnam War. Black people protested they weren't treated fairly. So Colombo decided to be hip. His complaint: Italians were being persecuted in this country. Our civil rights were being violated. Colombo shouted it for all to hear. Not everyone bought in.

Truth was, there were hoods who didn't like the scam. It wasn't becoming. Bad optics, they'd call it today. Some hoods, such as those on President Street, didn't want to go to the rally. We went.

The Gallo crew, and me a six-foot teenager. We were told it would be disrespectful to not be there.

Hoods were tepid at best when it came to the movement, Colombo's slogans resonated big-time with Italians in the legit world tired of being thought of as mobsters just because their names ended in a vowel. Everyone had their own take on Colombo's unusually bold form of hypocrisy.

It was called the Italian Pride Rally, and attendance surpassed Colombo's largest dreams. The crowd grew until it stopped traffic on the West Side. The entertainment was out of this world. Frank Sinatra and Sammy Davis Jr. rat-packed their way through a set. Jimmy Durante played piano and told jokes.

Colombo's tub thumpers said there were 650,000 people there. Cops said 40,000. My estimate was in between, about 100,000 people. More than five-hundred charter busses delivered Italians to the city, coming from as far away as Florida. Some of the piers were shut down because of absent longshoremen. In Italian neighborhoods, shops were closed. It was a holiday, a big party. At the rally, someone handed out little American and Italian flags, so everyone was waving something. The previous summer 300,000 kids gathered on a farm in upstate New York for three days of rock and roll and anti-Vietnam chanting, so the Columbus Circle rally was dubbed in the tabloids as "Italian Woodstock."

"Come on, FBI, stop harassing the Italians!" That was the rallying cry. A stream of speakers assailed the practice of equating Italians with criminals. Joe Colombo was in charge, of course, but the real *energy* behind the movement was his son Anthony, V.P. of the IACRL ad hoc committee. When Anthony took the podium, the band played "For He's a Jolly Good Fellow." *Goodfellas* wasn't yet a movie title back then, and only a few got the joke.

"Are we one? Are we united today?" Anthony asked. Most of the crowd cheered enthusiastically. But others did not. Carmine and other old-fashioned gangsters thought it was too much. To be facing prison and appeal for sympathy from those who weren't in the life was downright castrating.

Joe Sr. spoke last. At first disregarding the self-serving nature of the protest—after all, this entire event was about Joe's son not going to jail—the crowd gave Joe an enthusiastic hand. He told the gathering that he was just a real-estate salesman. Why should his family be subject to federal investigation?

Enthusiasm waned as Joe's hypocrisy went from implied to in-your-face. When festivities were over, only about one out of ten at the rally stayed for the march on FBI headquarters. Two cops on crowd control duty at FBI HQ were stabbed with ice picks, but there were no arrests. Both cops were taken to the hospital with non-life-threatening wounds.

Blowback was harsh. Some journalists weren't afraid to call Joe Colombo out. He was the boss of a crime family, after all, the very guy who most made all of those innocent Italian-Americans look bad. The FBI, the papers said, was not trying to persecute Italians, but was rather intent on getting killers off the streets.

Karma was instant. The day after the rally, Joe was arrested and indicted, along with twenty-four others, by Nassau County D.A. William Cahn and charged with criminal contempt for refusing to answer grand jury questions about organized crime. Colombo pleaded not guilty and paid his $5,000 bail. Predictably, the IACRL sent about one-hundred protesters out to the Long Island courthouse where Colombo's hearing took place. Signs referred to the D.A. as a "stoolie" for the FBI.

Colombo denied refusing to answer questions. If he seemed evasive it was because he wasn't feeling well and may not have communicated well. Cahn called Colombo the head of a "Mafia crime family." Colombo said Cahn was going to have to prove that.

"If there's anything we can do to help Mr. Cahn fight crime, we want to do it," Colombo said.

Carmine Persico must've felt like he was going to puke. Mr. Profaci had maintained that he was a legit businessman as well, olive oil, but he didn't go around rubbing people's noses in it. Some newspapers, astoundingly, printed Colombo's Dyker Heights, Brooklyn address.

A year later, as the anniversary of Italian Woodstock approached, Joe Colombo made plans to hold the second annual. But things had changed by then. I know the boys in the Gallo crew were told not to go to the 1971 Italian-American Civil Rights League rally, again to be held at Columbus Circle, because that would have been construed as showing support for Joe Colombo, which by this time the crew did not want to do. Support for Colombo had degraded from begrudging to non-existent. The crew had gone to the first one but didn't like it and left early. The League scored a major victory in November 1970 when they held a benefit at Madison Square Garden and Sinatra again showed up to sing. By this time though, it wasn't just the Gallo crew that wanted to steer clear of Colombo's party. Carlo Gambino ordered all of his people to stay away as well. So both the crowd and the energy level was down at Italian Woodstock II, June 28, 1971.

Colombo's activism had been interrupted as of late by African-American agitators. Guys from the ghetto, Nation of Islam guys with sharp black suits and skinny ties but no dough, were wondering out loud just what the fuck this millionaire was talking about. Colombo assumed the pushback from blacks was Joey Gallo's work. Crazy Joey was getting the brothers agitated. Colombo had heard that Joey had, counter-intuitively, gotten tight with some of the inmates from Bed-Stuy while in prison.

Now this Gallo crew doctrine—"don't go to the rally"—became very important, because things did not go well for Joe Colombo that day. As he was on his way to the podium to give his speech, a mini-skirted black woman with a large Angela-Davis-style afro flirtatiously said hey.

Colombo's face twisted languorously into a wolfish grin. The guy escorting the woman, a press-credentialed filmmaker toting an expensive camera—in actuality Harlem hustler Jerome Johnson—took advantage of a stationary target, pulled an automatic, and fired three shots into Joe Colombo's head.

Colombo's kid and a bodyguard wrestled Johnson to the ground, at which point another man stepped forward and shot Johnson to death. The second shooter escaped. His identity (as well as that of the flirtatious woman) remained forever unknown—officially, anyway.

Only moments after the shootings, a reporter found Colombo's son Anthony, who was already processing dad's shooting in an historical context: "It was a nut—the same kind of a nut who killed President Kennedy and Bobby Kennedy," Anthony said.

As police tried to secure the area, which had turned into a wild scene, people running and screaming and falling and being trampled upon, Colombo—blood pouring from his mouth down onto his shirt—was loaded onto a gurney and rushed by ambulance to Roosevelt Hospital where a team of three brain surgeons battled for hours to remove bullets and fragments from his gray matter.

Afterward, one surgeon said that Colombo remained close to death. He described a blood clot in Colombo's brain that had "burst like a boil" during the operation. Eventually, doctors said he was probably going to live, but Colombo was brain dead.

Back at Columbus Circle, there was a half-hearted attempt to continue the show, but just about everyone split after the shooting. Colombo didn't die, not technically, and not right away.

As Joey Gallo liked to say, "Colombo got *vegetabled*."

At the 54th Street police station, Kid Blast and Joey Gallo, who admittedly had a reputation for questioning authority, were among the first to be questioned by investigators.

Joey was adamant: "It was not me. Someone tried to make it look like it was me, but it was not!" Joey explained that he wasn't a major fan of Colombo's style, but his beef was with the previous administration. Investigators tended to believe him. But not everyone did. Joey made friends with black men in prison. Black guy bumped Colombo.

Some city authorities were avoiding the question of culpability by going to the Warren Commission playbook: Daniel P. Hollman of the NYC Joint Strike Force to Combat Organized Crime said he didn't think rival mob families were behind the shooting, that Jerome A. Johnson was (like Lee Harvey Oswald and Sirhan Sirhan, referenced by Anthony Colombo minutes after the shooting, before him) a lone nut, a psychopath, who acted alone for reasons unknown. Hollman said he'd studied Johnson's background and came to the conclusion that no one would ever have hired Johnson as a pro killer.

The NYPD didn't leap on the "lone nut" bandwagon. They knew better. Johnson might have been a psycho, Chief of Detectives Albert A. Seedman said, but that didn't mean someone didn't hire him.

Sal Polisi, an insider, has pondered the question. He's asked himself, who gained the most? And he thinks it was Carmine Persico and Carlo Gambino that had Colombo vegetabled. The boss didn't die until May 22, 1978. Polisi backed up his theory by pointing out that following the Colombo shooting, the Colombo and Gambino families displayed a downright cooperative relationship, including joint endeavors, which would have been out of the question when Joe Colombo was animate.

Of course, the Colombos were not known for their ability to read between the lines. They reacted spontaneously and blamed Joey Gallo and his crew. There was more violence on the hori-

zon, and again Carmine Persico moved up a wrung on the ladder
of power.

With the boss incapacitated, underboss Joseph Yacovelli and
Tommy DiBella technically took control of the Colombos—but
in reality the Persico family overwhelmed Yacovelli and DiBella
at that point. Yacovelli, it was noted by insiders, did not have a
crew of his own but had allied himself with Carmine Persico's
crew.

There was no insubordination involved. Yak was smart enough
to let Carmine do his thing.

Carmine would have been an almost automatic choice as the
new boss if it wasn't for the hijacking beef that wouldn't go
away. The boys didn't want a new boss who was going to go
away any day for a decade or more. Or did they? Maybe having a
boss in stir was workable.

In 1971, there were indications that Carmine, undeterred by
the tightening perimeter of justice around him, had upped the
earning ante, diversifying from the usual mob rackets into the
world of WASP white-collar crime. We know this because of
statements made that July by forty-year-old Edward H. Wuenesche, a government informant with immunity, testifying before
the Senate Investigations subcommittee. Wuenesche said that he
handled $50 million in stolen stocks and bonds, and was in-
volved with certain mobsters in the "counterfeit security racket."
He listed many names of mobsters he'd had dealings with, and
one of them was Carmine Persico Jr. Some of the fraudulent
transactions were made with the "Sheikdom of Kuwait." Now
that is the white-collar crime big time!

Yacovelli was a short stocky man with slicked-back black hair,
a bachelor, rare in mob circles, and known as an expert wine-
maker. He was hauled in front of a grand jury in September 1971

and asked questions about organized crime's influence on New York City's legitimate businesses. He refused to answer. Newspapers noted that, "like Carmine Persico," Yacovelli was moving up the Colombo ranks like a hit single, going from soldier to capo to consigliere in quick order. Yak was acting boss with Colombo in a coma.

The older men of the mob, the traditionalists, thought sixty-seven-year-old Frank Fusco, who had run gambling operations in Brooklyn forever would make an excellent choice to replace Colombo. But they were behind the times. The family was filled with strong and youthful up-and-comers. A sixty-seven-year-old man was not going to lead.

The other pretenders to the throne were Joe Colombo's kids, Anthony and Joe Jr., known as Jojo. They, as princes, thought they were destined to be kings. In the mid-1970s, FBI informant Joe Cantelupo, a Colombo guy, reported that Joe Colombo's sons had tried a coup but failed. The Colombo brothers had plenty of juice when the old man was in charge. Now, not so much. "The wheel is turned," Cantelupo said. "The Colombo boys are on the bottom and the Persicos are on top."

How big was Carmine Persico's domain? What was the scope of his power? Investigators wanted to know. Cantelupo said Carmine's wealth and influence was now tremendous, the scope broad. The Colombo crime family, with Carmine in charge, was taking protection money from every business in Bensonhurst, as well as other Brooklyn neighborhoods—a vast region. The protection racket worked, just as it had in the old days, with raw intimidation and terror.

"They put the fear into a guy and then they shake him down," Cantelupo explained.

And the government knew it.

So, even though Joe Yak was technically the acting boss, for all practical purposes, Carmine took charge of the Colombo family in 1972 at the youthful age of thirty-nine. The official switch probably occurred some time in 1973.

America's relationship with the mob, along with the mob's vision of itself, changed drastically in 1972 with the release of Francis Ford Coppola's masterpiece, *The Godfather*. That movie cast a deep spell over America and the world. It was a wildly romantic vision, and an incredible artistic achievement. Just maybe the greatest movie ever made. It presented the American Mafia the way people wanted it to be—hell, it presented the mob the way mobsters wanted it to be.

Everyone loved the movie, even though some of the inside guys said its notions were imaginative. "I can't see an American kissing another American's ring, no matter how Italian they are," one hood close to Carmine Persico commented, but added that the music was the best he'd ever heard.

On the impressionable, the movie had a startling effect. There was now a new crop of hoods and hood wannabes that dreamt one day of living *just* like those guys in the movie, but most of them never did. The film presented a world of familial dynasties in which bloodline was king—instead of money being king, which was the way it was in real life.

During production of *The Godfather* and after its release, there was interaction between the movie's players and real gangsters, like Carmine Persico. The actors were drooling to get some inside tips on playing real-life gangsters, and it was Carmine Persico who said if the Hollywood boys wanted to learn about the life, they were free to hang out with him and his crew. According to Eric Pooley, writing in *New York* magazine in 1992, Carmine was a "technical advisor" on the movie and had allowed the actors, James Caan in particular, to hang around with him to "soak up real mob color."

Coppola had no more than called "Action" for the first shot when Joseph Colombo himself and a small crew, one of them as big as a house, visited the set and told the director, along with producer Albert Ruddy, that the word "Mafia" was *not* to appear in the movie. *La Cosa Nostra* either.

"Why not?" Coppola asked.

"It is demeaning to Italians and Italian-Americans," Colombo said.

And so those words were deleted from the script, but . . .

"Okay," Coppola said. "But I want *him* in my picture."

The director pointed at the middle of the chest of the man-mountain standing over Colombo's shoulder. Colombo nodded and turned to leave.

"Lenny, talk to the man. He wants to make you a star," Colombo said, unaware that he'd never have a chance to see the picture.

The man was Lenny Montana and he played Luca Brasi in the movie. Truth was, Montana—all six-six, three-ninety of him—had some show-biz experience. In fact, Montana was a stage name of sorts. He'd been born Lenny Passofaro in Brooklyn in 1926. He'd been in the pro wrestling biz. Starting in 1953, he'd worked under many names: Lenny "The Bull" Montana, Chief Chickawicki, Zebra Kid, Mighty Sico. He once won the NWA World Tag Team belts with Hard Boiled Haggerty. Things went bad in 1960 when Montana broke a leg in a match against Verne Gagne. After that he went to work for Mr. Colombo. Not just as muscle, either. He was an innovative arsonist, too—used to tie kerosene-soaked tampons to the tails of mice, light 'em up, and release them into a structure.

So Hollywood and South Brooklyn broke bread. The relationship was not always a smooth one, mostly because Caan could be an asshole. He thought he was funny, but someone could've gotten hurt. After one uncomfortable interaction with Carmine, Gi-

The Red Hook section of Brooklyn
during the 1950s, where men had two
choices: work on the piers or go into
the life. The Gowanus Canal can be
seen cutting through left to right.
That's Governor's Island on the left,
Manhattan on the right, New Jersey
at the top. Drawn line indicates proposed
path of the Brooklyn-Battery Tunnel, the
entrance to which would further cut off
Red Hook from the rest of the borough.
(Brooklyn Eagle photograph,
Brooklyn Collection,
Brooklyn Public Library)

Fifth Avenue and Garfield Place,
Ground Zero for Carmine's first gang,
the Garfield Boys—and also the corner
where ill-fated jockey Albert Grillo used
a nightstick on a cop during the raid of a
friendly corner crap game. *(Author photo)*

When Carmine's mom was a
pregnant lady with a shiner,
she and Carmine's dad brawled
above this garage on Eighth Street,
on a block that's a mix of houses
and warehouses. By the time the kids
came, they'd moved to better digs.
(Author photo)

The Persico boys really were
better off than a lot of the street
hoods they hung out with.
Dad was a legal stenographer
and they lived in this beautiful
building on a different part of
Carroll Street, on a steep portion
of the aptly named Park Slope.
(Author photo)

The Prospect Park Boathouse, scene of the famous and deadly rumble between Carmine's Garfield Boys and their rivals, the Tigers. Since 1972, it has been listed on the National Register of Historic Places and in 1993 was the setting for a scene in a Martin Scorsese picture, *The Age of Innocence. (Author photo)*

James Fortunato represented the Tigers at the great Prospect Park rumble of 1950. When his crew and the Garfield Boys scattered, he was left behind, dying with two bullets in his belly.
(Brooklyn Eagle photograph, Brooklyn Collection, Brooklyn Public Library)

The morning following the Prospect Park rumble, the *Brooklyn Eagle* splashed the news across its front page in a type-size usually reserved for V-J Day or FDR's death.
(Brooklyn Eagle photograph, Brooklyn Collection, Brooklyn Public Library)

After Fortunato's death, cops sought to return to the fistfight era and called for the Garfields to turn in their weapons. Guys who were turning in their slingshots and clubs had probably just built a zip gun in shop class. *(Brooklyn Eagle photograph, Brooklyn Collection, Brooklyn Public Library)*

Carmine Persico at age seventeen, under arrest for the murder of Steve Bove,
and being questioned by Assistant District Attorney Louis Andreozzi.
(Brooklyn Eagle photograph, Brooklyn Collection, Brooklyn Public Library)

The Red Hook saloon where Steve Bove drank his last. *(Author photo)*

The gutter where Alphonse left Steve Bove's dead ass after shooting him repeatedly in the backseat of Albert Grillo's car. This is how it looks today. It didn't look any better back then. *(Author photo)*

In 1952, six guys running numbers for Frankie Shots' policy bank were rounded up and taken to the police precinct where they turned camera shy when a photographer from the press appeared. Carmine was caught peeking.
(Brooklyn Eagle photograph, Brooklyn Collection, Brooklyn Public Library)

On July 28, 1959, Carmine Persico and his crew hijacked a truck with $50,000 worth of piece goods in it, from this location, the Akers Motor Lines Terminal, hard against the Gowanus Canal. That hijacking would plague Carmine for the rest of his life.
(Author photo)

Giuseppe "Joe" Profaci, largest distributor of olive oil and tomato sauce in the U.S., and already a very rich man when he branched out into organized crime. It was Profaci who pulled Carmine out of Frankie Shots' crew before it was too late, Profaci who made Carmine.
(Brooklyn Eagle photograph, Brooklyn Collection, Brooklyn Public Library)

The Olive Oil King's mausoleum in St. John Cemetery, Queens. The woman with flowers in her hair holds a cross and a skull. *(Author photos)*

Carmine made his bones when he whacked this man, Albert Anastasia,
who was in a barber chair in a hotel shop. The hit was big because Anastasia was big,
controller of the waterfront and Lord High Executioner of Murder, Inc.
(Brooklyn Eagle photograph, Brooklyn Collection, Brooklyn Public Library)

Abbatemarco was buried in Holy Cross Cemetery in East Flatbush, Brooklyn.
His grave features a statue reminiscent of Michelangelo's *Pietà*.
The small print reads: "Blessed are the dead who die in the Lord." *(Author photo)*

Carmine's attempt on Larry Gallo's life was unsuccessful and Larry died of natural causes.
Brother Joey was not as lucky, and died in a hail of bullets.
Both are buried in Green-Wood cemetery. *(Author photo)*

In 1999, William Cutolo was called to a meeting with Allie Boy Persico at this spot, John Paul Jones Park in Brooklyn, commonly known around Fort Hamilton as Cannonball Park, for obvious reasons. Cutolo never returned home. *(Author photo)*

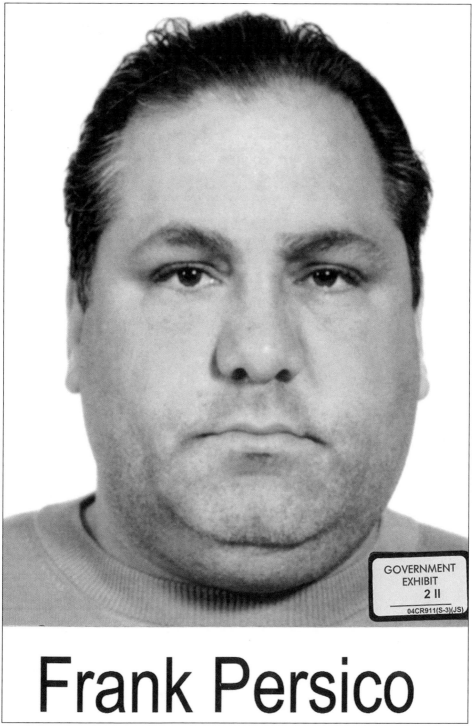

Frank Persico

Only days after Cutolo's disappearance, union pension administrator Kathleen Joseph refused to turn over the $50 million fund to the mobsters, earning her a personal visit from this man, cousin Frank Persico. *(Courtesy U.S. Attorney's Office, Eastern District of New York)*

GOVERNMENT
EXHIBIT
2C
04CR911(S-3)(JS)

Alphonse "Allie Boy" Persico

Carmine's son, Little Allie Boy. Just like his namesake uncle,
this Alphonse figures to die in prison.
(Courtesy U.S. Attorney's Office, Eastern District of New York)

Carmine "Junior" or "The Snake" Perisco

Carmine Persico will be remembered for the swath of destruction he left behind, a street kid who started out beating up children for their lunch money, and who carried that same "born to extort" manner into adulthood, where he accrued fantastic wealth and power but lost his freedom. *(Courtesy U.S. Attorney's Office, Eastern District of New York)*

This Green-Wood mausoleum holds the remains of Carmine's dad,
Carmine Persico, Sr. (1909–1976), his mother, Susan (1911–1989),
brothers Alphonse (1929–1989) and Theodore (1937–2017),
Carmine's mother-in-law, Gertrude "Lubilee" Smaldone (1911–2002),
and nephew Daniel (1962–2016).
One day it will hold the remains of Carmine Persico Jr.
(Author photo)

anni Russo—the actor who played Carlo Rizzi in the movie, the real-life godson of Frank Costello—came to hate Caan and could never again be in the same room with him. During the second week of filming, Rizzi said, sometime in the summer of 1971 before Carmine went away for hijacking but after the attempted assassination of Joe Colombo, cast members were having drinks at Jilly's, a west-side tavern known for being Frank Sinatra's favorite. Caan, ever the smug prankster, told Russo that Carmine Persico was in the back room with his daughter, that he should go back and pay his respects. So Russo went back to see Carmine, and sure enough there he was with a beautiful woman.

Russo said, "Your daughter is gorgeous. What a beautiful girl."

Carmine's face dropped.

It wasn't his daughter, it was a broad he was with, and Caan had purposely lied to Russo. Some of the boys at Carmine's table got up to teach this idiot a lesson, but Tommy Bilotti stepped in: "Honest mistake, honest mistake. The woman is beautiful."

So Russo didn't get a beating, but he has hated Caan's guts ever since.

Bilotti was best man at Russo's wedding, but his peace-keeping days ended on December 16, 1985, when he came down with a serious case of lead poisoning outside Sparks Steak House in the same hit that killed Big Paul Castellano.

Despite that one faux pas, Carmine and the film people got along. Caan and Andy Mush Russo became life-long friends. Carmine allowed Coppola access to genuine locations that lent the film supreme authenticity.

There are solid indications that Carmine shared some of his favorite stories with the Hollywood boys. In *The Godfather Part II*, which came out in 1974, there is a scene in which the character Pentangeli is being garroted in a dark and empty bar when the murder is interrupted by a cop on the beat—a clear reference to the attempted murder of Larry Gallo in the Sahara Lounge.

* * *

The feds didn't give up on Carmine just because he was facing serious hijacking time. They knew he was a killer and went after him harder than ever. On November 11, 1971, Carmine went on trial for thirty-seven counts of usury, coercion, extortion, and conspiracy. The charges, in a nutshell, were that Carmine had been running a loansharking business out of a Manhattan fur shop.

As was often true in cases with multi-indictments, there was a lot of repetition from charge to charge, and before the trial Judge Postel trimmed the indictment down to ten counts.

During the trial's first day, with the jury outside the courtroom, Justice George Postel of the New York State Supreme Court began to act strangely. By this time Carmine knew more than the average joe about courtroom machinations. There was something about the judge's tone, his mannerisms, his body language that made Carmine feel good inside. The judge, with just a touch of paranoid fervor, warned the reporters in attendance that they were to confine their accounts to the indictment and the testimony, and to eliminate any descriptions of the defendant's background, which might serve to bias the jury.

"I don't want anything in the papers that doesn't come out of this courtroom. If you repeat it tomorrow, you'll be in the can," His Honor exclaimed.

In particular, the judge objected to usage in print of Carmine's nickname "The Snake," mention of his designation by the feds as a member of organized crime, or the word "hijacking."

Judge Postel's pronouncements were in response to Carmine's defense attorney, Maurice Edelbaum, who'd asked for a mistrial based on news stories that ran in *The New York Times* and *Daily News* describing Carmine's past as a criminal and member of organized crime. The judge ceremoniously polled the jury, and each said they hadn't read the articles. Judge Postel denied the motion for a mistrial. For purposes of the record, Prosecutor Samuel A. Yasgur asked the judge upon which law he was basing his ruling. Judge Postel replied "Postel's Law," and informed the press of the new ground rules.

The incident caused the managing editor of the *Times*, A. M. Rosenthal, to issue a statement saying that the paper was sensitive to fair-trial issues, yet believed under the First Amendment that the decision as to what to print must rest with the newspaper "in accordance with responsible journalistic standards."

As the trial proceeded, and public interest grew, Carmine's notoriety approached superstar status. Judge Postel in response took further steps to prevent his courtroom from being contaminated by Persico fever.

Counsel on both sides were forbidden to make statements to the press. The court transcripts, legally the possession of the court stenographer, were by the judge's order sealed until the jury verdict was in.

He eventually barred the public and newsmen from the trial. Five reporters—Richard Oliver of the *Daily News*, David Burnham of the *Times*, Jack Robbins of the *Post*, Howard Rieser of the *Long Island Press*, and Edward McCarthy from UPI—tried to sit in the courtroom in defiance of the ruling, and the judge promptly had them removed. Reporters and photographers began peeking through the windows in the courtroom's outer doors so Judge Postel had green blotters placed over the windows. The public trial would go on in essence privately.

That privacy was most controversial. The Sixth Amendment provides that a defendant shall have the right to a public trial. The counter to this was that, although this might be true, the removal of the public and press was done because of complaints by the defendant and his defense team that he could only get a fair shake if the trial was held in private, so Carmine Persico had in essence waived his right to a public trial. To this, members of the press argued that the right to a public trial was not at the discretion of the accused alone. The right of the people to know was also to be considered. A public trial is necessary in all cases, the press argued, because a trial held "in camera," that is outside the public's view, always, justifiably or not, gave rise to suspicions that the proceedings weren't on the up and up. The press, after all, was not at trials just to inform the public but also as a guard against miscarriages of justice. It was that role that was being denied by Judge Postel.

All of the fuss about who was and wasn't supposed to be in the courtroom proved to be beside the point. The defense really had nothing to worry about as the prosecution's case fell apart regardless of the fact that no one was watching.

First of all, one of the prosecution's witnesses vanished just before he was supposed to take the stand. This, purposefully or not, served as a message to the others scheduled to testify against Carmine.

The prosecution's key witness, Mrs. Sylvia Winograd, was supposed to implicate Carmine in a loansharking operation. Although she endured six grueling days on the stand, she somehow failed to ever incriminate Carmine Persico.

Judge Postel overruled prosecution objections and promised Winograd that, in exchange for her truthful testimony, not only would her guilty plea for loansharking be wiped out, but her amnesty would include a guilty plea in another case involving possession of stolen furs. Mrs. Winograd and her husband Joseph owned a fur shop and had pleaded guilty to thirty-seven counts of possession of stolen goods. They were scheduled to be sentenced in December.

Before Mrs. Winograd's testimony, prosecutor Yasgur asked that she be considered a hostile witness, a designation that allowed the prosecutor to ask leading questions. The judge refused to do so, but finally relented several days into Mrs. Winograd's testimony.

During her testimony, Mrs. Winograd said that she had known the defendant for seven to ten years. She and her husband knew him as "Junior." Yasgur played for the jury a recording of a 1968 wiretap, a phone conversation between Mrs. Winograd and Samuel Lessner, a fourth defendant in this case that had disappeared. Mrs. Winograd admitted that it sounded very much like her voice on the tape. She admitted that Lessner worked with her in a loan-shark operation. She said that Lessner had been missing since April 30, 1969, last seen getting into a car with one of Carmine's crew.

On the tape Lessner, who Winograd accused of stealing $30,000, was fearful for his life. Mrs. Winograd assured him that he had nothing to fear from either her or The Kid, an apparent reference to Carmine.

Yasgur asked the witness: "When you say Lessner stole $30,000 from you, you meant that he stole it from your business, a business that Mr. Persico has an interest in, correct?"

"No."

"Mrs. Winograd, during the course of the conversation did you not tell Mr. Lessner that Mr. Persico, in your language, 'feels like a jerkoff' if you could do this to him and he'd do nothing about it?"

"Yes, I said that."

"Now, when you said that, 'if you could do this to him' in the context of the conversation, isn't it a fact that you were referring to what Lessner had done when he had stolen the $30,000?"

"He stole that money from me."

"Mrs. Winograd, what I'm asking you is, in the context of the conversation, when you said that to Lessner, 'if you could do this,' isn't it quite clear that you were referring to the fact that Lessner had stolen the $30,000 from the money-lending business?"

"I was talking in the heat of anger, I don't know exactly what I meant."

"Did you ever discuss your business with Mr. Persico?"

"No, never."

"Have you ever discussed with Carmine Persico the fact that Lessner has, as you previously testified, stolen money from you or the lending business?"

"Absolutely not . . . I think I told Mr. Persico that Mr. Lessner had robbed me but not from my money-lending business."

"Did Mr. Persico ever warn Lessner to stay out of the fur market?"

"No, that was a figment of Mr. Lessner's imagination."

And on and on it went. Not just with this witness, but with all of the other prosecution witnesses as well. No one could testify that Carmine did anything illegal ever. So it came as no surprise that, on December 8, 1971, the jury found Carmine not guilty on all charges.

When Judge Postel first prohibited the press and public from the courtroom, Carmine's defense team filed suit. The courts being the way they were, by the time a court got around to looking at the suit, Carmine's trial was over. In January 1972, the Court of Appeals briefly considered Carmine's request for a retrial, but he was acquitted so no new trial was necessary.

The subject didn't go away completely however, as legal efforts were made to prevent Judge Postel's rulings from happening again. In March the seven-man New York State Supreme Court unanimously decided that Judge Postel had been wrong when he closed Carmine's trial to the press and the public. Right to a public trial meant just what it said. However, again because of Carmine's acquittal, the Supreme Court dismissed a lawsuit brought by the five reporters who'd been kicked out of the courtroom. The dismissal was not because the reporter's claims were without merit, but because the trial was long over and "the relief requested now served no purpose."

In his decision, Chief Judge Stanley Fuld explained that it was up to the judge to prove there was an imminent threat to the integrity of the trial before taking action to limit the First Amendment's guarantees, and Judge Postel had not done that. You don't bar the press, Fuld wrote, you sequester the jury.

The 1959 hijacking still hung increasingly heavy around Carmine Persico's neck, a bloated and blindfolded albatross. When Carmine was first in the case years before he'd been offered a deal: plead guilty, do three years, parole in one.

Instead, Carmine fought and fought and fought, good news for the lawyers he hired but not so great for him. He was eventually sentenced to fourteen years. As he listened to the judge, his first thought was of how much he'd changed, grown, since the crime was committed. At the hijacking he'd been a dour-faced street punk. Now he was a dapper and wealthy man. He'd played cards with billionaires and fucked movie stars.

He'd been offered three, got fourteen. Was it a blunder? Best bet is that he felt he'd done the right thing. It was worth it just to tell those federal fucks to go fuck themselves.

"Mushy, you and Tommy are boss while I'm gone," Carmine said to his cousin Andy Russo, referring to Thomas DiBella.

According to sources close to Carmine, he ran the Colombo family from behind bars, using his brothers Alphonse, Teddy Boy, and Hugh McIntosh as messengers to Mush. As boss, Carmine demonstrated a new level of cooperation with the Gambino family, making himself indispensable to the Boss of Bosses.

Just as Carmine was going into prison, Joey Gallo was getting out. Crazy Joey was angry and suffering from a genuine personality disorder. He just wanted to kill everybody.

Once again war was in the wind. Tensions grew between the family—now known as the Colombos—and that old thorn in their ass, the President Street Boys. Carmine, as he adjusted to prison life, came to understand that there could be no peace on the outside until the Gallos were dead.

On April 7, 1972, "Crazy" Joey Gallo was killed at Umberto's Clam House. Because my dad worked with Joey and the guys who were supposed to guard Joey, I learned a lot of inside dope on what went down that night, and still none of it makes much sense.

Earlier in the year we'd noticed that Joey wasn't on the block as much as the old days. We'd still see him once or twice a week, but that was it. He'd moved on. He had a new wife and a new life in the city. He had to know he was a target, yet he'd walk around without protection.

He thought the Colombos were too chickenshit to shoot him. Kid Blast tried to convince Joey that being careful out there wasn't a sign of weakness, it was a sign of wisdom. Joey heard him and didn't hear him. He had my Godfather Bobby Darrow and Pete "The Greek" Diapoulis watching his back, and he said that was enough for him. But it wasn't. Once the bullets started flying, Bobby and Pete did him no good at all. Bobby had met a girl that night and Joey sent him off with her to have fun. Pete was a guy no one liked because he was all muscle and no brain, but he'd been a pretty good bodyguard, up there until the very end. Joey got shot dead and Pete the Greek got shot in the ass. According to the stories we heard, the hit was ordered somewhat spontaneously. A guy named Joe Lupacelli spotted Joey and his family coming into Umberto's, and quietly slipped a dime into a nearby payphone. He called Yak. Yak said he'd take care of it.

Pete the Greek maintained his innocence with a desperate fervor right from the start, but was eyed suspiciously from then on.

That same weekend when Joey was whacked, one of the New York dailies ran an "expose" on the Colombo family. It said that Carmine was in charge, but that Joey's death was not a Colombo hit. Not that hitting Joey in retaliation for the vegetablization of Joe Colombo didn't occur to Carmine. He must've wanted Joey dead very badly, but he reportedly decided against it because he didn't want it to interfere with one of his perpetual upcoming court appeals—another refrain that would follow Carmine from cell to cell. (If this story was true, Yak apparently didn't consider Carmine's plight when he decided Joey Gallo had to go, knowing well that Carmine would not be heartbroken by the news.)

On April 7, 1972, the same day Joey Gallo was murdered, Gennaro Ciprio, a Brooklyn restaurateur, was shot to death by a rooftop sniper as he exited his place onto the sidewalk. (This sounds like the same Persico sniper who later took out a couple of Gallo guys on President Street, shootings to which, as you'll see, I had an uncomfortable proximity.) We don't know if Joey Gallo and Ciprio were friends, but interestingly, Ciprio was rumored to have been the guy at Columbus Circle that killed Colombo's shooter and disappeared. Officially, the case of the shooter of the shooter was wide open, without suspects. So many had a motive, apparently, that it was hard to narrow it down.

Police investigators learned that, since Joey's death, members of the Persico crew had been hiding out in Upstate New York in the town of Saugerties. There, Carmine had an impressive compound where it was cool and quiet in the summer, a nine-bedroom villa built on fifty-nine acres of land. The farm was called the Blue Mountain Manor Horse Farm. It was Carmine's even though, for tax purposes, the on-paper ownership shuffled around, at one time technically belonging to Donnie Shacks.

Watching the farm from afar with really good binoculars, investigators could see that the men at the farm always carried long arms, either shotguns or rifles, whenever they went outside. Seventeen days after Joey's death, Allie Boy (just now entering the scene after spending two decades away for the murder of Stephen

Bove), Gerry Lang, and Colombo-captain Charles Panarella and his girlfriend, twenty-three-year-old April Ballanger, were arrested as they drove away from Carmine's farm. Feds had the impression plans were—again—being made to eliminate the Gallo crew. Not that they could charge them with that. Not yet. What they did was charge Alphonse with "making a false statement in application for a bank loan." Lang was charged with possession of fireworks. Panarella and his *goomada* were charged with state weapons violations.

Agents from the FBI, and the Treasury Department, as well as state policemen, raided the farm a second time on August 12, 1972. Only Allie Boy and his family and brother Teddy were home. Allie Boy was picked up on a previous arrest warrant. This was a disappointment as agents were seeking Joe Yak and Carmine DiBiase in connection with the Joey Gallo hit, and had hoped they were in Saugerties.

DiBiase, a.k.a. Sonny Pinto, was a bad drinker. Pete the Greek from the Gallo crew said of him, "He was no big earner or mover. Sober, he was nothing, but drunk he'd blow your head off."

In December, DiBiase was indicted by a Manhattan grand jury for Joey's murder. DiBiase promptly disappeared and was never seen again. Best bet is that, sooner or later, he was victim to the White Death.

It was one thing to be a target, another to be a target and everyone knows it. A couple of weeks after Joey Gallo was killed, the Associated Press released a story to newspapers everywhere that Kid Blast and the remaining members of the Gallo crew were next on the Colombo family's hit list. The papers said the Gallo upper rank was "marked for assassination." The deposition said that the Colombos had thus far been responsible for two Gallo losses, Joey Gallo and Gennaro Ciprio. The source was an FBI nameless informant with "known reliability." The information went public when it was included in a Kingston, New York, State

Supreme Court deposition in application for a search warrant for Carmine Persico's farm.

A confessed participant in Joey's killing, Joseph Luparelli, turned himself in to the FBI because he thought his accomplice was going to rat on him. He told the FBI, contrary to what un-named sources were telling the New York newspapers, that Yak ordered the Joey hit. He said that he'd been in Umberto's when Joey came in, and quickly ran to a nearby restaurant to inform four members of the Colombo Family.

Joey was buried in Green-Wood Cemetery not far from the grave of Albert Anastasia. At the funeral Joey's sister screamed, "The streets are going to run red with blood, Joey!"

Despite denials in the papers—which sounded like they might've come from Carmine directly, or someone close to Carmine—the Colombo family had another Civil War on its hands, Persico vs. Gallo—a grudge match!

This time, there was still a riches gap, with Carmine's crew having far more assets than the Gallos, but in terms of manpower the numbers were surprisingly close: one hundred eighteen Colombo men compared to ninety-eight Gallos, according to *The New York Times* anyway. (I would've put the number at around fifty. I don't know who did the counting. Reporters, I guess. Maybe it was the Pizza Squad, the cops who needed to file some-thing after a day's surveillance at the end of President Street.) Those numbers, it said in the paper, were evened out by the fact that more of the Gallo men were combat-ready, veterans of the Profaci war. Profaci's men were replaced, many of them, by Colombo guys that had never been to war.

When Carmine finally went into a federal pen for hijacking, Hugh McIntosh made frequent trips down to Atlanta to visit him. The FBI monitored McIntosh's visits but gathered no evidence that their conversations involved Colombo business.

Now that Colombo was out of commission, would the Profaci

guys who'd had to step aside when the olive oil king passed away be allowed to return, guys like Harry Fontana, John Oddo, and Sal Mussachio? Best guess was that who was in and who was out was entirely up to Carmine. Importantly, there had also been an upheaval at the top of the Gallo family since the last war. Larry died in 1968. Joey got whacked, and Blast was in charge, smartest of the brothers, sure, but not an aggressive man by nature.

Time magazine, among other media outlets, followed the Persico/Gallo wars closely, and used "inside" sources, never named, to prognosticate future casualties. Blast and Punchy were said to be on the Snake's hitlist. On the Gallos' list was Allie Boy and Yak. The Gallos were also looking to bump off their old buddy Nick Biano, who had a big mouth.

While Carmine and his buttons holed up in an apartment building on Fifth Avenue in Brooklyn, once again chicken wire had been put over the windows of the President Street social clubs, and the boys were hitting the mattresses in the basement, some of them right where the lion used to be caged.

The two sides approached the war in purely military terms. Their outposts were well-guarded. They had scouts and spies that went on reconnaissance missions into enemy territory. And of course, they had guns that went out to plug any enemy soldier with his ass exposed.

One set of piers not controlled by the five families was on the west side of Manhattan. On that waterfront, it was Irish mob all the way—the Westies, in particular. I heard that the Westies were supposed to be even deadlier than their Italian counterparts— dishing up big plates of corned beef and carnage. The Westies were the Lords of Hell's Kitchen, a neighborhood that no longer exists, that then consisted of rotting tenements, shadowy rat runs, and elevated trains, and is now a sun-drenched and gentrified community called Clinton.

The Westies' leader during the bad old days was a guy named Mickey Featherstone, who lied his way into the Green Berets and fought in Vietnam. He came home, but continued to wage war, now as a soldier-of-fortune nicknamed "Jungle Killer," a broken-sidewalk mercenary.

Each hit created a power vacuum, one that the Westies would promptly fill. Featherstone once walked into a west side bar and sprayed the joint with machine-gun fire. The Westies looked at the battle for the streets of South Brooklyn as a money-making opportunity, and earned big by hiring out their services to *both sides*.

And this gang-for-hire arrangement was nothing new. The Westies had been carrying out hits for Carlo Gambino for years in exchange for money and power considerations. Featherstone was convicted in 1979 of counterfeiting, and in 1986 of murder.

On Friday, August 11, 1972, Carmine was seven months into his hijacking sentence and word was out that brother Alphonse, along with bodyguards Gerry Lang and Hugh MacIntosh were going to be in a meeting at the Neapolitan Noodle, a small restaurant on East 79th Street in the city. At the meeting, those men were joined by Ernest LaPonzina and Joseph Gentile, who that spring had allegedly attempted to bribe an IRS agent with $4,000 and free golf lessons. The men had gathered to discuss a possible expansion of Colombo rackets.

Special for the occasion, an outside hitman named Ted was imported from Las Vegas to kill them all, right there in the eatery. According to an FBI report, Little Allie Boy, Carmine's teenaged son Alphonse, was also there but his name was withheld by the police because of his age.

Ted might have been technically a professional, but he didn't act that way. There were a couple of issues. For one thing, Ted didn't exactly blend. He was a stocky guy wearing shades (at 9:30 P.M.), and a wig of long black straight hair hanging down his back. Every other guy in the joint was wearing a tie. Not Ted. He sat down at the bar on the end stool, placed a ten-dollar bill on the bar and ordered a scotch.

Ted also entered the bar having *no idea* what his targets looked like. So a kid from the crew had been added to the op. His *only job* was to point out for Ted where Allie Boy and the others were sitting.

Trouble began when, after the kid pointed out the targets, they moved, quietly exiting the bar area and switching to a table to eat. Result: Ted set his drink down, pulled two pistols and fired nine shots. He hit four kosher meat wholesalers—total innocents. Two of them died.

Mistakes like that were *very* bad for business. But they did, nonetheless, intimidate the opposition. Some say it was the shooting in the Noodle that convinced Joe Yak to leave town and leave Carmine Persico officially in charge of the Colombos.

Because Carlo Gambino was the most famous of the city bosses, he took the brunt of the bad publicity. New York City Mayor John Lindsay ordered the NYPD, thirty thousand strong, to drive the hoodlums into the sea. He said the shootings were an "outrage which demands the romanticization of the mob must be stopped."

No strategy was offered. The violence, authorities opined, was the result of a booming narcotics market, and an influx of impatient and hot-blooded buttonmen unwilling to let natural causes take out the mob's elderly dons.

The Saturday after the Noodle, Big Allie Boy, a man who had spent his twenties and thirties in prison and was just now adjusting to freedom, was arrested for unlawfully receiving firearms in interstate commerce. One goddamn rifle. By Tuesday he was in U.S. District Court in Foley Square in Manhattan, pleading not guilty. The head of the fed strike force against organized crime, Edward M. Shaw, asked that bail be set high.

"Alphonse Persico, as of late," Shaw told Judge Arnold Bauman, "has been avoiding his usual hangouts and seldom goes home."

Allie Boy was defended at the hearing by the very pregnant Nancy Rosner, who argued that the police version of events was under question and Allie Boy should be allowed to remain free "in his own recognizance."

Judge Bauman and the prosecution both alluded to the fact that there'd been a recent attempt on Allie Boy's life and perhaps he was safer in jail.

Rosner would have none of that. She said that there had been *no attempt* on her client's life. The mere fact that Allie Boy was in a restaurant during a shooting did *not* mean he was involved in any way. To believe that Alphonse was a target in the shooting, one had to believe in a gunman three-quarters blind. Rosner found it hard to believe that Allie Boy—tall, nattily dressed, black hair slicked back—could be mistaken for a middle-aged butcher.

Allie Boy was released on $100,000 bail and posted bond through the Public Service Mutual Insurance Company of New York.

Later that year, *The New York Times* published yet another mob story based on "inside info." It said Carlo Gambino was plotting to reduce the number of families in New York from five eventually down to one, with himself as the lone boss of New York City mob business. That notion must have put a damper on the bromance between Gambino and Carmine Persico. Further indication that the two families no longer had a cooperative relationship came when the Gambinos openly tried to recruit men they admired to jump ship and join them. As always, Gambino was firm that anyone who spoke out of turn—or sold drugs—was going to be thoroughly ventilated.

In Red Hook, snipers were climbing to the rooftops and taking shots at members of the Gallo crew down on President Street. This is an important part of the story for me, just eighteen at the time, because twice I was standing out on the sidewalk when friends of my dad's and mine were gunned down.

On September 2, 1974, I was on the sidewalk on President Street and Louie "The Syrian" Hubela was shot. Louie was a gunman who owned a joint on Atlantic Avenue where you could gamble or borrow money. I had turned my back to him for a second, heard the shot, and turned back to see him on the ground bleeding from the head. He was taken to Long Island College Hospital and reported in poor condition.

Nine days later I was standing at the corner of President and Columbia Streets when Punchy Illiano was shot in the neck and shoulder as he was buying a hot dog from the hot-dog guy on the corner.

Louie the Syrian and Punchy were both in the hospital for more than a month. Punchy was never the same, suffered nerve damage that would affect him for the rest of his life. He died in 2014 after a long illness.

One of the ugliest incidents in Colombo family history came in 1974 when underboss Sonny Franzese discovered that a Colombo soldier named Carmine Scialo was nailing his wife. Scialo was found under a cellar with his severed cock and balls stuffed in his mouth.

Allie Boy was back in trouble in 1974. He was subpoenaed to appear before a federal grand jury (Eastern District of New York) investigating the effects of racketeering on legitimate businesses. Racketeering in this case being defined as patterns of criminal activity that cannot be perpetrated profitably by small criminal systems. Only a few years had passed since J. Edgar Hoover's death, and the feds were just starting their 1970s publicity campaign about the dangers of the mob and how crushing organized crime needed to be prioritized. They said that the mob ran all but a pittance of the nation's illegal gambling, that they were the principal importers of narcotics. They had monopolies in seemingly legitimate businesses, such as coin-operated machines like juke boxes and cigarette machines. And the mob controlled the government far more than the government wanted to admit. They had guys in their hip pocket at all levels, in the legislative, executive, and judicial branches of government—local, state, and federal. There was a need to have new legislation to plug in the loopholes in the mob's system. Mob bosses were difficult to prosecute because there was always a couple of strata between the guy who ordered the crime and the guy who did the dirty work. Up till then, the feds had had the most success nabbing hoodlums because they had extravagant lifestyles but didn't like to pay their taxes. What was needed was a law that made it illegal to be part of an organization that committed crimes. (Of course they were describing what would become known as RICO.) They decided to have a hearing, gather intelligence on how the mob was making life harder for the average joe.

Allie Boy waived his rights regarding self-incrimination, was given "testimonial immunity," and agreed to testify in the Cadman Plaza courthouse.

Robert Del Grosso asked the questions. He was a former Marine who earned both a Purple Heart in Vietnam and a law degree at Fordham. Del Grosso identified himself to the court as a "Special Attorney of the Organized Crime Section of the Justice Department's Criminal Division, appearing on behalf of the U.S. Attorney."

Del Grosso asked, "Mr. Persico, do you run a gambling business?"

"Sure."

"In what sort of gambling do you deal?"

"Horses. Sports. Numbers."

But that was as far as he was willing to go. Allie Boy refused to identify any employees in his business. They asked him about specific conversations he'd had with those employees.

During this exchange the witness learned more than the questioner. Allie Boy realized by the way the questions were worded that there had been a bug, either at a location or on a person, so he said, "I refuse to answer on account of illegal electronic surveillance."

The court ruled that that wasn't an adequate excuse and ordered Allie Boy to answer the questions. But Allie Boy still refused. The judge found Allie Boy in contempt and ordered him to sixty days in the custody of the marshal.

Allie Boy served his sixty days stoically—if there was one thing he knew how to do, it was time—and when he walked out free he rolled his eyes as he was instantly subpoenaed again to appear before the same grand jury.

The whole process was repeated, Allie Boy again clamming up when it came to his employees. This time, with a couple of months to plot, Allie Boy and his attorney had a new excuse. Alphonse was refusing to answer because he didn't think Del Grosso had the right to ask him questions at all, due to Del Grosso's convoluted association with the U.S. Attorney's office. That excuse didn't fly either. But hearings were held to justify Del Grosso as Allie Boy's questioner, and while that was going on, it was realized that Allie Boy was never going to talk about the employees in his illegal gambling operation, and he was allowed to get off the legal merry-go-round.

By the mid- to late-1970s the Gallos were through as their own entity. What was left had its own war—a Civil War within a Civil War—of Blast versus not-Blast guys.

Blast in the meantime started talking to the Chin, turned Genovese, and our gang in Red Hook dispersed. The Colombos and Gallos had been at war off and on for a quarter of a century, and finally, with the break-up of the President Street crew, that conflict ended.

On October 15, 1976, Carlo Gambino died, and the effect on the New York mob scene was dramatic. Few new buttons had been given out during Gambino's time in power, and now that he was gone new members were once again being inducted into his family. Gambino stopped recruitment of made men because Albert Anastasia had been selling buttons. Sure enough, it wasn't long after Gambino's death that the practice of selling buttons resumed.

The initiation to get into the Colombo family included a watered-down version of making one's bones, which now meant you either had to commit or participate in a murder. If you think the word "participate" smacks of a downgrade in balls, you're not alone. That meant that the queasier guys could make their bones as innocuously as digging a grave that a body would later be dumped into. Not the same.

On the morning of December 11, 1978, as Carmine served the last few months in prison, almost $6 million was stolen in cash and jewelry from the Lufthansa Terminal, Building 261, at JFK Airport in Queens—the biggest cash robbery in U.S. history, and the subject of many books and movies.

One of the guys that cops suspected of being involved in the heist was thirty-seven-year-old Angelo "Angie" Sepe, known as a Lucchese guy. He became a suspect when FBI informants overheard him talking about the heist, so they slapped a tail on him, and followed him as he distributed the alleged tribute money from the robbery. One stop was the social club of Carmine's brother Alphonse, where Sepe gave Allie Boy an envelope containing an estimated $20,000. Sepe then drove upstate to Saugerties and presented a second envelope to Carmine's wife.

Agents bugged Sepe's car but were foiled when Sepe always had conversations in his car with the radio blasting.

Like many involved in the Lufthansa heist, Sepe didn't have long to live. He and his eighteen-year-old girlfriend were found shot to death in his Bensonhurst apartment on July 18, 1984.

CHAPTER NINE

From Behind Bars

*All he ever wanted to do was have his own gang, and now he
did. And what a gang: one of the five families, the mighty
Colombos. But the joy was soon tainted by arrests and court
hassles. Bombs couldn't stop Carmine. Bullets couldn't stop
him. Only law enforcement had an effect. The government did
what the Gallos couldn't. They took Junior off the streets.*

THE GOVERNMENT DID NOT LET UP on Carmine. They believed him
to be not just a mass murderer but a guy who remained leader of
the gang despite being in prison a great deal. There was tape-
recorded evidence to support this.

The tapes were recorded in January and early February 1978.
Carmine was the subject of a recorded conversation between his
dear old friend, Hugh McIntosh, and a guy named Richard Annicharico, who was a tax agent "posing" as corrupt, willing to
pull some strings that might help Carmine in exchange for information and cooperation. (This and other recordings discussed
here were secret until 1985, when Carmine was a defendant in the
so-called "Colombo case" and the tape recordings went public
when they were played for the jury. See Chapter Ten.) Annicharico was on to Carmine Persico with this particular play
because he'd previously learned of the Colombo family's willingness to pay bribes. All he had to do was put it in the wind that
Get Out of Jail Free cards could be purchased.

The tapes were made at Junior's Restaurant on Flatbush Avenue. Carmine at that time had been away for years but the conversation's tone made it clear that Carmine remained, even
behind bars, a very powerful figure—one who held true to his

oaths. Bribes were being paid so that Carmine could be transferred from a prison in Atlanta to one in New York, where he
could more easily operate his outside business.

Two things McIntosh got across on that tape. One: his friend
Carmine would rather remain behind bars for the rest of his life
than be labeled an informer. Two: Mr. Persico did not engage in
drug trafficking. Period.

"Not now?"

"Not never. He never had nothing to do with junk. You know
his record. Anything else but junk. If you have a plan to get him
out of prison early, do not mark him [as an informant]."

"Yeah. Yeah, okay."

"That's very important, see? Because the guy will rather go to
jail and do whatever time he's got left to do." It was, in fact, the
crux of the man.

Other subjects were discussed on the tape, a few tax evasion
investigations needed quashing—Mush Russo wasn't known for
his accurate accounting—and on that subject the families stood
as one, cut out the tax bullshit.

But the great bulk of the conversation was strategizing to get
Carmine's transfer to the New York jail to be permanent and
thinking of a way to gain Carmine's freedom ahead of schedule,
which currently had him eligible for parole in late 1979, still almost two years away.

According to Annicharico, the offer was $200,000 to move up
the parole date, as they put it, to "fix his release." The "do not
mark him" comment was in response to Annicharico's suggestion
that Carmine deal for his release by telling the feds what they
wanted to hear. The plan was for Carmine to come forth and say
that he had information regarding the killing of Vincent Papa in
the Atlanta prison where he lived. That would prevent him from
being sent back. Carmine nixed it without consideration. He didn't
give names to feds, true or not, and he didn't want *nothing* to do
with drug dealers.

On a January 18, 1978, recording, Carmine was on furlough in a meeting with Annicharico and Joel Cohen, a prosecutor who knew of Annicharico's undercover role. Carmine gave an example of his eloquence on this tape. He said he was *tired* of being Carmine Persico. Sure, he did some stuff when he was a kid, he was a tough guy, but that was a long time ago. Ancient history. It was all different now. He was a businessman, and it was hard when everyone assumed you were calling the shots all the time.

Carmine explained that his reputation led to the government picking on him, that he was going to end up in prison for life whether or not he ever committed another crime, just because he was Carmine Persico, *the* Carmine Persico, and they wanted him caged.

He'd had enough trouble since 1959 and that hijacking that went really really bad, enough for a lifetime. Carmine felt it was time he caught a break, and Joel Cohen said he was a "believer" in Persico's cause.

Annicharico later recalled that the meeting took place in Cohen's office, and the purpose of the meeting was to come up with some excuse to keep Carmine out of his penitentiary home and in New York City for another month or so, which was what Carmine wanted. Annicharico said that he communicated to Carmine Persico through Victor Puglisi, a Long Island restaurateur and alleged conduit for Colombo family payoffs.

Carmine said he knew nothing about the Papa killing in Atlanta. Maybe some rumor he'd heard around, he caught wind of things through the prison grapevine like any other inmate, but nothing you'd call *evidence*. Whatever Carmine might have known or not known about Papa would remain a mystery as he wasn't about to give these guys—cops—that kind of information.

On a tape recording made January 24, 1978, again at Junior's Restaurant, there is a conversation between Annicharico, and Victor Puglisi. Puglisi showed Annicharico a bag filled with currency. The bag was on the floor. Puglisi said, "That's $100,000—deposit on two-fifty."

"What a character," Annicharico said to Puglisi. He looked in the bag. "I don't want to count it. Take me three years to count."

The next tape was made the following day, again Annicharico and Puglisi at Junior's.

"I hope you have the money in a safe place," Annicharico said.

"Don't worry about it," Puglisi replied. "I got it hidden at my cousin's house. Have faith in me, brother."

On that same tape, Puglisi was heard acknowledging that he was passing $7,000 to Annicharico, and in return expected a fix in Mush Russo's pesky tax investigations.

Annicharico would later claim he was only pretending to be corrupt on those tapes. He had decided "sort of on my own" to go undercover, and did not inform his supervisors regarding his deception. He had accepted many thousands of dollars from Puglisi. Annicharico said that, in return, he had arranged for Carmine to be temporarily transferred on two occasions from a penitentiary in Atlanta to one in New York where it was easier for him to meet with friends, relatives, and lawyers. Carmine was a busy guy, and the visits to New York greatly cut the cost of meetings.

In 1978, Michael Franzese, the legendary Sonny's son, came up with a lucrative plan. Bootleg gasoline. He told Carmine Persico, "I will show you more money than you've ever seen." Michael Franzese eventually left the life. While producing a movie in 1985, he met a beautiful dancer named Camille Garcia, fell in love, and changed his ways. Today he is a legit motivator who speaks to at-risk kids and church groups. He is, he says, the only high-ranking mob figure to walk away without a new identity and survive. Good for him.

In 1979, Carmine was granted parole and released from prison, having served almost eight of the fourteen years in his hijacking sentence. As Carmine resumed his life with his three sons and one daughter in their stately home in Hempstead, Long Island, he set up his business headquarters in a South Brooklyn social club called Nestor's on Fifth Avenue at the base of Park Slope between President and Carroll Streets, within blocks of where he grew up.

He also had the farm in Saugerties. The compound wasn't just about quiet, coolness, and equine breeding, of course. Cops raided the horse farm and confiscated fifty rifles and forty bombs.

At the 1979 Commission meeting there was a discussion to decide what to do about Carmine Galante, who had his eye on becoming boss of the Bonannos. Carmine refused to sanction a hit on Galante. Carmine and Galante had once shared a cell in Atlanta, played cards, bonded. Carmine considered him a friend. To a confidant, Carmine later said, "Quite frankly, I voted against him getting hurt."

History tells us that Carmine was outvoted by the other commissioners, as Galante died with his cigar still in his mouth on July 12, 1979, just as he finished eating lunch on an open patio at Joe and Mary's Restaurant in the Bushwick section of Brooklyn.

Carmine might've gotten out of prison but at no point was he out of trouble. In November 1980, he was indicted on twenty-six charges involving the attempted bribery of the IRS agent. He was held briefly and released on $250,000 bail.

His troubles were compounded and his parole violated on May 6, 1981, when a meeting in a Brooklyn home went bad. The meeting was between Carmine and Gerry Lang and the leaders of New Jersey's crime family, the DeCavalcantes, held to discuss ways for the Colombos and the DeCavalcantes to work together and divvy up turf in Florida.

Carmine later said that the meeting involved a guy named

Johnny Irish. Donnie Shacks was assigned to pick up the guy at the airport and bring him to the meeting.

"Donnie, make sure you're not followed," Carmine said.

"I got this, Junior," Donnie Shacks replied.

Trouble was, Johnny Irish rented his own car, and he wanted to drive it. So Donnie told him to follow him, and the two-car convoy went to the Brooklyn meeting. Donnie was greatly troubled by this. With Johnny Irish's rental in his rear-view mirror, there was no way to tell if he'd picked up a tail. Donnie took the guy to the meeting and then split to attend his own birthday party at the Maniac Club.

A few minutes later Gerry Lang arrived with dire news. "Junior, there's a car parked outside with two guys in it. I think they might be feds."

Carmine replied, "Then why did you come in?"

Lang practically stammered. "I was already in, practically in, so I decided to come in."

The guy who owned the house where the meeting was being held said he'd go outside and take a look. Upon return he said, "They don't look like feds to me. I think they're watching the house across the street."

And so the meeting went on.

Minutes later, a team of FBI and U.S. Marshal's Service agents raided the meeting. Carmine and Gerry were arrested while attempting to escape out the back and charged with a parole violation, associating with known criminals.

Carmine blamed the owner of the house. "They don't look like feds to me." "Watching the house across the street." Bullshit. About their host on May 6, Junior said, "After getting me violated like that, that guy deserves to get hurt." Surprisingly, "that guy"—sniper Anthony "Tony Fats" Regina—lived another two years.

*   *   *

In July and August, Gerry Lang was called before a grand jury to talk about the meeting with the DeCavalcantes. He said he didn't know anyone who belonged to the Colombo crime family, that he didn't remember how he knew other hoods that attended the meeting. He said he hadn't worked in a dozen years due to health problems.

"Was Carmine Persico in the house at the time of the meeting?"

"He was. But he stayed upstairs and didn't attend the meeting."

Lang would later (September 1984) be charged with making false statements to a grand jury based on those responses.

On August 11, 1981, Carmine pleaded guilty in Brooklyn Federal Court to a conspiracy charge in the IRS bribery case. Carmine had admitted paying the bribe to a man he thought to be corrupt but who instead was wearing a wire. The money was to go to expedite his own release from prison and to shut down the tax investigations regarding Carmine's friends.

Carmine's sentencing hearing on his criminal conspiracy case was held on November 9, 1981, Judge Eugene H. Nickerson presiding. In court, Carmine, now forty-eight years old, wore a three-piece black suit, white shirt, and patterned tie. The whole thing was over in a half-hour.

Carmine had originally been charged with robbery, conspiracy, and obstruction of justice. All but the conspiracy charges were dropped however in exchange for Carmine's guilty plea. He was sentenced to five years for the bribery, four for the parole violation of associating with known criminals, but those sentences were to run concurrently.

The length of the sentence had been known to Carmine in advance, yet he was still rankled at the hearing, which he felt portrayed him incorrectly. He was referred to in a pre-sentencing report prepared by the U.S. Probation Department as the "head of the Colombo crime family."

Carmine and his attorney Barry I. Slotnick were up in arms over that characterization. Slotnick was a grad of NYU law and had started out as an appellate attorney, but was transitioning into a mouthpiece for high-profile clients, such as subway vigilante Bernie Goetz and Panamanian dictator Manuel Noriega. He had previously defended Joe Colombo and won, so he was the family lawyer. By this time in his life, Carmine was loath to relinquish power under any circumstances but begrudgingly allowed Slotnick to do the talking for him.

Slotnick, who understood the new conspiracy laws and the new strategies he would need to use to circumvent them, said, "Mr. Persico is not only *not* the head of a crime family, he is *not* in organized crime at all."

The conspiracy laws were known as "Racketeer Influenced and Corrupt Organizations Act" (RICO), which said that long prison terms could be given to those convicted of committing acts as part of an ongoing criminal enterprise. They'd been around since 1970, but it was a decade before the government figured out just how devastating they could be when applied to organized crime. The law was drafted by Notre Dame Law School professor, JFK-assassination theorist (he says the mob did it), and advisor to the U.S. Senate Government Operations Committee, Robert Blakey. To the mob, the RICO laws, especially after Rudolph Giuliani started using them as a weapon, were like Kryptonite to Superman. The law was potentially mob-busting, but it was most certainly *omerta*-busting. Guys facing life in prison were far more apt to disregard their vow of silence.

The RICO laws were the beginning of the end for organized crime as it was defined and functioned in the twentieth century. RICO okayed guilt by association. It became a crime to be a member of a group that was known to commit crimes, even if you, the individual, could not be proven to have committed any crimes. It was a crime to be a made man. It was a crime to be a respected elder of a family. The laws—named after the lead character in the book *Little Caesar* by W.R. Burnett, later turned into a gangster picture starring Edward G. Robinson—only had to demonstrate that a racketeering crime had occurred, that a certain organization carried out that crime, and that the defendant belonged to that organization. Significantly, a figurehead boss was every bit as guilty as a boss who was pushing the buttons.

Slotnick's argument flew in the face of earlier statements made by the federal prosecutors, who told Judge Nickerson that they were "prepared to prove" that Carmine Persico was head of the Colombo crime family.

If the sentencing had been anything other than a done deal, the fireworks at this hearing most certainly would have thrown a wrench in the works, but as it was, the arguments were moot. Carmine was going away for five years, and his status in organized crime wasn't going to change that one way or the other.

Slotnick's complaints did not go completely unheeded. The U.S. Probation Department agreed to re-write their pre-sentencing report. Instead of referring to Carmine as head of the Colombos, the report now read that he was an "upper-echelon member" of the crime family.

Slotnick wanted to make it clear that this in no way meant he was conceding Carmine's membership in the crime family or in any facet of organized crime. They had agreed to this compromise in the report's wording in order to avoid having Carmine go to prison with a report in existence that "tarnished" him as the head of a crime family.

Slotnick's point was that the tag of crime boss would potentially hurt Carmine's chances of winning early parole or qualify for work-release programs.

Prosecutor Cohen said that the government agreed to the compromise because he didn't see that there was a significant difference between "head" and "upper-echelon." Not big enough to argue, anyway. If they were happy, he was happy.

Cohen also pointed out that proving something like who was or wasn't the head of a crime family involved using a lot of undercover surveillance stuff, and it was difficult to present that evidence in court without potentially outing an undercover informant or a useful surveillance system.

Regarding the changing of "head" to "upper-echelon," Judge Nickerson, with a real ha-ha sense of humor, quipped: "Do you use the word echelon on the theory that no one in prison will understand it?"

In 1975, a woman named Arlyne Brickman began her career as a call girl/informant for the Fort Lee, New Jersey, police after her daughter got in bad with a Colombo loanshark whose standing with the family deteriorated once Gerry Lang was in charge of his operation. Brickman was so good at her job that she found steady work, making serious money spying for the DEA and FBI, taking advantage of hoods that talked in and out of bed. Her crowning achievement however was the part she played years later in the RICO investigation of top Colombos, namely capo (and Prospect Park killer) Anthony "Scappi" Scarpati, Little Allie Boy, and his dad Carmine. She got people to mention the Persicos and their longtime brain trust by name, on video, but did it in such a foul-mouthed *puttana* manner that the FBI was worried schoolmarm jurists might disapprove. (Not a problem, as it turned out.) Of concern to Brickman was her daughter, who used drugs, was sweet on the shylock who'd victimized her, was hip to mom's government job, and didn't like being related to a rat. Brickman ended up paying off her daughter to keep her quiet.

According to an FBI report, in January 1982, Carmine allegedly put a hit on a pair of guys who were keeping more than their share of the profits from the hit porn movie *Deep Throat*. The guys were Joseph Peraino Sr. and Jr., who had financed the making and distribution of the number-one all-time blockbuster XXX movie and didn't feel like paying the tribute. "I'm being robbed by my own family!" Peraino Sr. had been overheard complaining. So it was the Frankie Shots deal all over again. The Perainos had to go.

The hit was exceptional, sadly, because of its collateral damage. In fact, for a God-fearing hoodlum, it was the worst that could happen. One of the members of the hit team was Salvatore Miciotta, and it's his version of events (told after receiving a new I.D.) that follows.

The plan was hatched in an Avenue U social club. Two sawed-off shotguns arrived at that location by a discreet messenger. Both the targets and the shooters were on foot in the Gravesend section of Brooklyn. Others were there, Miciotta said, but it was he and Jimmy Angellino with the guns. The Perainos knew they were targets. In fact, Sr. had one arm in a sling, a remnant of a previous gunshot wound, as he and his son stood on the south edge of the Gravesend Cemetery on Village Road. They spotted men approaching, bearing sawed-off shotguns. They made a run for it, the gunmen in pursuit. The Perainos ran about one-hundred yards before picking a random two-family house around the corner on Lake Street. The fleeing men galloped up the outdoor stairs toward the front door of the second-floor apartment. The gunmen stopped at the base of the stairs and gathered themselves.

Two shotgun blasts echoed down the street. Buckshot blew a hole in Jr.'s chest, killing him instantly. Buckshot tore through Sr.'s spine, through a window into the upstairs apartment, and through the head of fifty-three-year-old, Brazilian-born Veronica Zuraw, a former nun of the Pallottine order that ran a Bensonhurst storefront helping arriving Italians just off the boat. She had left the convent to get married, but had once been known as Sister Mary Adelaide, a teacher for the Brooklyn Catholic Diocese school system. She was a beloved character to whom children flocked, and was folding and putting away the laundry when death came suddenly.

Miciotta said he shot and killed Peraino Jr. in those stairs, while Angellino shot and wounded Sr., leaving him forever paralyzed. The FBI report noted that it was allegedly Angellino's shot that killed the innocent bystander. There was no one to disagree with Miciotta's story.

By the time Miciotta told the story in 1999, Angellino was dead, himself a victim of a hit allegedly carried out by Carmine Sessa in November 1988 in a reputed mobster's home in Kenilworth, New Jersey.

Veronica's husband, Louis Zuraw, was in his mid-sixties and became despondent after his wife's death, drank himself sick, and died in the VA Hospital next to Fort Hamilton in 1986.

In 2012, the story of that notorious hit was again told, this time in a Brooklyn federal courtroom with a different cast of characters. On trial was Tommy "Shots" Gioeli. Prosecution witness Big Dino Calabro was all set to say he heard Tommy Shots confess to killing the nun, adding the lament, "I'm going to Hell." Gioeli was charged with six murders, none of them the nun or Peraino Sr. She only came up because the prosecution wanted to hear evidence regarding the Gravesend hit in front of the jury, but Judge Brian Cogan said no, stick to the six in the indictment. That ruling was overturned as the defense announced its plans to call character witnesses on Tommy Shots' behalf, at which time the prosecution would be allowed to use the nun-killing evidence in cross-examination. Calabro was called to the stand, but only to discuss Gioeli's involvement in the six murders with which he'd been charged. The closest he came to mentioning the shooting of the nun was to say Gioeli had taken up prayer, and was frequently seen on his knees in a Long Island church's outdoor grotto.

Reportedly, Gioeli vehemently denied having anything to do with Veronica Zuraw's death.

During 1984–85, three mob commission meetings were held, the Colombos repped by Donnie Shacks and Gerry Lang. According to the April 29, 1988, Washington, D.C. testimony of Fish Cafaro, the third meeting turned into a bit of a comedy when fed agents were spotted and the hoods took off. Anthony "Fat Tony" Salerno, Cafaro testified, took after his nickname and got stuck in a window while trying to escape. The fat man was pulled to safety in the nick of time.

CHAPTER TEN
The Grim Reaper

*"I love the smell of gunpowder," Gregory Scarpa would say
with eyes dancing.*

BY THE TIME CARMINE MATURED out of his youthful reputation as
an up-close-and-personal killer, his days of freedom were down
to a few and he chose as his battle leader a true psychopath, a guy
who would kill his own grandmother if she looked at him
funny—or if the price was right. He was Gregory "The Grim
Reaper" Scarpa, a stylishly dressed ladies' man who carried thousands in cash on him at all times in case he needed to pay out an
emergency bribe. Scarpa was a trip and a half, happy as a clam
with a gun in his hand.

He was nuts, thought he was James Bond, and told his kids
that he worked for the government. In a sense it was true, but
holy shit. He was a tough guy, five-ten, 210 pounds, with a heavy
build and pitch-black hair. Dating back to the 1960s, he'd been a
Colombo, involved in extortion, loans, and reportedly narcotics,
getting his instructions from the boss, be it Profaci, Colombo, or
Persico.

By his willingness to take on the most difficult and distasteful
hits, he had made himself a wealthy man, with homes in Vegas
and in three of the five New York City boroughs. He once
bragged that killing enemies was such a gas, he wished he could
ghoul the bodies from their graves and snuff them one more time.

Scarpa HQ was the Wimpy Boys Social Club on Thirteenth Avenue in Dyker. His record was long, but he always walked, sometimes with probation, other times with the charges dropped outright.

Scarpa may have had some personality traits in common with Carmine Persico, but unlike the stoic Junior who would rather do time than rat every single time, Scarpa was not averse to cooperating with authorities.

In fact, almost bizarrely, Scarpa was a rat from the get-go. According to FBI documents, Scarpa was initially contacted in August 1961 at the start of the Gallo-Profaci War. At that time Scarpa lived in a freestanding house on a quiet street on Staten Island. The feds came to visit him at the social club he owned. They came back two or three times. Scarpa was friendly with the agents, but he didn't give up any info. He told the feds not to contact him again because people were starting to talk about why agents kept visiting his club. The agents agreed and told him that if he changed his mind about supplying info, there was money to be made, and they gave him a number to call. Scarpa's actual cooperation with the U.S. Government went at least as far back as 1964 when the feds used him to help solve the "Mississippi Burning" murders of three civil rights workers in 1964. Somewhere there's a tape of Scarpa cajoling a KKK member to disclose where the bodies were buried—and by cajoling, I mean he beat the shit out of him and stuck a gun in his mouth.

FBI documents seem to indicate that, at the time the FBI recruited Scarpa, they didn't know he was a killer. They saw him as a white-collar mobster, running various scams while calling himself a self-employed clothing salesman. They did, however, know that Scarpa had been "consorting with others with evil reputations." Carmine Persico was mentioned. Hugh McIntosh, too.

Scarpa's deal with the feds placed him in deep, deep cover. Only his handlers knew of the arrangement. It was kept a secret from the rest of the FBI and federal prosecutors. The deal was that Scarpa's information could be used to help the feds bust racketeers, but Scarpa was never, under any circumstances, to be called as a witness before a grand jury or at a trial.

On September 24, 1984, the elder Alphonse Persico's thirty-one-year-old ex-girlfriend, the stunningly gorgeous Mary Bari was found murdered and dumped in the street, all identification removed. She was ID'd by her sister, who recognized the tattoo of a peach on her ass. Bari was called in the papers Allie Boy's "longtime paramour."

She'd thought she was going to a job interview for a cocktail waitressing gig in a Bensonhurst tavern. The joint was called the Occasions Bar and run by Carmine Sessa. Bari was dressed to impress, wearing high-heeled boots, designer jeans, and a black halter top.

But there was no interview. According to the *New York Post*, it was a father and son job. Gregory Scarpa Jr. put Mary in a bearhug while dad, Greg Sr. pumped three bullets into her head.

Senior would be dead before he could be prosecuted for this murder, but his son went away to the fed pen in Florence, California, in part because of his role in the Bari hit. (In 1988, Scarpa was suffering from a bleeding ulcer and received a gift that kept on giving, a transfusion from a member of his crew, a body-builder who shot steroids with a dirty needle and died of AIDS. Scarpa was himself diagnosed with AIDS in 1991, a fact kept private. Everyone noticed his emaciated and ravaged appearance, however, as he lost fifty pounds.)

Mary Bari's body was cocooned in canvas and dumped in a street two miles away, where it was found only hours later. Scarpa had been tipped off that Bari was talking to the FBI by his FBI buddy Roy Lindley DeVecchio. Scarpa and DeVecchio, as we'd later learn, had a very strange relationship. Scarpa would help DeVecchio with his investigations, and DeVecchio would help Scarpa with his mob business, including allegedly at least five hits. Both were paid on the taxpayer's dime.

Later, Carmine Sessa, proprietor of Occasions Bar, told the FBI that he'd witnessed Bari's murder. Sessa said a member of Scarpa's crew lured Bari to the club where Scarpa shot and killed her. Bari was murdered, Sessa said, because she knew where Allie Boy was (he had been on the lam for four years after skipping his sentencing hearing for extortion) and, now that she was cooperating with the feds, was apt to disclose his location.

That was what Sessa said, but the FBI only partially agreed. The mere suspicion that she was an FBI informant was enough to order her murder, regardless of the other factors. For one thing, they didn't think Bari knew where Allie Boy was hiding. She was his ex-girlfriend. Allie Boy moved from place to place. He and Bari had been out of touch for years.

"Not even his family knew where he was," said Victor Oboyski, the deputy U.S. Marshal in charge of the search for Alphonse Persico. "His wife and daughter would drive toward Connecticut, but a meeting would be set up at a neutral site, usually a diner."

Oboyski was troubled by Bari's murder because it was, in essence, one FBI informant rubbing out another. Oboyski had asked for permission to question Bari regarding Allie Boy's whereabouts but had been told no because of the FBI's "special relationship" with her.

Larry Mazza, who admits being a Scarpa gunman, was at the shooting of Mary Bari and its aftermath, aspects of which he found extremely troubling. After the killing there was a "celebration" at an Italian restaurant on 13th Avenue in Dyker Heights. Scarpa and his crew, including Mazza, were there. So was Sessa and his wife. Some of them had a big laugh about the hit. It was a joking, festive type of atmosphere. Someone said that when Bari was shot her ear went flying off. Mrs. Sessa then joked that a dog found the ear lying on the ground and couldn't figure out what it was. Scarpa pulled the trigger himself he said because it was hard to find someone to kill women. A lot of guys didn't have the stomach for it. But it didn't bother Scarpa—or, apparently, his kid.

In my crowd, this whole Mary Bari thing was very disturbing. Best guess is that Scarpa was fucking her and caught her stepping out on him. Allie Boy had nothing to do with it. It was personal. To tell the truth, it wasn't even a mob hit. It was sick twisted shit, more like something that would be done by a father/son serial-killer team. I wonder about that "festive" atmosphere after, too. A lot of people will play along because they don't want to enrage a psycho killer, but once alone they feel differently. It was fucked up. Even the most desensitized hood had to see that.

In the meantime, Mary Bari's ex, Allie Boy, was not captured for another three years, in November 1987, hiding in West Hartford, Connecticut. (More about Allie Boy and his time on the lam in Chapter Eleven.)

Karma had a field day with the truly evil Scarpa. By December 29, 1992, Scarpa was wasted with AIDS to the point of being barely recognizable. And, yet things *still* managed to turn drastically worse for him. In what was described as a drug transaction near his Brooklyn home that had nothing to do with Colombo business, Scarpa took a bullet to the left eye but lived to die a wasting death.

One of the weak points in Scarpa's deal with his fed handler DeVecchio, was that the rest of the FBI had no clue about him, and if they wanted to prosecute him for his many crimes, there was nothing DeVecchio could do to help him.

"If they catch you, I don't know you," DeVecchio said.

Scarpa was confident that he'd never be caught. But by 1993 he was sick, and the feds were closing in. Racketeering charges ensued. Scarpa took a plea. Even after the bust he continued to inform to DeVecchio, even as he was begging for a way out.

DeVecchio knew he could outwait the situation. Scarpa looked like he was about to keel over at any second. "The Grim Reaper," a nickname now swollen with irony, just barely managed to stand for his sentencing. Judge Jack B. Weinstein said he was "worse than a wild animal," gave him ten years, but the actual Grim Reaper visited Scarpa weeks later in a prison hospital.

Scarpa ended up causing the justice system just as much trouble in death as he had in life. DeVecchio was arrested, his behavior having gone above and beyond his legal role as handler of an informant. They offered to a grand jury plentiful evidence that DeVecchio, even when around other feds, seemed to have forgotten his role as an FBI agent and was thinking of himself as an active player for Carmine Persico's team.

He, they said, was an accessory to murder. The initial attempt to prosecute DeVecchio didn't take. The Justice Department concluded there was insufficient evidence to indict. The agent agreed to retire with his pension. He swore up and down that the info he collected was a one-way street—and he asserted that working as a catalyst for mob mayhem, dividing and conquering, was good for the bureau, because the resulting chaos begat defectors and backstabbers, canaries and rats. Being a provocateur, therefore, was in the best interests of the bureau as well.

The problem with that statement was that it made DeVecchio's and Scarpa's evidence harder to use in a courtroom. Guys arrested on Scarpa's info grew harder to prosecute, as they could now say there was an undercover fed in the works tipping the scales to make them look guilty. Nineteen hoods were acquitted or had their convictions reversed in Appellate Court. Juries were willing to believe that an agent of the FBI and an agent of Carmine Persico would work hand-in-hand in the underworld if they had a common enemy. Nineteen men returned to the streets— although many were re-prosecuted for similar crimes, this time successfully, when new vocalists discovered their voice. (Jumping ahead for a moment, the justice department never forgot about DeVecchio. He was indicted many years later in 2006 for helping Scarpa on four hits, and spent eighteen months free on $1 million bail before the case against him fell apart when Scarpa's live-in girlfriend contradicted herself, saying she both did and didn't know details of the relationship between Scarpa and De-Vecchio.)

CHAPTER ELEVEN
Operation Star Quest

*Scarpa went out ugly, sure, but the damage he did to the
Colombos was uglier. The feds had already known most of the
games the boys played. Scarpa told them who did what and how
the organization was put together. Feds asked Scarpa: "Who's
the boss?" "Junior," Scarpa said. Wasn't it obvious?*

ON OCTOBER 14, 1984, Carmine Persico—just out of prison for
parole violation—and the entire *upper echelon* of the Colombos
were indicted on racketeering charges. The indictments, announced
by straight-laced Attorney General William French Smith, claimed
that the Colombo crime family, operated by Persico and others,
was engaged in the usual nefarious activities, i.e., a "pattern of
racketeering." Smith added that the Colombos had strong "influ-
ences" within New York City's construction and restaurant industries.

Smith's accent betrayed him as originally Bostonian, when he
said the investigation was called Operation Star Quest, a three-
year federal investigation in which an undercover FBI agent used
a yacht to entertain the mobsters. The agent posed as a purchaser
of stolen goods and, aided by a hot female companion, recorded
the men on the yacht discussing illegal activities.

Carmine was still adjusting to freedom, and was again a
wanted man. To the government's chagrin, however, Carmine
was tipped off by Jerry Capechi of the *New York Post* that a bust
was imminent—so he went into hiding, at first staying at a hotel
out on the eastern tip of Long Island, a place owned by Nick
Monte, proprietor of Carmine's favorite restaurant. While there,

Carmine had meetings with his brain trust: Gerry Lang, Donnie Shacks, and Anthony Scarpati. The Garfield Boys had grown up and become middle-aged men, but the cast of characters remained largely the same. They discussed whether Carmine should turn himself in, and if he did who should pay his bail.

First to be arrested was Scappi, who was arriving at his Bensonhurst home in the passenger seat of a red Cadillac when he was nabbed by two FBI agents. Scappi stepped out of the car with hands up, and the driver squealed out of there and made his escape, the passenger door still swinging open.

A week later, however, Gerry Lang was arrested, then Tommy DiBella. William French Smith held press conferences to announce he was taking down "the entire leadership of the Colombo family." The captured Colombos were arraigned before U.S. District Judge Robert Carter.

Carmine remained mobile, staying with a guy nicknamed Frankie Highway for a few days, then below a restaurant. He gained access to some of the tapes that would be used against him in what would come to be known as the Colombo case. They were recordings of Colombo bigs, including Lang, discussing Colombo family business. In addition to the stuff on the yacht, there were tapes recorded with a bug in the Casa Storta Restaurant, on 21st Street near Fourth Avenue in Brooklyn. The bug was placed on the ceiling directly above the boys' regular table.

Carmine was in prison when the tapes were made, but his name did come up in incriminating ways. The thought of capture was terrifying. Being on the lam and transient was stressful. It was like trying to run a floating crap game. He needed a more permanent hiding place, so Carmine took up residence in his cousin's attic in a private house in Wantagh, Long Island.

The cousin was Katherine Russo DeChristopher, sister of Mush. Katherine's husband since 1973 had been Fred DeChristopher, a guy born in East Boston, but raised in the Navy Yard section of Brooklyn. His dad was a Pinkerton detective, but Fred left school after the seventh grade, before joining the Navy at age seventeen and serving in the Pacific Theater during World War II. Fred started out legit, working for his dad in plastic heat sealing. The business went kaput in 1963, and Fred switched to selling insurance. It was around this time that he met Mush Russo, met him through Mush's friend, the famous pro wrestler Antonino Rocca, who was hanging around because he worked in the ring with Lenny (Luca Brasi) Montana.

Mush, Fred learned, was a guy who could be helpful if you had trouble with your union. Through Mush, Fred met Carmine and came to understand the power of Carmine's organization.

Fred had been one of the guys to hang around in Nestor's. According to DeChristopher, they called it "Junior's headquarters." Also hanging out or floating in and out were brother Allie Boy (after he got out of prison but before he went on the lam), Hugh McIntosh, Mush, and Scappi, of course, Sally Albanese, and John Minerva.

All sorts of stuff went down there, stolen items for sale, shylocking, numbers. DeChristopher knew Mush to be a guy who always had a lot of irons in the fire. Fred once asked Mush if he wasn't worried about the feds cracking down on loansharking. Mush told him feds don't do loansharking, that was state, and the state needed two corroborating witnesses, which was always hard to get. Fred had an office only a few doors away from Nestor's. He was the treasurer for a chapter of Joe Colombo's Italian-American Civil Rights League with offices also on Fifth Avenue in Brooklyn.

DeChristopher remembered a time back in the late 1960s when Colombo had a rule not to drive on the Gowanus Expressway through Red Hook because of Gallo snipers. Even during the spring of 1971, there was concern. Carmine and Fred remembered the block party they threw that season to raise money for

Colombo's civil rights cause, and how they had guys with rifles on the roof for that, too, just in case the Gallos attacked. DeChristopher married Katherine Russo on December 28, 1973, and they moved into Mush's old house in Farmingdale on Long Island, while Mush moved to Old Brookvale.

Point is, Fred had been around, he married Carmine's first cousin, and Carmine had no reservation about crashing at Fred's house now that he was on the lam. Fred said he could have his daughter's attic room. She just got married and didn't need it. Carmine took a look at it and laughed. It was nicely furnished . . . for a teenage girl: single bed, white furniture. Every square inch was as adolescently frosty as a princess tiara. Carmine had everything moved out and ordered new furniture for his new attic digs.

Going into hiding at the same time was Gerry Lang, who grew a beard as a disguise but was nonetheless picked up quickly in Brooklyn.

By 1985, whether true or not, it was the common perception that Carmine Persico thought murder a suitable solution to any business problem. There was no glitch in the system, large or small, that couldn't be alleviated by bumping a guy off and burying him in a shallow grave. That was the man's reputation.

So you have to wonder what Steven Piazza, owner of a Brooklyn moving company, was thinking when he received the great honor of marrying Carmine's daughter, and then slapped her around when she didn't listen. Reports of the physical abuse allegedly made their way to Carmine, who already didn't like Piazza because he was into drugs and prone to flapping his lips. Carmine allegedly instructed Little Allie Boy—who would be convicted in this case years later—to take care of it.

The thirty-two-year-old Piazza was last seen alive on June 6, 1985. His body was found on June 13, wrapped in plastic bags and stuffed into the trunk of his 1980 Cadillac, which was parked in the Nathan's Restaurant lot on 86th Street, across the street from the Dyker Golf Course.

Twelve days after the indictments, the FBI announced that it was launching a nationwide manhunt for Carmine Persico Jr. Three of the other indictees—Donnie Shacks, John J. DeRoss, and Frank Melli—were also missing, but Carmine, as usual, was the headline.

U.S. Attorney Rudy Giuliani was in charge for the government, a guy with tremendous leadership skills and a boner for wiping out the mob. He was Italian, obviously, and Catholic—and yet he had his eyes on national power. So, take out the mob. Proves to the world that he isn't mob, see?

Giuliani blamed the *New York Post* for the mess. Jerry Capechi's article. The reporter called Carmine to ask for comment before he even knew he was in trouble. Damned suspicious, Giuliani said.

The future mayor wasn't alone in his opinion. The Justice Department was looking into it also. Somebody from the government had to have leaked the news to Capechi. Giuliani swore the leak had not come from his office.

A reporter from the *Times* asked, "Rudy, do you have any idea where Carmine Persico is?"

"He's not at any of his usual haunts," Giuliani said. To tell the truth, he added, he didn't even know if Persico was still in the country. "He could be in Timbuktu," Giuliani said with an elaborate shrug.

The prosecutor in charge of the case, Bruce A. Baird, softened the focus, took the spotlight off Carmine in particular. "They are fugitives from justice and we are looking for them," he said.

Unbeknownst to Carmine, he had picked the worst possible place to hide. Fred DeChristopher had been an FBI informant for years, making a deal to turn while facing a twenty-five-year prison term.

The FBI couldn't believe its good fortune. They knew where Carmine was going to be hiding before he even got there. But they decided not to take him right away. There were things to be learned.

They announced the nationwide manhunt just to help Carmine relax and to protect DeChristopher's cover. Meanwhile, Fred and Carmine found themselves having a good time, having long, deep conversations about nothing and everything.

Carmine told DeChristopher that money was never going to be a problem because he had enough cash stashed away to last ten lifetimes. Carmine said he voted against a hit on Carmine Gallante. He talked about the old days, man, they were the best, and how he'd been a gunman at *La Mafia*'s Greatest Hit, Albert Anastasia in his barber chair. What a day that was. He could still feel the adrenaline pumping. He'd been a member of the "barbershop quartet."

While staying at his cousin's, Carmine didn't just lay around and get waited on. He had a function in the home: the house cook. Carmine loved to make pasta with a simple oil and garlic sauce.

On October 29, 1984, Judge Charles L. Brient held a bail hearing for the Colombo men they did have in captivity, they being former Garfields, Lang and Scappi, plus sixty-four-year-old Frank Falanga of Staten Island, and forty-eight-year-old Dominic Cataldo of Valley Stream, Long Island. At that hearing the prosecution argued that the men should continue to be held without bail because they represented a threat to the community and were a flight risk as well. Earlier in the month co-defendants Ralph Scopo of Queens, who was in the hospital, and fifty-seven-year-old Vito Pitta of Brooklyn, were arraigned and released on $300,000 and $500,000 bail respectively. Another man named on the indictments was Thomas DiBella, who was described as a "top leader" of the Colombos by one source and as "the group's advisor" (i.e., *consigliere*) by another, was also in the hospital, and his lawyer Frank A. Lopez said he would appear in court for arraignment as soon as he was well enough to leave the hospital.

On January 31, 1985, Carmine's career as a crook might've peaked, for that was the day he cracked the FBI's Ten Most Wanted list. His face lit up in a smile when he heard that news. The glow of pride faded somewhat when Carmine learned it was all a show to reinforce his belief that the FBI was clueless.

During Carmine's time at the DeChristopher's, he only left twice, once after Christmas dinner to go to a meeting in eastern Long Island with a couple of guys, including Donnie Shacks, to discuss just how much trouble he was in. They concluded he was fucked. At the beginning of February 1985, DeChristopher drove Carmine to his attorney's house for a secret meeting.

Carmine did receive visitors at the DeChristophers', most frequently his son Allie Boy, who delivered legal papers for his dad to read. When Allie Boy came over, father and son would sit together at the dining room table and talk for two or three hours. DeChristopher didn't listen in on the conversations but did hear Carmine say his son's visits should be infrequent at most, because Allie might be under surveillance. Another visitor was out-on-bail Donnie Shacks, who came twice to the DeChristophers' to visit the boss, once in December and a second time on the day of Carmine's arrest. DeChristopher spotted Carmine's good buddy Scappi hanging around outside his house, but the guy never came in. DeChristopher asked Carmine what he was doing out there and never received a good answer.

At 4:30 A.M., February 15, 1985, twenty federal agents and Nassau County police officers surrounded DeChristopher's Wantagh home. An agent called the phone inside the house.

DeChristopher answered: "Hello."

"Hi, is Junior there?"

"Just a sec. Junior, it's for you!"

Carmine took the phone. "Who's this?" he asked.

"This is Special Agent Taylor of the FBI. We have the house surrounded. Please tell the others that you should all step outside right now, hands up."

There was no stand-off. The occupants of the house complied with Agent Taylor's instructions, and Carmine and the others were promptly arrested. In the car with the feds, Carmine cracked jokes. He autographed a copy of his Top Ten Most Wanted poster for them.

According to the FBI, Fred, Donnie Shacks, and Joseph Russo were arrested for harboring fugitives. DeChristopher had to spend the night in the Metropolitan Correctional Center, but in the morning they very, very quietly let him go without ever formally charging him with anything.

Carmine was arraigned on February 16 in Federal District Court in Manhattan. The prosecutors in charge of his case were Bruce A. Baird and Aaron R. Marcu.

On July 2, 1985, Carmine's dire legal situation grew worse. Much worse. He was indicted, along with other mega-powerful underworld figures in what would be called the Mafia Commission Case. These indictments were the product of the FBI's Operation Star *Chamber* (not to be confused with Operation Star Quest, i.e., the Colombo case). The charges: "Engaging in an enterprise which operated, supervised, and promoted crime, activities in Interstate commerce and did unlawfully, willfully and knowingly combine, conspire to participate in the conduct of the affairs of that enterprise through a pattern of racketeering activities. It was a pattern of racketeering activities to unlawfully, willfully obstruct and affect commerce by extortion by use of actual and threatened violence and fear of economic loss."

Gerry Lang was a co-defendant—again. But not all of Carmine's co-defendants were compadres. Setting a precedent, expanding the scope of RICO, the defendants, to be tried together, represented a sampling of mob power from across the families: Anthony "Fat Tony" Salerno, seventy-three-year-old Tony "Ducks" Corallo, head of the Luccheses who wore a golf shirt and a cardigan in court, Sal "Tom Mix" Santoro, Christy Tick Furnari, Ralphie Scopo, and Anthony "Bruno" Indelicato.

If you could show that an organization existed to commit crimes and that a person belonged to that organization in a specific capacity, you didn't need to show that the person committed the crime. That had clicked in court in the past, with a crime family used as the unit of organization. But the feds were greedy fucks. They had caught the leaders of the families meeting, forming one super-organization, membership of which would be, they hoped, considered an automatic crime. In that way they would take out the bosses in one fell swoop.

To the delight of the press, the fifty-three-year-old Carmine Persico announced that he was going to do something he had dreamed of since the first time he ever saw the inside of a courtroom back in his days with the Garfield Boys, when he watched the trials of Scappi and brother Allie Boy with such fascination. He was going to defend himself at the Commission trial—that is, do his own talking, without a lawyer. He respectfully informed the court that he was qualified, based on the long list of defense attorneys who'd gotten him convicted. He referenced his own "considerable experience with the criminal justice system."

Persico's co-defendants were dead set against it. Fat Tony Salerno was particularly vocal. He was cranky anyway because he wasn't eating as often or as well as he liked, and he'd recently had eye surgery, so one eye was red and swollen throughout the trial. His body language always suggested aloofness. If he could have, he would have perched on a riser, above his co-defendants. Salerno and the other co-defendants feared that Carmine's mistakes would hurt them also. They didn't see how Carmine defending himself helped them in any way.

Presiding over the Commission case was Judge Richard Owen, a man of multiple talents. He flew bombing missions in World War II, went to Harvard Law, and eventually was appointed a U.S. judge by Richard Nixon in 1973. But he was also a musical child prodigy, one of those spooky kids who could play Beethoven when he was six, and is perhaps best remembered as the composer of the opera *Abigail Adams*, based on the life and times of America's second First Lady.

Judge Owen didn't like this defending-yourself business either. It was a mistrial waiting to happen, potentially a big fat waste of time. He warned Carmine that men who represent themselves in criminal trials often have incompetent counsel.

The judge may have moaned when he first heard of Carmine's intentions, but there was a part of him that admired Persico as well. What balls the guy had. He knew the spotlight was going to be on him, and he couldn't wait to take the courtroom stage.

Carmine could be smart and charming, absolutely—but Judge Owen had to be practical. As incompetent counsel was such a common appellate theme, he offered Carmine a deal: if he were allowed to defend himself, he waived the right to appeal any potential conviction on those grounds. Carmine said whatever.

Folks who'd known Carmine since the old days understood that this was perfectly in character for him. He was not the sort to relinquish control, and for years had been badmouthing lawyers, saying he could do a better job than they did and do it without a single day of law school.

Carmine's stubbornness grew when he saw he was alone in his

desire. Fuck everybody. If he wanted to defend himself, he was going to defend himself.

So Judge Owen upped the ante. He would grant Carmine his wish only if his co-defendants, grumpier than ever, also waived their right to appeal on the grounds of incompetent counsel.

Judge Owen thought that would put an end to it, but no. It was a power struggle, and as usual, Carmine proved to have the stiffer spine. His co-defendants and their attorneys—among them Anthony Cardinale representing Fat Tony, Gerald McMahon for Gerry Lang, Albert Gaudelli for Tony Ducks, Samuel M. Dawson for Sal Santoro, James LaRossa for Furnari, John Jacobs for Scopo, and Thomas Nooter for Indelicato—had no shot of changing Carmine's mind.

Carmine Persico remained, as always, the immovable object.

So they all waived that right, and Carmine prepared his case. The spotlight, already on Carmine anyway, intensified.

The judge had lost, but he wasn't done. He insisted that Carmine have a legal expert of some sort on hand to give him advice during the trial. Trials were a complicated thing and Carmine didn't want to make any unintentional mistakes, right?

Carmine begrudgingly agreed, so a hearing was held to determine Carmine's advisor. Carmine testified briefly, telling the judge that his regular lawyer, Frank A. Lopez, was free to represent another defendant in the case if he chose. (Lopez did pick up a new client. Gerald McMahon was fired and Lopez repped Gerry Lang.)

Carmine said, "I will be using the advice of attorney Stanley E. Meyer."

Judge Owen said, "I gather, presumably, we will not hear Mr. Meyer's voice during this trial. We will only hear your voice, is that right?"

Carmine replied, "Your honor, the truth of the matter, I am only having a lawyer sit by me because you directed me to have a lawyer sit by me. I am trying to follow your rules or else I would sit there alone."

Jury selection for criminal trials is usually conducted in a courtroom, with prospective jury members sitting in the jury box during voir dire. For this case the process, beginning on September 8, 1986, took place in the jury room with only the defendants and the lawyers present.

Prospective panelists were interviewed individually, without any other candidates present. All were assured that their names would be kept secret, and they would be referred to if necessary during the proceedings by number only.

When no prospective juror was in the room, Carmine asked Judge Owens to instruct future prospects that the Mafia was not a criminal organization and that to be in the Mafia did not necessarily mean that you were a criminal.

Judge Owens refused.

The men and women from the jury pool were questioned by the prosecution and the defense, and often by the judge as well. During voir dire, Carmine repeatedly expressed concern about the jury pool's attitudes toward the "so-called Mafia," whether they believed in it, feared it, etc.

When Judge Owen asked one prospective juror what she thought about the Mafia, Carmine complained that His Honor's line of questioning was too brief and did not dig deeply enough into the prospective juror's belief systems.

Judge Owen became impatient with Carmine's complaints and said, "I really thought I exhausted that."

The judge asked a male member of the pool who worked as a word processor, "Do you have any impressions as to anything called a Mafia or a *Cosa Nostra*?"

The man replied, "I have no impressions at this time as to whether this exists or not. It is up to the Government to prove it in this case."

This man ended up on the jury.

Asked the same question, another man replied, "It is my belief that Mafia is an organized crime kind of proposition that is involved in all kinds of questionable activities."

He was excused.

Not all of the citizens marching through Judge Owen's chambers were picked or not picked based on their opinions on organized crime. The jury pool was a cross-section of society and as such contained the young, the old, the male, the female, the big, the little, the loud, and the quiet.

One memorable fellow was released immediately after telling Judge Owen that he was an actor and often had trouble distinguishing fact and fiction.

After the person left, Judge Owen said he smelled a malingerer. "Now there goes someone who just doesn't want to serve," the judge said.

One of the trial players quipped, "There goes our chance to be rated by a pro."

A retired social worker was excused from jury duty when she revealed her marriage to the NYPD's deputy inspector.

And on and on it went. It was tough to sit a jury in a case like this, but not impossible, and by being methodical and reasonable, they got the job done.

Carmine asked that extortion charges against he and Gerry Lang be dismissed because of double jeopardy. Persico and Lang had a whole second trial going on for extortion in the construction industry, charges that were practically indistinguishable from the charges here. Why the redundancy? Who did it serve?

The request was denied.

Men who represent themselves in trials, especially complicated conspiracy trials such as this based on laws that were relatively new, never do a great job. Civilians who can do an adequate job are few and far between, and Carmine, to his credit was better than most.

Assistant U.S. Attorney Michael Chertoff delivered the opening statement for the prosecution. He was thirty-two years old and looked younger despite a substantial moustache. He told the jury about the commission system, the heads of the various families, or their representatives, meeting to discuss the business of the Mafia.

Chertoff said, "What you will see is these men, these crime leaders, fighting with each other, backstabbing each other, each one trying to get a larger share of the illegal proceeds. You are going to learn that this commission is dominated by a single principle: greed. They want more money, and they will do what they have to do to get it."

The commission, he said, had been around for years, ever since the five-family system in New York was set up by Lucky Luciano in 1931. He planned to prove beyond a reasonable doubt that the commission approved three murders, including that of Carmine Galante.

Chertoff noted that only four of the five families were represented on their distinguished panel of defendants. The Gambinos were missing because Aniello Dellacroce had died of cancer and Paul Castellano was gunned down outside Sparks Steak House, or else they would have been invited to the party as well. (Ironically, one of the tapes the government would have used against Castellano had he been alive was of him griping about Sparks Steak House. Castellano complained that Sparks wasn't paying him, and the steak house was going to have to be closed unless Sparks paid up.)

If you've ever been to the fights—boxing, MMA—you know the tension in the air just before the bell rings. Adrenaline you could smell. Well that was the way it felt in that courtroom, the gallery full. The stars came out to watch. James Caan and Robert Duvall were there, stars of *The Godfather*. Caan and Carmine were buddies from back in the days when Caan was studying to play Sonny Corleone.

The tension grew as the defense attorneys took turns getting the jurors in the correct frame of mind to acquit, as it finally came time for the boss to address the jurors. Carmine wore a black pinstripe suit, white shirt, and red tie. He was balding and had heavy bags beneath his eyes.

With a small nod, Judge Owen said, "Mr. Persico."

Carmine rose, and stepped up to the lectern. He gave the jury his most pleasant smile, and there was nothing reptilian about it. The jurors felt a warmth. It was surprisingly difficult to see him as a monster.

"Judge, gentlemen of the defense, ladies and gentlemen of the jury. By now I guess you all know my name is Carmine Persico, and I am not a lawyer. I'm a defendant. Sitting at this table.

"You've heard all the lawyers before me talk to you and tell you what your oath was as a juror, what you promised us in the jury room and what we expect of you. We're going to hold you to them because I believe you gave those answers in good faith and honestly. So I'm going to hold you to it.

"What I'm going to talk about is the witnesses that will be called in this case and the defendants' obligation. As a defendant I have no obligation. I could have sat down in that chair and not say a word. I don't have to call a witness. I don't have to produce a document. They have to prove I'm guilty. And I tell you they *can't* prove it. When the witnesses take the stand, at the end of the case, they will have no evidence against me, Carmine Persico. They will have *none*.

"They're going to bring a lot of witnesses here. A lot of FBI agents they're going to bring. They're going to bring a lot of another type of witness. They're going to get up here witnesses that committed murder. Committed extortion. Bribery. Every crime you could think of. Dope dealers, polluted the city with dope.

"These witnesses are going to get up on the stand and tell you they reformed, that they are here to tell you the truth. They want to be believed. You look at them. You watch them when they talk. Not only what they say. Watch how they carry themselves. How bold and brazen they are. And the reason they are so bold and brazen is because they have contracts with these people. They signed contracts. They entered into agreements with the government. They paid them for that testimony.

"You know what they paid them. They paid them *your* money. Your money and my freedom is the payment these witnesses got. It will all come out on the witness stand. They had contracts. Written contracts. They'll get up there and tell you how honest they are and how they are reformed. You'll find some of them are doing life in prison. They want to come home. They want to be free. You'll get others who got six-thousand, seven-thousand a month. They pay them to come here. That's the kind of witness they're going to bring in here.

"I don't have the power to do that. I can't pay a witness. I could pay a witness to come here for one day, for his testimony here for that one day, but I can't afford to pay a witness five-thousand a month. That's illegal for me to do it. But it's legal for them. They could do it. I can't tell a witness that's in jail come and testify for me, I'll give you freedom. I can't do that. But they could do it. The government could do it. And they did it. They're powerful people. Not me. Not the people sitting at this table. They're not powerful. The government is powerful and they'll tell you, the witnesses that get up there, who they fear. They don't fear us. They fear the government. Not us. Not me.

"That's the type of witness they're going to ask you to believe. But I also tell you bring your common sense into court. Use your every day common sense when you listen to them people talking from that witness stand. Don't let them blind you. All the other lawyers told you about Mafia and labels and all that. I'm not going to go over that. You just listen to their witnesses. You'll see when Mr. Chertoff questions them, they'll be right direct, yes, answer every question. But when there is such a thing as cross examination, on cross examination these witnesses here, you'll hear, 'I don't remember. I don't recall. I don't remember.' Count the times they say I don't remember. But when Mr. Chertoff asks them questions, they will remember everything. They'll go back twenty years and remember. We'll ask them what they had for lunch and they may not recall.

"That's evidence. All kinds of evidence. Not just words. Watch how they act on the stand. That's evidence, too. That's the kind of evidence that the government is going to want you to send somebody to jail on.

"Labels? Labels, I tell you are a smokescreen. Mr. Chertoff told you to keep your eye on the issue, not the labels in the indictment but the charges in the indictment. Keep your eye on the issues. I say that, too. Keep your eye on the issues.

"Mr. Chertoff says this Mafia, Cosa Nostra, whatever he wants to call it, is all about making money. Orders go down, money went up. I'd like to know where that money went. You won't see it coming to me. They're going to present evidence but they won't prove the money went to me. Orders went down, money came up. That's okay, but they can't try me on gossip, on rumors. You're going to want proof. Let them prove it to you. That's their job, to prove it to you. It's not my job to prove anything.

"They tell you I gave Ralphie Scopo orders. You won't hear me on the tape talking to Ralphie Scopo. You won't hear Ralphie Scopo on one tape speaking to me. You won't hear Ralphie Scopo utter my name. You won't see me in a picture with Ralphie Scopo. The government can't put Ralphie Scopo with me. The witnesses will come here and they'll try to do it. All right. Let them prove it. Let them try to do it. Call the witnesses.

"Besides the witnesses that will take the stand, besides the money they paid them, there is such a thing called immunity. Immunity, the judge will explain it to you, but immunity is the witness will get up there and testify to all his past crimes, behavior, all his bad acts, and he won't go to jail because they told him, 'Tell us, you won't have to go to jail.' They gave him immunity, the people with the power gave them immunity. I can't give them immunity. If I call a witness, if I choose to call a witness, he will not have immunity. He'll sit up there and have to talk and tell the truth. And they'll be watching him. See if he makes a mistake. You can bet if he makes a mistake he'll have problems. I don't know about his witnesses, what happens if they make a mistake. I don't have the right to give immunity but he has. That's another thing you should consider.

"Now, you have a lot of FBI agents going to take the stand. Every time they get on the stand, Mr. Chertoff will ask them what is your job and they will say I'm a special agent of the Federal Bureau of Investigation assigned to the organized crime task force. There you go again with the labels. Special label. Special agent, every one of them is a special agent. They mean nothing more than anybody else. They have a motive. They get paid to do what they do. Just because they say they're special agents or they belong to an organized crime task force doesn't mean they are any more sincere, any more honest. You must study them and watch how they testify. I say them special agent and organized crime task forces are just another form of labels. Because they know they are going to come here and testify and they want to impress all you people.

"I hope to God that you do bring your common sense with you. After you finish hearing everything in this courtroom you'll know what the government is trying to do. You'll figure it out.

"Bear with me please. I have so many notes here, I don't know. I'm getting a little confused. I'm a little nervous, too. I'll try not to be too long.

"Well, I don't want to repeat myself but again you will not hear me on tape. You won't see a picture of me. They'll show you a lot of pictures, but you won't see one of me.

"They talked about my son. I want to see what they say about him.

"They say they are going to try to convince you that I was not around and when I was not around I gave Gerry Lang orders to carry out for me. These men sitting at this table are individuals. We're all responsible for our own actions. I gave no orders to Gerry Lang and I think Gerry Lang is man enough to take care of himself. He doesn't need any orders from me. You'll hear that on the stand, too. Gerry can take care of himself. None of these people need me to do anything.

"You'll hear talk about the construction industry. I own no construction company. I never worked in construction. I have no interest in concrete companies. You wouldn't hear me speaking to any concrete construction owners of companies, ready mix cement companies, no union delegates. I have no interest in concrete. If they say I have, let them prove it. I have no interest.

"Don't let them blind you, ladies and gentlemen, with all the labels, with Mafia, Cosa Nostra. That's not what the case is all about. All the lawyers told you that. I'm not going to take up too much of your time but I have to tell you, listen to the evidence. Listen to it the way they told you, with clear conscience and common sense and I'm sure after you hear all the evidence you will acquit me and find me not guilty.

"Thank you."

Carmine's opening had been far better than Chertoff had expected, but there were elements he thought he could score points with. Each time he called a witness that was an innocent crime victim, he always made sure to point out to the jury how "bold and brazen" they weren't.

During the trial, the *Chicago Tribune* claimed to have an inside source, a lawyer who knew Carmine well, and from him they offered insight into what made Carmine tick. The source said Carmine was "Intuitively intelligent. While he's so far not doing the job a good lawyer would do, he is doing a fantastic job for an organized crime guy." Regarding Carmine's scruples, the guy opined, "As mob guys go, he's loyal to his friends and he won't kill you unless he has a reason."

The government carefully laid out its case for the jury: the men on trial were bosses and underbosses of different but affiliated criminal enterprises, and they ran organizations that individually, *and sometimes in conjunction*, committed an assortment of crimes including scores of murders.

Carmine ran the Colombo family, they said. To demonstrate this, the prosecution showed the jury videotapes, played audiotapes. As promised, Carmine didn't appear on the tapes, but he was mentioned frequently, and always with reverence. Junior was the guy in charge.

Carmine remained alert and active in the courtroom. He was always quick to interrupt when he thought a witness wasn't speaking clearly enough to be heard by the jury, or if the lawyer's legalese was above the jury's head.

He sat mute however as the prosecution entered into evidence exhibit after exhibit of bills paid in connection with the Persico compound in Saugerties and noted how the conspicuous spending was impossible unless Carmine was the master criminal they said he was.

Some of the liveliest moments in Carmine's courtroom performance came during his cross-examination of prosecution witness Joe Cantelupo, who had identified Carmine in his direct testimony as boss of the Colombos.

Cantelupo told the court he was forty-three years old, born in

Brooklyn, raised in West Islip, way out on Long Island, graduated from high school there in 1961, served in the army for four years, and went to work for his dad's Dyker Heights realty company. Although he had never been convicted of a crime he admitted illegally finagling finances for friends. Back in the day he was also involved in fencing and shylocking. Those were the days when everyone worked for Joe Colombo.

During Cantelupo's direct examination, the government used him to explain how shylocking worked, so he carefully explained that debtors paid two percent weekly, that this was called the vig, for an indefinite period of time—until such a time that they could pay back the balance of the loan as a lump sum.

Cantelupo testified that he'd seen Carmine Persico having face-to-face meetings with Joseph Colombo, in a fashion that led him to believe Carmine was a key man in the Colombo family—even all those years ago.

When it was time to cross-examine, Carmine rose and moved to the questioning lectern. He wanted to make it clear to the jury that the whole notion that his meeting, sharing a meal, with Mr. Colombo was evidence of any kind of guilt was ludicrous. This witness simply didn't know him well enough to say these things about him.

Carmine said, "Mr. Cantelupo, you saw me in a public place. This is a public place, right? It's not a back of a restaurant, and the office that Joe Colombo worked in there was a big glass window, is that right?"

"Yes," Cantelupo replied.

"So you could see me, right. You could see from the outer office, you could see into the back?"

"Yes."

"And I came there to speak with Joe Colombo?"

"Yes."

"Did you know what I spoke to him about?"

"No, sir."

"Describe for these people my relationship to you."

"At that particular time or through the years?"

"At that time and at any time after."

"Our relationship was only to say hello, shake hands, goodbye, nothing formal."

"And you never heard what I spoke to Joe Colombo about?"

"No."

"You never sat down in the back office with us, did you?"

"No."

"Did you ever buy me dinner?"

"No."

"We ever go out partying together?"

"No."

"So everything that you spoke here in this courtroom about me was knowledge you picked up from other people?"

"Correct."

"Let's talk a little bit now about your cooperation. When did you first start cooperating with the government?"

"Nineteen seventy-three."

Carmine took Cantelupo through his criminal record. He was arrested for perjury in 1969 and for filing a false loan application in 1971, but nothing came of it.

"Did there come a time when you did not go to jail for burglary, for robberies, because you had a deal with the government?"

"Yes."

"How much were you paid for information in total between 1973 and 1978?"

"Twenty-four thousand dollars, approximately."

Carmine's eyes went wide with surprise, and he turned to the jury to make sure they heard that startling number. He returned his attention to the witness and bore down.

Cantelupo described life—his ratty, ratty life—as an FBI informant, one that came out in the open only in 1978 because his cover was blown.

"Didn't you testify at one time that the FBI threatened you, told you that they would get you killed, drop your name in the street and have you killed if you didn't come out?"

"Yes."

"And then you went into the Witness Protection Program, right?"

"Correct."

Cantelupo testified that his contract with the government was on a sliding pay scale, and that he was paid by the "value" of the information he testified to. The implication was clear. Carmine was a big fish and no doubt commanded top dollar.

Carmine wanted to demonstrate that Cantelupo was biased against him because of a previous beef with the Persico family, but in doing so he may have done his cause more harm than good.

"Do you feel a bookmaker, a shylock, somebody that deals outside the law is fair game for you to go and borrow money and keep it?"

"No."

"You felt if you borrow money from a shylock you would be obligated to pay him back?"

"Definitely."

"Alphonse Persico, you owed money to, didn't you?"

"Your brother?"

"Yes, Alphonse Persico my brother, not my son."

"Your brother I paid off."

"Who didn't you pay off?"

"I left owing money to Dominic Sidoti."

"Who else?"

"I don't recollect."

"The marshals didn't garnish your pay and go pay those people, did they? They arrested them and sent them to jail on your testimony?"

"As far as I know Sidoti was never arrested and went to jail."

"Didn't Alphonse Persico beat you in order to get you to pay the money back?"

"Yes."

"Didn't he treat you like a piece of garbage? Didn't he treat you that way, punching you in your face in front of people?"

"I didn't feel like a piece of garbage."

"You didn't feel like a piece of garbage? You hated him for punching you?"

"No."

"And you wouldn't go to the law to get even with him?"

"No."

"You went to the law because he was doing something wrong, he shylocked you and you went to the law on that?"

"That was over a period of time."

"Did he shylock you?"

"No."

"You took the money."

"No, I didn't."

"You took the money. He didn't give you the money."

"He gave me ten-thousand dollars. But not for me. To give to another guy."

Cantelupo identified the "other guy" as the publisher of pocket-sized paperback books. The publisher, Cantelupo said, didn't want the money so he took it back. This might not have made much sense to the jury, but Carmine followed with no problem.

"No interest?"

"Two points a week."

"Didn't he know you couldn't pay nobody?"

"I don't know what he knew."

"Did he know that you owed lots of money out and didn't pay anybody?"

"I paid for many years."

"You had to lie to my brother to get the ten-thousand dollars, didn't you?"

"I don't know."

"You know."

Carmine's tone was very sharp now. He was intimidating the witness. The jury didn't like it. Regardless of the tone, this exchange did as much to help the government's case as any of the prosecution's witnesses. His brother, Carmine had made clear, lent people money and beat them up if they didn't pay it back.

"Mr. Cantelupo, you said Anthony Colombo became a made member in what year?"

"1977."

"And you was told this?"

"Yes."

"You weren't at the ceremony or anything?"

"No, sir. But I heard he'd been made, and I congratulated him."

"And this is a secret organization, don't talk, and he comes and you congratulate him?"

"I knew Anthony was made and I congratulated him."

"And when you meet these people, they are introduced as so-and-so from the Genovese family, this guy's a good fellow with the Gambino family. Is that how they were introduced?"

"A lot of people confided in me."

"A lot of people got hurt for confiding in you. You testified against them," Carmine said. "When you wanted to borrow money from my brother, you could've walked away, right?"

"Yes."

"Nobody put a gun to your head and forced you to take the money?"

"No, sir."

"You took it because you wasn't going to pay it back so you didn't care how much interest they charged you."

"I took it because it was a good deal."

"Nothing else," Carmine said.

Cantelupo breathed a sigh of relief. He still had to be cross-examined by the other defense attorneys, but he felt the worst was over.

On the other hand, Carmine was kicking himself. He'd gotten caught up in the argument and his questions exposed the business.

Defense attorney Samuel Dawson grabbed the headlines for a day when he acknowledged the existence of the you-know-what: "The Mafia exists and has members. Just because someone is a Mafia member, it doesn't mean that he committed the crime in the case."

This was not helpful to his cause. It was as if Dawson didn't get it. RICO was very clear on that point.

Dawson told the jury that the commission existed as well. But it wasn't a war council. It didn't start trouble. Being a member was not a crime. It was more like the United Nations. The members met in an attempt to avoid conflict and prevent violence.

The photos placed into evidence by the government were perhaps the most damning of all. They showed the defendants exiting a May 15, 1984, meeting on Staten Island, proof that the bosses got together as a crime commission to run organized crime in New York City and elsewhere. (Carmine wasn't there, but only because he was incarcerated. He was represented at the meeting by Lang and Scopo, prosecutors said.)

One of the most damaging tapes was of Fat Tony and Tony Ducks having a conversation in the Palma Boys Social Club. In a nostalgic tone, doused with braggadocio, they discussed the current state of the mob.

"If it wasn't for me," Fat Tony said, "there wouldn't be any mob left. I made all these guys." He also said, "Tell him the commission from New York—tell him he's dealing with the big boys now."

Ducks added to the prosecutorial goldmine by discussing professional killings as something that needed to be carried out without emotion. A disabled target needed to be rubbed out the same as a healthy one. No difference. "He's crippled, but we do it," Ducks said. Some of the tapes the feds used against Ducks were from a bug planted in his chauffeur-driven Jaguar.

Of course, mob trials being what they were, many of the prosecution's witnesses had questionable credibility. Not only did these wiseguys admit on the stand that they had lied during previous trial testimony, but also that they were there because they'd cut a, for them, sweet deal with the government. These guys were like human bugs, flesh-and-blood surveillance devices, soaking up the details of how operations worked in the mob and spitting it back on cue under oath.

Fred DeChristopher was one of them. A rat among rats. He told the jury about how he had offered Carmine a place to hide and immediately called the FBI to tell them about it. DeChristopher described in detail how Carmine ran his business.

"And what was his business?" Chertoff asked.

"His business was running a crime family."

"Did he actually use the words 'crime family'?"

"No. He would never say that."

Chertoff asked, "Mr. DeChristopher, do you recall a conversation you had with Andrew 'Mush' Russo not long after the attempted assassination of Joseph Colombo?"

"I do. Russo told me that with Colombo out of commission, Carmine Persico was the boss now. Not long after that, Persico went to jail, but he stayed boss. The only thing that changed was they moved Junior's headquarters to the Diplomat at Third Avenue and Carroll Street." He testified that Carmine was boss, and that Lang and Scopo were Carmine's "key men."

"Was there an acting boss when Carmine Persico was in jail?"

"Yes."

"And who was it?"

"Tommy DiBella was the acting boss of the Persico family, uh, I mean the Colombo family."

"Did Carmine Persico have a nickname for Tommy DiBella?"

"Yes, he called him the Old Man."

According to DeChristopher, Scopo controlled the cement and concrete workers' union. The concrete workers' union, in fact, was Carmine's biggest skim. All deals of under $2 million, the Colombos got two points, anything over $2 million, they had to share the booty with the other families. You couldn't pour cement anywhere in the five boroughs without Carmine getting a cut. It was called The Concrete Club. After spending the bulk of the 1970s in prison for hijacking, Carmine emerged into the light to discover that a lot of people owed him money. Deals he had cut had been allowed to deteriorate. Carmine, for example, was supposed to get a third of the Tampa docks, but had only been getting ten percent. One guy was giving him ten percent of fifty percent. He had debts to collect, something he'd always been very good at. As soon as he got out of prison he sat down with the other bosses and explained the deals he had made and the amount he was owed. The percentages returned to those originally agreed upon and the retro debt was paid with a combination of cash and future power and turf considerations.

"Did he have comments regarding the other bosses?" Chertoff asked.

"Yeah," DeChristopher replied. "He said Tony Salerno was a big earner. He told me, 'The guy has more money than me.'"

The gallery looked to Fat Tony at the defendant's table, but he looked as miserable as ever with his inflamed eye and gnawing hunger pangs.

"When Mr. Persico got out of prison in 1979, how did he refer to the other bosses?"

"He always called them 'my friends.'"

"How did it come about that the defendant Carmine Persico came to stay at your house?"

"My brother-in-law, Andrew Russo, said Junior needed a quiet place to stay away from the limelight. My daughter's wedding had just ended, so she had vacated her attic room, and he said Junior only needed a place for two weeks. So he stayed up there."

"You were to be compensated?"

"Yes."

"How much?"

"Seven-hundred dollars a week."

"Did Junior offer to pay you for your hospitality?" Chertoff asked.

"He told me he had a lot of money on him and I should tell him if I needed anything. I was welcome to take whatever I needed. And I declined. But he is a very generous man. He is. He said all of the companies he had an interest in, I should sell them insurance. He was sure they would be receptive."

"What did he tell you about money?"

"He told me he wished his money was his only problem, that he had enough money to last ten lifetimes."

"Is that his words?"

"That's his words."

"How long did Carmine Persico live at your house?"

"Three months."

"Did he have a set schedule?"

"He got up about three in the afternoon, had breakfast and read the newspapers, *Post*, *Daily News*, and *Newsday*. He'd catch some early news on TV. Then we'd cook dinner. After dinner we would sit around and he'd read a little more or watch the news until about midnight. Him and I would generally play cards and about two o'clock there was a game show that would come on and he'd watch that and go to bed."

"When watching the news, was there any particular news that you observed him paying particularly close attention to?"

"Yes, anything that had to do with organized crime and the indictments, the arrests."

"Did you leave the house for any extended period of time while Junior was there?"

"I didn't. I had been advised that Junior did not like to be alone."

Carmine, DeChristopher said, talked about the indictments against him. He said he learned about them when a reporter for the *Post* called him and told him about them. He talked about his 1972 to 1979 prison stint and how for part of that stretch they had him cooped up in Marion where it was hard to do business because of limited visitor- and phone-privileges. Carmine told him about how much easier it was to run things when he was on the street. Problems had come up when he was in jail that would have been solved like that, snap of the fingers, if he'd been out.

DeChristopher recalled a time when attempts were made to serve a subpoena on him to testify regarding his brother-in-law Mush's taxes. The government wanted to talk about the house in Farmingdale that he was living in, the one he'd gotten from Mush. Instead of testifying against his brother-in-law, DeChristopher "went away for awhile." He hid out in the Boston area for a couple of months. He moved out of Mush's house and into his current home in Wantagh in 1979.

During the direct examination of Fred DeChristopher, Carmine on several occasions became concerned that the jury would hear references to Carmine being involved in a second trial, the Colombo case. He did not want the jury to know he was being tried twice at once in the same building but with different judges. Also, a previous witness had described him as a "fugitive," a characterization he thought prejudicial to the jury.

This just delayed the inevitable. Carmine had gabbed away about this and that while living in DeChristopher's house, and now it was all going to come back to slap him in the face. Carmine told Fred that Donnie Shacks was a tough guy, a guy who did things correctly when doing them for himself but ass backwards if he did them for anyone else. He said Mush was a guy for whom he had "tremendous respect," as a relative, a friend, and a top guy in the organization. He said Anthony "Scappi" Scarpati, a guy DeChristopher had spotted lurking outside his house while Carmine was staying there, was a friend from childhood. He told Fred about how teenaged Scappi did time, but when he got out Carmine immediately gave him a key position in his crew. He said he had great affection for his brother Alphonse, another guy who did a long stretch but had a job waiting for him when he got out. Carmine never put brother Allie Boy in charge of anything too complicated. His son Alphonse, on the other hand, was a person whose ideas Carmine respected. Little Allie Boy was allowed to give counsel.

Chertoff said, "Mr. DeChristopher, directing your attention to the period 1981 to 1984, when Carmine Persico was in prison," for parole violation, "what if anything did he tell you about his activities at that time?"

"He said when he went back to prison a second time he had no problem running his family. He said he had almost complete access to phones, visitors, as often as he wanted. He ate what and when he wanted to eat. He said it was pretty comfortable for him the second time."

"Did he say anything else about the running of his family during that time period?"

"Yes. He said that Gerry Lang and Donnie Shacks had the biggest role in running the family while he was in prison."

"What, if anything, did Mr. Persico tell you about Ralph Scopo?"

"He said Scopo was his front man in the Cement and Concrete

Workers Union and not a yard of concrete was poured in the City of New York where he and his friends didn't get a piece of it."

One thing about a trial with multiple defendants, after a witness had been questioned by the prosecution, each defense attorney had an opportunity to cross-examine. Although Judge Owens made it clear that he would not tolerate redundancy. As a rule, each witness affected one of the defendants more than the others, and many of the off-point lawyers waived cross-examination. Before the first witness was called, Carmine sat down with the attorneys defending the other so-called commissioners, and they had agreed that Carmine, should he choose, could be first to cross-examine. When it came time to cross-examine DeChristopher, Carmine Persico was practically licking his chops.

Just as any lawyer might, Carmine attacked DeChristopher's credibility, pointing out contradicting statements he had made in the past. He added that there was no credible evidence supporting the charges he faced.

The prosecution objected vigorously. Judge Owen sustained.

"Mr. Persico, please refrain from giving your closing argument until the appropriate time."

"Isn't it true that you made up lies about me to get the $50,000 reward?" Carmine asked.

"No, Junior, it is not," DeChristopher said.

"Isn't it true you're a liar? That you lied about me to cash in?" He snuck a glance at the jury. DeChristopher's answers didn't matter. It was the questions he wanted the jurors to hear.

"Objection, asked and answered."

"Sustained, Mr. Persico, please."

Judge Owen frowned, and banged his gavel.

"I beg your pardon, Your Honor," Carmine said.

Judge Owen added, "Mr. Persico, I am going to ask you to address yourself in the third person."

Carmine blinked twice, and said, "Such as?"

"Such as, 'Did you say this to Mr. Persico?' 'Was Mr. Persico there?' You have in the past said to a cop, 'Didn't you put the gun to my head?' The proper form of the question, in my judgment, because you are a lawyer when you are standing at that questioning lectern, would be to say to the officer, 'Didn't you put the gun to Mr. Persico's head?'"

Carmine said he understood. But the lesson only partly took. Most of the time the witness continued to call Mr. Persico "Junior," while Mr. Persico referred to himself in the first person.

Mr. Persico knew why DeChristopher was so desperate to work for the government. Money. Fred was in debt to an unhealthy degree. Carmine had a list of people to whom DeChristopher was rumored to owe money, and he ran down the list with the witness, asking how much he owed. Legal decorum went out the window, and no one objected.

"Did we forget any other money that you owe people?"

"That's possible, Junior."

"You need time to think? I'd like to know who else you owe money to."

"I don't know, Junior. You tell me."

Carmine attempted to draw out DeChristopher's hypocrisy. Didn't DeChristopher get $500 a week from restaurants to keep the union out? Didn't he threaten them with a black mob throwing things through his windows? Didn't he use Lenny Montana to intimidate people? Did he say things like, "If you wasn't our good friend, we would kill you"? Didn't he use certain restaurants as a personal check-cashing service, because they were afraid of him? Didn't he sic the union on businesses that didn't pay? Didn't he arrange for a food critic to give a restaurant a favorable review in exchange for a piece of the place? Didn't he do that knowing full well the owner had cancer and not long to live? Didn't he try to get a life insurance policy—no physical, of course—for the dying guy with the agreement to split the payout with the widow? Didn't he assault the widow?

DeChristopher denied some of it. The rest he said he couldn't remember.

"Why did you shake them down?"

"I shaked them down, Junior?"

"Yes, you shook them down."

"Why did I shake them down?"

"I'm asking you."

"I never shook them."

Judge Owen interrupted, "Are you finished, Mr. Persico?"

"I'm not finished. I've got a lot more to go," Carmine replied, as if he were describing his life.

Judge Owen threw up his hands. "There is a lot of back and forth going on here that I can't control," he said wearily.

The jury looked annoyed. Carmine's bully side had again surfaced.

It is common practice during trials to have "sidebars," meetings of counsel with the judge at the front of the courtroom, conversations not for the jury's ears. The defendant is usually left alone at the defense table during this process, so it was an odd sight when Carmine joined in the sidebars, arguing a point in a hushed tone.

Carmine continued to grill DeChristopher. Didn't a certain restaurant owner come to him for a favor when one of his waiters was blackmailing him? The witness said it was sort of true. They really were trying to get in touch with Mush, and he was a conduit.

"Isn't it a fact, sir, that four months after you married Katherine Russo you got in touch with the FBI to inform upon her brother?"

"That's true, that's true."

"And at that time, February and March of 1974, did you have

any specific problems with Andrew Russo? Did he intervene in your marriage? Did he try to meddle in your personal and family affairs?"

"No, sir."

"Yet you called the FBI and started giving them information about Andrew, is that right?"

"Yes, it is."

"What was your reason?"

"I think they are despicable," DeChristopher said, apparently referring to gangsters in general. "They are the most despicable people on the face of the earth and that's why I began to do it."

"And knowing that Andrew Russo was one of those despicable people, you nonetheless married into that family, is that right?"

"I married Katherine, not the family."

"You chose Andrew to be your best man."

"She chose him to be best man."

"When you hooked up people with beefs with people who fixed problems, did you say, 'Stay away from those people, they are despicable'?"

Chertoff: "Objection. Argumentative."

Judge Owen sustained.

The cross-examination had become a toe-to-toe fight with both men landing solid blows, neither playing defense. To the referee, Judge Owen, it had started to sound like a family argument, and he stepped in.

During a recess, attorney Frank Lopez, the man who would have represented Carmine had he not been repping himself, spoke with a reporter in the hall. Naturally, Carmine's performance came up.

"He's coming off like a human being," Lopez said. "The jury understands that he's not a lawyer."

"Witnesses are afraid of him," the reporter said.

Lopez laughed lightly, a "ya think?" laugh. "He is placed in an advantageous position when there are witnesses affecting him. He's not only an attorney in this case, they tell me he's also a boss."

When the government rested, Carmine called only one defense witness, his cousin Kim Roggeman, Fred's step-daughter, the original occupant of the attic room Carmine had lived in for three months. She said she was a teacher, that she'd just had a baby. She testified that she was fourteen years old when Fred DeChristopher married her mother. She'd known Carmine Persico her entire life. She'd seen him three of four times a week during the time he was living with Fred and her mom. Her understanding was that cousin Carmine was staying for a while because he had some problems he was working through. She hadn't asked what the problems were. She never heard Carmine say any of the things Fred said he said, and as far as she knew, Cousin Carmine was a highly successful legitimate businessman.

"Did you ever hear your father and Mr. Persico or anyone discuss the construction business?"

"No."

He listed his co-defendants. Had she ever heard Fred and Carmine mention any of them. She hadn't. During the time that Mr. Persico lived at the DeChristophers', did Roggeman ever see his wife Joyce or son Al. She had not. She remembered Carmine's stay as a fun time. They played cards and Trivial Pursuit. She heard some business talk from the men, but all legitimate stuff, like getting together and opening a coffee shop.

As Roggeman stepped down from the witness stand, Judge Owens said, "Mr. Persico, will you be calling another witness?"

"No, Your Honor," Carmine said. "The defense for Carmine Persico rests."

While Michael Chertoff handled the opening statement and much of the questioning of witnesses during the trial, it was his youthful prosecution teammate, U.S. Attorney John F. Savarese who delivered the closing argument. It was an artful speech that helped win Savarese the Attorney General's John Marshall Award for Outstanding Legal Achievement. Regarding Junior, Savarese said, "Persico would like you to accept his smoke screen and believe that the money that furnished an estate like the one in Saugerties just came out of thin air, it didn't come from any of his criminal activities. Remember what he told Fred DeChristopher: 'I've got enough money for ten lifetimes.'"

Eventually it came time for Carmine's closing argument, and he didn't pass up the opportunity to raise his own voice in one final plea for common sense.

CHAPTER TWELVE
La mia voce

"YOUR HONOR, ladies and gentlemen of the jury, at the beginning of the case I told you I wasn't a lawyer. I guess you found out that's true. I don't think I could speak as well as all these people did, but I am going to try to make you understand what the facts are in this case. I am going to try to tell you what I think: To me, it is like a bus ride in a sightseeing tour. You came here. We had the opening statements. The government told you what they intended to prove. The gentlemen of the defense told you what they said they couldn't prove. We had the witnesses take the stand, direct, cross. Now we come to the summations. And that is the tour. That is the sightseeing bus tour.

"Mr. Savarese, the other day, put us all on the bus, the whole bunch of us, and he was going to take us through the tour and show us what the evidence was, as he has seen it. We got on the bus. And where did he take us? He took us to tinseltown, Hollywood town, cardboard town. Big maps, big signs, theater marquee.

"In a movie, in a Hollywood production, you always try to use top names, stars, to attract attention, Genovese family, Gambino family, names that have been around for a lot of years and everybody is familiar with it.

"So that is part of the tour. That's what I think the case is. But on that bus tour you come to a rest stop, a rest area, and that is the defense summation. At that rest area, we try to go over what he told you on the tour, what case happened, because there is a return trip. You have to get back on that bus and come back the other way and they are going to put another tour guide on that bus.

"Mr. Savarese got on the bus right in the front and, as all tour guides do, started to tell you what he had seen and what he built on the way. I quote from Mr. Savarese's summation, 'Put aside any preconceptions or prejudice you might have about the Mafia.' And, 'It's true that you should not convict just because a defendant is a member of the Mafia.' And, 'Sure, membership alone is not enough. It is not in itself a crime.' You have been told that a couple of times, while you were being picked, selected as jurors. Mr. Savarese acknowledges it and of course the defense asks you to keep that in mind.

"Not only is it not a crime to be a member. You have to prove in this case that somebody not only agreed to commit a crime, but did commit a crime. We are going to look for that agreement. I don't think you are going to find it as to Carmine Persico. As I stand here, I only talk about Carmine Persico. I am going to try not to mention any of the other defendants in this case because they will defend themselves.

"Another thing he said at the beginning of the summation that I want to bring to your attention. The government spent a lot of time on membership and proving who was boss with big charts and everything. We will go through it a little bit. I want to bring your attention to another thing Mr. Savarese said while we were going through this town on this tour: 'Now, the government has not charged these other men with involvement in the murder because we have no direct evidence.' Direct evidence. I say he has no direct evidence not only to the murder case against Carmine

Persico. I say in the concrete and extortion case he has no evidence.

"You remember Fred DeChristopher—we will talk about him later—he says Carmine Persico voted not to kill Galante. The government didn't even consider that direct evidence or else they would have indicted me in the murder. They didn't indict me. They chose not to indict me in the murder because they had no direct evidence. Without Fred DeChristopher, Carmine Persico wouldn't be in this courtroom.

"There is another kind of evidence—circumstantial evidence. We will talk about that, too. But direct evidence, Mr. Savarese admits that he can't indict us because there was no direct evidence in the murder.

"They have to prove two predicate acts in order to convict me of a RICO count. I say they can't prove even one act, let alone two acts. There is no direct evidence and there is no circumstantial evidence. A lot of smoke, a lot of cardboard scenery, a lot of big charts. Fake towns.

"They spent a lot of time trying to prove who was the boss of the Colombo family, who was the boss of this family. They went back to 1957 to Apalachin. Brought in pictures of the farm up there. 1957. Lawyers all objected. 'Your Honor, objection. Objection.' The judge said, 'I will let it in for history.' I say that is history, all right, *ancient* history. It doesn't bear on anyone in this courtroom. Mr. Savarese didn't say anybody at this table was at Apalachin."

"And who do they bring in? Who did they bring in to prove Carmine Persico was a boss? Cantelupo. Well, we can talk about him, Cantelupo. Cantelupo is one of them witnesses I told you about in my opening. Immunity. Paid substantially. Called him back whenever they needed him. Threw him out of the program whenever they didn't want him. Brought him back again. I hope they don't try to say he is my friend because I never received a

Christmas gift off of him. I never went out to dinner with him. You heard who went out to dinner with him. He told you that. You heard who he sent gifts to for Christmas. He got so good at it he negotiates his own deals, He didn't even need a lawyer. They didn't even give him a list of lawyers to pick from because he had been testifying, wheeling and dealing with the government since 19—what did he say, '72, '73, '71? I forget. But it's in the record. Yes, he asked him did you make a deal with the government for this to come here and testify? Did you have a lawyer make the deal? No, he made it himself. He told you all about how he lied to all the agents. Full immunity. Bold and brazen—and he was *bold and brazen*. You seen it. I told you to look for it. And I think I proved that. If not, he helped me prove it. All the stickups, all the robberies, narcotics he sold. They didn't put him in jail. They kept putting him on the stand to testify against everybody. And every time he got on he had more to tell. He forgot to tell them. They didn't write it down. He remembered it here. If an agent wrote something in the record, he said I didn't say that, that's not my words.

"Let me read you some of his testimony."

Carmine read from the court transcript an exchange in which Savarese, referring to a time after the shooting of Joe Colombo, had tried to get Cantelupo to say the phrase "acting boss" to describe someone. Cantelupo wouldn't do it, and insisted on the word "boss" instead. Carmine's thinking was that the government was trying to program the phrase "acting boss" into the jury's collective mind.

"You see, you have to get programmed to using the word acting boss. Because he has to act for Carmine Persico. Because Carmine Persico is never around. All these years talking about, all these things going, driving through the town, can't put Carmine Persico on the scene, so he has to put in the word 'acting.' And that's not the last acting boss he's got. He has got plenty of them. They change. Like they take them up and put them down like the names they put on that chart, the marquee we will call it. When the movie changes, they take the sign down and that's what they did. Acting. Misstating.

"Talk about the Colombo family, about the boss, about this, which is not necessary, they say, because that's not a crime. But let's see what they did. They went back to Apalachin. They brought in pictures and cops about an arrest in LaStella's restaurant in Queens, happened sometime in the sixties. It's a restaurant open for the public. A couple of people went in there to eat. They were arrested. Mafia meeting. House of Chan, a few more people got together to have dinner. They didn't hide. They went in restaurants, public places. Again, a Mafia meeting. Everything. Say they are going to take you through the dark worlds of the underworld. Restaurants, House of Chan. You heard me ask the FBI agent that surveilled me there. Were there other customers? Was the place closed? Was the place open? A lot of people in the restaurant, he said.

"After Cantelupo, they brought another witness in. This one is a good one. Angelo Lonardo. *Bold and brazen*, drug dealer, lonesome in prison. Wanted to come home. So he called up the agents, told them everything he knew. They went back to that judge in Cleveland, promised to help Lonardo get him bail so he could get out, help the agents clean up organized crime. The judge wouldn't give him bail. That judge denied him. What's he have to do? Tell him you have to do better than that. The only one you can talk to. That is Giuliani, the U.S. Attorney in New York, somebody important in the Justice department. They tell him you have to do better than that. That's on page 711 of the transcripts. Good number. Lucky number. It was lucky for Lonardo. He got out. He's not living in jail any more. He said he can't go where he wants but he's eating a little better. They told him they could make a deal but they couldn't write it down. I don't know why they couldn't write it down. They were hiding anything? Was that in the darkness? Or was that in the light? Whatever it was, he spoke to the right person because he's not there no more. He's not in jail no more. And you know what happened? That judge in Cleveland did cut his sentence—only after he spoke to Mr. Giuliani. That's the power I spoke about in my opening, so I guess I kept my promise to you on that.

"Let me talk about Lonardo just a little bit more. I don't want to bore you with him. What did he come up here to say? Did he come up here to say anything about the construction? He don't know anything about construction, he says that. Does he know Carmine Persico? No, he don't know Carmine Persico. But he came up here to talk about Mafia and rules which Mr. Savarese said that alone can't convict. You got to have direct evidence. You don't have no direct evidence of Carmine Persico. He never met him. He said he met my son, Alphonse Persico, Carmine Persico's son. When he met Carmine Persico's son, they didn't talk about construction, they talked about helping Alphonse Persico, his uncle, if he could come in and surrender and get five years—five years for slapping Joe Cantelupo. That says he was a shylock. Joe Cantelupo says that. They didn't talk about construction.

"How many people did Lonardo say he killed? Admitted? He had a hundred years, life plus twenty-five. It's a lot of years. Talk about prejudice. That's what they brought him here for: prejudice, to use the Mafia. He went back to 1927, how he killed a doctor because a doctor operated on his cousin, his cousin died with appendix and he went and killed the doctor. He says he's a boss. Him. You have to take his word for it. There was no other evidence for it. I'll talk no more about Mr. Lonardo.

"Now they are going to bring the big evidence in this case. Mr. Chertoff, again in summation, said, you've seen the checks. Joyce Persico and Michael Persico's check, two checks. He showed you the two checks but he didn't tell you what the checks are. They just showed them, endorsement, nobody said what they are. They didn't say they are supposed to be a pay to me through my wife. Mr. Savarese said the Mafia, they don't write checks to the Mafia. You pay them cash, hundred dollar bills. That's what they said. But if you write a no-show job check, bring it to Carmine Persico's wife, Joyce, she'll cash it. And then they bring it here. Ask them on that ride back. Ask them to tell us what the checks are for. What are they here for? Are they evidence? Evidence to what? Evidence that Gerry Langella knows Carmine Persico and knows Joyce Persico? What is it? What do they want you to believe from this? What inference do they want you to draw from this? Is this direct evidence? I don't know. They showed them to you but they haven't told us what they want us to believe from them. Maybe on the trip back they'll tell us."

Carmine complained about the attention the government gave to his farm in Saugerties, how they made it seem like something out of a James Bond novel, a fortress. One thing they didn't do. Show the jury photos. Carmine took care of that. "Smaller than you thought, huh?" he commented. "See how sinister." That got a small laugh. Carmine reiterated that he didn't even own the farm, not even a piece of it. It was owned by his son, Alphonse T. Persico. The attention the government paid to the property "since it was bought" was more "tinseltown, another cardboard front. What does this got to do with this case? Let them prove I own that farm. They did not." They did the same thing with the cost of Joyce Persico's two automobiles. They were gifts from sons Little Allie Boy and Michael. "Nothing was hidden from the government," Carmine said.

He discussed the meeting he'd attended that was raided and violated his parole. "I was running out the back, they said, and there with this person and this person and this person. I did five years for that. What does it have to do with this case? Nothing.

"Another label: acting boss. Everybody acts for Carmine Persico but you never see Carmine Persico acting or doing anything. You see Little Allie Boy or Gerry Lang doing this or that, and the government infers that they are following orders. Oh-oh, here's a picture of Ralph Scopo and Alphonse Persico talking. They spent fifteen minutes together in Dyker Heights. They didn't mention that Allie Boy has an office near there, that his mother lives near there. They'll have you think everything Alphonse T. does is for his father. They had a theory that trouble started because Donnie Shacks went off on his own and did something without Carmine Persico not knowing about it. Theories. They didn't bring up one witness that said he talked to me, except Fred DeChristopher. They told you about all the phones they got tapped and Fred DeChristopher says I'm running a family through the phones. A prison phone is not an easy place to talk about criminal activity. The government has access to a list of every visitor I ever received in prison, of every phone call I made or received, and they introduced none of that into evidence here. I'll leave it up to you to figure out why.

"They come up with records from 1957, hotel bills from 1957. No phone records, no taps. Donnie's phone was bugged, Gerry's phone was, and Tom DiBella's house was, Donnie's club, Casa Storta, the restaurant, Scopo's. Tell me something: why in 1982 if Tom DiBella is retired, they say he is, why would they be bugging his phone? If Carmine Persico is the boss and he is giving orders to his son, don't you think they would tap the son's phone? Get a court order and put a bug in his house? They don't do none of these things. And they don't have my voice on tape."

He'd been revving up, but now paused, took a sip of water, and when he started again he spoke softer and more slowly. Carmine told the jury he had heard and appreciated the cleverness of Mr. Chertoff's using the phrase "bold and brazen" against him, as he presented legit witnesses who'd been victimized and had really suffered. He trusted the jury knew which of the government's witnesses the phrase was meant to describe.

"Fred DeChristopher was bold and brazen," Carmine said. "The million-dollar roundtable man, insurance man. His wife, son, and son-in-law all said he couldn't hear too good. While on this stand, seventy-seven times Mr. DeChristopher asked Mr. Chertoff to repeat the question. 'Didn't hear you,' he said. Right after he married Katherine DeChristopher, for no other reason than to be a good citizen, he says, he went to the FBI and started giving them information. He says I went to his house on November 12. He accepted me at the house. He didn't tell me I had to leave. He accepted me. He took me in the house and I stayed there for three months. He decided, the first time I went there, to give me up, but only after he goes to the post office and sees my wanted poster and the $50,000 reward.

"It's true. I fled. I came home from jail after four years, first time eight years, second time four years, and I ran away. Maybe, again, I was tired of going back and forth to jail. Maybe I was tired of being pulled into these courtrooms, being tried on my name, my reputation. Maybe I was afraid. Not again. For what? What could I have done being in jail for so long, so many years? When does it end? When do they stop? When do they leave you alone? When do they stop inferring? Why don't they get proof, direct evidence?

"So I went to Fred and Katherine's house and I stayed there. Then I got caught and they put me on trial. Who comes to testify? Fred DeChristopher. The government puts him on the stand and he tells you, 'Carmine Persico spoke to me.' He says I knew Carmine Galante. Met him in jail. Played cards. That's evidence? He got in all the key words though: boss, top man, organized crime family, control. He only came here to testify, do his duty. If you noticed, he never remembered. 'I can't recall.' But as soon as you shook a piece of paper at him, he remembered. He only testified to what you showed him. And he talked about the things he says I told him. They never even tried to prove it was true. *They took his word for it*. Did he say, 'Persico told me there are ten guns in this house,' and they went there and found ten guns? No. It was just conversation. Even though there was always someone else in the house, Fred is the only one who heard these conversations. He owes a lot of people money, can't pay it back, but he paid $800 a month for his girlfriend's rent, paid for his daughter's wedding, $20,000, $30,000, says he got scared seeing people come to his house, Anthony Scarpati outside his house, he's not family. After I came, he left his house with six dollars and no teeth, owing money to everybody, without a dime in the world, and he wants you to believe he didn't want the $50,000 reward money for turning me in, that he is here testifying because he's a good citizen. They told you to bring your common sense with you to this courtroom and I pray to God you brought it with you as we talk about Fred DeChristopher. When he came here to testify the government was paying him $3,000 a month. That is bought-and-paid-for testimony. He did pretty good for a man who ran away from home with six dollars and no teeth. The government gave him a new life, a new life to start with his girlfriend. Dedicated family man, worried about his children, left his whole life behind, never even called them, never even bothered to find out how they were doing, never bothered to send them money, didn't care if they had money or not. Despicable? How much more despicable can you be than Fred DeChristopher?"

Carmine paused for a drink of water and steadied himself for the final push.

"Mafia, Mafia, Mafia. Take Mafia out of this trial, there's no case here. Mafia and my past and that I have been in jail. That's what they depended on to convict everybody here. How much longer do they want me to keep on paying for that mistake I made"—referring to his hijacking conviction—"to go to jail. Mafia, Mafia, and jail."

He came home from prison and they tailed him every second.

He was on parole. Why didn't they call his shadow to the stand? Because they never saw him doing anything, that was why.

"Ladies and gentlemen, I can't say that I never did anything wrong, because you know I have been to jail, but you can't send me back to jail because I've been in jail. They have to prove I did something else. And the only thing in this country that makes anybody have faith in this justice system is the jury. Ask someone that knows. We have no faith in the prosecutor. We have no faith in the courts. We have faith in the jury because the jury is people with no ax to grind. They come in here, they promise to judge the evidence as they see it, and thank God for the jury system in this country. That is what makes us separate and apart from any other country. And our faith is in the jury.

"You gave us your promise that you won't be prejudiced, that you will look for the evidence, and I say if you look for the evidence, you will find no evidence against Carmine Persico that he extorted any money from any contract companies or had anything to do with the concrete companies.

"Thank you, ladies and gentlemen."

He had spoken for ninety minutes.

The lawyers for the other defendants didn't have Carmine's advantage. Their clients had not been in prison when the crimes occurred. And their voices and images appeared in much of the surveillance footage the jury watched for more than two months. They argued that things were not as they appeared and sounded on those tapes. Their clients had not been extorting anyone. They'd been given a fee for mediating business deals. That's all. Sure the defendants had met in Staten Island, sure they had a club of sorts, but that didn't mean they were masterminding anything.

The only defendant not in the club was Bonanno capo, Bruno Indelicato. He was in a different club, altogether. The jury had seen Indelicato in a surveillance video taken in Little Italy at the

Ravenite Club—Neil Dellacroce, your host—only hours after the 1979 hit on Bonanno boss Carmine Galante, a death that hastened Indelicato's criminal success. The video showed Indelicato being congratulated on the "good job" he did. On that evidence—and the fact that he left a palmprint on the getaway car, and was promoted from soldier to capo soon after the hit—he was on trial for Galante's murder. Even if Indelicato did leave his palmprint on a getaway car, that didn't mean he was an agent for any so-called Commission. It was all the government's active imagination.

The last word to the jury came from Assistant U.S. Attorney Michael Chertoff. He said that he disagreed strongly with the defense's claim that belonging to the Mafia should not in itself be considered a crime. "The Mafia is very relevant in this case. The Mafia is relevant because it is the Mafia that makes possible this kind of concerted criminal activity," Chertoff explained. The Mafia itself *was* on trial here.

The jury deliberated for five full days, repeatedly asking for tapes to be shown to or played for them one more time. The last tape they asked to re-hear was the one in which Salerno took credit for "making" all of the mob's current members, and Tony Ducks said that killing firm and infirm men needed to be done with an equally cool dispatch.

Early on the sixth day of deliberation the jury foreman informed the court that the jurors had reached a unanimous verdict—151 of them, in fact. The jury convicted the eight defendants on all counts. The defendants took it without outward emotion, all but Indelicato, who giggled inappropriately.

January 13, 1987, Carmine was sentenced in the commission case to one hundred years in prison. He was the only defendant to make a statement following his sentencing. Carmine addressed the court, "This case was prejudiced from the first day, and that is because of the slanted and unfair publicity the case received, all of this Mafia-mania that's been flying around. Your honor, I urge you to focus on a defense accusation of prosecutorial misconduct instead of attempting to satisfy the public that he's sending Mafia people to jail for one hundred years."

Looking at it from a gang-busting point of view, this had to be the best day ever. Here was the Mafia's "board of directors." Fat Tony Salerno, Genovese; Tony "Ducks" Corallo, Lucchese; and Carmine Persico, Colombo—all gone forever. Seven of the eight drew a century. Bruno Indelicato got forty years.

The only defendant to sass the judge was Sal "Tom Mix" Santoro, seventy-two years old, Lucchese underboss. The evidence against him consisted of tapes of him mediating a loan-shark dispute with Tony Ducks.

As the judge was about to read Tom Mix his sentence, "You are in the driver's seat, Judge. Give me the hundred years."

"I'm just doing my job, Mr. Santoro," Judge Owen said.

"And you're doing a good job," was Santoro's sarcastic reply.

When Judge Owen was about to sentence Gerry Lang, his lawyer Frank Lopez pointed out that Lang was already doing a stint. "He doesn't have that much more time to give to his country, Your Honor," Lopez said. Lang nonetheless was sentenced to one hundred years, and would die at age seventy-four at the U.S. Medical Center for Federal Prisoners in Springfield, Missouri, on December 15, 2013.

The judge was calm and efficient except for when he sentenced Fat Tony Salerno, who during the trial had spent more time thinking about his own discomfort than the legal matters being bandied about. Salerno was allowed to snack on cookies and candy while court was in session but still complained about getting a sandwich instead of a hot lunch at the noon break. There was a fuss when co-defendant Indelicato tried to slip Salerno a sandwich during court, but the transfer was spotted and the food confiscated. That stuff had annoyed the judge, but it was Fat Tony's career synopsis that really pissed him off: "You have essentially spent a lifetime terrorizing this community to your financial advantage," Judge Owen said.

Carmine, somewhat ludicrously, was on trial twice at the same time. Justice would seem to indicate that a guy facing life in prison should be able to take on his trials one at a time, so he could properly prepare for both. But Carmine was not given that consideration, mostly because he had co-defendants. Unless Carmine was to be tried separately, and the government did not want to do that, he was going to have to endure overlapping trials.

While he was doing an admirable but imperfect job representing himself at the commission trial, the "Colombo trial" was also devastating Carmine's chances for future freedom. Because there was overlap, both trials were held in Federal District Court in Manhattan.

At the Colombo trial, U.S. Attorney Aaron R. Marcu, a Harvard Law graduate, offered the jury a short bio, saying that Junior killed his first human being in 1951, when he was seventeen years old. While it is true that Carmine was arrested for murder in March 1951, those charges were dropped and his brother Alphonse took the entire rap for shooting Steve Bove in the backseat of the Blue Beetle's car. This wording on Marcu's part, put together with Carmine's arrest following the Prospect Park rumble, may have been the origin of the story that Carmine as a teenager beat a kid to death with his bare hands.

In November 1985, at the Colombo trial, with Judge John F. Keenan presiding, the first and star prosecution witness was Richard Annicharico, the bribable IRS agent that wore a wire while meeting with Carmine and others back in 1978. He was on the stand for four days.

Annicharico had been allowed to listen to the tapes earlier and had initialed them. He testified as to the authenticity of their content. The tapes were admitted into evidence and played for the jury.

The first tape was the clincher, the others window dressing. On that initial recording, jurors heard a meeting between Annicharico and McIntosh, in which McIntosh agreed to pay a hefty bribe, somewhere upward of $250,000, in exchange for Carmine's early release from prison. There were other tapes supporting the notion that the bribe actually took place. Annicharico was on all of the tapes, of course. He was the one wearing the wire. The final tape was recorded on February 2, 1978, and on it defendant Hugh McIntosh could be heard discussing the $250,000 and saying there was "more where that came from."

Carmine Persico, Victor Puglisi, et al. were arrested in connection with the bribery case, but Puglisi disappeared. The bag of money, Annicharico testified, was never recovered by authorities.

With the jury out of the room, the court heard testimony from Mush Russo's lawyer, George L. Santangelo, who said that he objected to Annicharico's testimony implying that witnesses before the 1978 grand jury hearing on Russo's taxes were going to be bumped off. Judge Keenan sustained the objection, and Annicharico was allowed to say instead that he sought back in 1978 "to insure the witnesses didn't have any problem."

Another key prosecution witness was Arlyne Brickman, the professional *goomada*/informant from New Jersey who cursed a blue streak as she induced men to talk about business. She rode to the courthouse on the morning of her testimony in a van containing heavily armed FBI men. The van drove directly into the basement of the Manhattan courthouse. She wore slacks and high heels. A bit of a hot mess to begin with, she appeared particularly disheveled. She was a nervous wreck, and heard Carmine and his co-defendants snickering at her as she entered the courtroom and took the witness stand. Her presentation was sprinkled with malaprops. She wanted to say asterisks and instead said asteroids. She told her story though: on Belmont Stakes day she'd borrowed money from a loanshark who told her the money came from Anthony Scarpati. She was humiliated during cross-examination when Scarpati's lawyer Jack Evseroff managed to work the word asteroid into his questions a few times and got a laugh each time. He asked her what she did for a living in 1981. She said she was a housewife, and that got a louder laugh. A more substantive cross came from Gerry Lang's attorney David Breitbart, who attacked Brickman's morality, and rattled her with detailed business questions. When Brickman was done, her ego in rags around her feet, FBI agents whisked her to an airport to start a new life.

Of Carmine's two simultaneous trials, the Colombo case—the one in which he used a real lawyer—ended first, as expected with a conviction. Also convicted in the case was Carmine's son Alphonse, who received twelve years. Marcu called Little Allie Boy "his father's trusted lieutenant, the future of the Colombo family." Lieutenant, in this case, was equivalent to captain, or capo.

At Carmine's sentencing hearing in the Colombo trial, Judge Keenan praised Carmine's performance as his own lawyer in the commission trial. As the trials were being held in the same courthouse, he'd sat in the gallery as a spectator for part of that trial. He then called Carmine a "tragedy."

"You are one of the most intelligent men I have ever seen in my life," Judge Keenan said. He then sentenced Carmine to thirty-nine years.

So Carmine's arrests and legal history culminated with his June 14, 1986, conviction for racketeering, extortion, etc. He has been incarcerated ever since. All that followed was the government thumping its puffed-out federal chest.

In November 1986, cousin Mush Russo was sentenced to fourteen years. He got out after serving eight, and was free for four years before going down again in 1999, for jury tampering and parole violation.

When both of Carmine's trials were finished, Rudy Giuliani was asked if Carmine was just going to run the Colombos from prison as he reportedly had in the past. Giuliani said no. Carmine had already appointed an acting boss and was "unlikely to retain power."

(And this, of course, is precisely what Carmine says happened. Just because some hopped-up torpedo said, "This is for Carmine!" when he hit somebody, didn't mean it was really *for Carmine*. The shooters were having a moment, glorying in the power of the Persico name. It was like taking an oath.)

With Carmine away for good, law enforcement let out a collective sigh of relief. They'd always had a feeling that Carmine was different, that killing wasn't just a matter of business for him, but a basic component of his problem-solving. Obstacles were to be removed, regardless of whether or not they were human. Alan Cohen, former chief of the organized crime unit under U.S. Attorney Giuliani, once said that if we removed the context of organized crime from Carmine's resumé, what remained would reveal him to be a psychopathic mass murderer.

To rub Carmine's nose in it, Judge Keenan specified that his sentence at the Colombo trial and the one from the commission trial were to be served back-to-back. Since the feds had no parole, if by some miracle Carmine survived the thirty-nine years, he would be ninety-two by the time he served it all, and would still have one-hundred years to go.

Carmine's wife Joyce was normally a very private woman, but following her Carmine's twin convictions she became bitter, angry, and fumed in public: "I know the kind of man he is. The love that Carmine and I have for our family and our home has helped us through the years of excessive punishment the government had inflicted upon us. We survived the ordeal, Carmine came home, and just when we thought it was safe to resume our lives again, along came RICO and Giuliani."

All of the prosecutors that put Carmine away made hay out of their success, but the spearhead of the investigation and prosecution, Rudy Giuliani, made by far the most—enough to fill a silo. He became New York City mayor, a national figure in the wake of 9/11, and an aspirant to the U.S. presidency.

Michael Chertoff parlayed his success into a position in the George Bush administration as assistant attorney general overseeing the Justice Department's Criminal Division. When informed of Chertoff's success in the Bush administration, Fat Tony Salerno, on his last legs, said, "He owes me a thank-you note."

The commission case defendants had waived their right to appeal their conviction on grounds of incompetent counsel, but there were plenty of other reasons to appeal—alleged prosecutorial misconduct, for example, desperation being first and foremost. Carmine, still working *pro se*, i.e., on his own behalf, filed an appeal for a rehearing on February 18, 1987. His primary argument was that RICO laws were unconstitutional. In court, RICO gave the prosecution a handful of cards it didn't deserve: immaterial evidence, illegal surveillance, etc. Trouble was, RICO was the law of the land. Lawyers objected that defendants who were charged with varying crimes should be tried together. The RICO laws, however, established that they could be tried together because they shared identical "patterns of crimes." The appeals process revealed only minor glitches in the Chertoff case, but nothing to overturn a verdict. The appellate court did say that evidence linking Persico, Salerno, and Corallo, to the murder of Carmine Galante was largely based on "speculation and inference." Other than that, the conviction was good.

Carmine's address on the paperwork was the Metropolitan

Correctional Center, a federal facility commonly referred to as MCC, 150 Park Row in Manhattan. For a time, Carmine was mostly concerned with being allowed to stay at MCC until the appellate process had run its course, rather than being sent to an out-of-town penitentiary. Not that MCC was nice. It was dank and overcrowded. Its nickname was "New York Guantanamo." But Carmine wrote that he wanted to stay close to his friends and family during this difficult time. Carmine's request was denied and he was shipped to the U.S. Penitentiary in Marion, Illinois, the very pen Carmine had reportedly complained to Fred DeChristopher about, the pen where it was "hard to do business."

Salerno (1992) and Corallo (2000) died behind bars, and the appeals, one by one, ran out for Carmine Persico.

The FBI had come a long way since the days when mob-controlled jockeys (including the Blue Beetle, no doubt) fixed races so J. Edgar Hoover could win at Santa Anita, and Hoover denied the Mafia's existence. In 1972, when Hoover died, Federal agents began to investigate organized crime for the first time since the Kennedy administration, especially in New York. At first the feds were happy creating stats that demonstrated they were on the job. They counted the number of arrests, without factoring in the success of the subsequent prosecutions. It wasn't until the 1980s that the FBI *really* went to war with the mob.

The Federal Government, armed with RICO, was hell bent on systematically destroying the Italian version of organized crime. As we know, the WASP version was going batshit and stealing billions, but investigating and prosecuting it was dangerous and not sexy.

The convictions already achieved by the feds were not enough to put the mob out of business, but they had a tremendous impact. William Doran, the FBI criminal division chief in New York, said that Carmine's removal from the streets created a "power vacuum." Shakeups would follow and offer cops opportunities to put undercover operations in motion. The question was, would the power void increase or decrease violence? Without someone like Carmine Persico at the top making the decisions—clear-headed, even-keel decisions—hoods might think with their guns instead of their heads. One effect was certain: mob leaders were no longer going to seek publicity and flaunt their mob power. John Gotti was boss for about three heartbeats before he was indicted. He might have earned the nickname "The Teflon Don" but they would get him. The best way to beat RICO was to keep your name off the list all together, so new methods of running rackets in secret were bound to be invented. Lower profiles would become the norm, Doran predicted.

ACT III

CHAPTER THIRTEEN
Cowboy Mike

What do you catch when the rat baits the trap?
Carmine Persico was a savvy guy with strong social skills,
but he was not perfect. As had been the case with Fred
DeChristopher, his flaw was his tendency to trust.

ONE OF THE FIRST PEOPLE Carmine met upon his return to Marion was thirty-eight-year-old Michael "Cowboy Mike" Lloyd, from Metuchen, New Jersey, a former rodeo bronco- and bull-rider, a small-time crook who'd gotten repeatedly busted until he was doing twenty years. He had been convicted of interstate cattle rustling, a federal crime, but he'd also been popped for bank robbery and counterfeiting. He once escaped from jail using a toy gun. He was first incarcerated at age twelve after he stole a luxury car to escape reform school. He was a relaxed man's-man kind of guy and had, while locked up, proven himself skilled at getting favors from his goodtime buddy corrections officers.

When Cowboy Mike and Carmine met, Mike brought the celebrated gangster a few gifts: a toothbrush, soap, and a pack of cigarettes (Pall Malls, biggest bang for your buck).

Carmine liked this guy, and they started to chat, a conversation that went on for months. One day the subject turned to the assholes that had taken Carmine's freedom, and his plans to get revenge. The stories gave the cowboy an idea.

In 1988, Lloyd wrote a letter to Carmine's arch-enemy Rudy Giuliani. He said that he'd been talking to Persico and was privy to a plot to kill Giuliani and Colombo-case prosecutor Aaron

Marcu. Lloyd reported that Carmine's men had found Giuliani's security daunting, and Marcu the easier target. The racket-busting bastard was being followed already and the hit could come at any time. Lloyd quoted Carmine as saying, "The one thing I wish is I could be there, see his face when they do it, I'd slap him, let him know what's gonna happen." Lloyd said Carmine had said lots of things, and that he, Lloyd, was willing to share that information. He'd served almost half of his term, had a parole hearing coming up in a while, and hoped to return to his wife and kid. He'd gotten his GED in prison and was ready to go straight.

After the plot to kill Marcu was verified and Marcu's security beefed up, Giuliani asked Lloyd if he was willing to take a polygraph. Cowboy Mike said bring it on. He passed, and Giuliani's chief organized crime prosecutor was sent to Marion to question him.

As it turned out, Lloyd not only gave the feds info about Carmine's past criminal life—Carmine reportedly said he was responsible for somewhere in the neighborhood of twenty-five murders, about half of which he did himself—but also about ongoing projects on the outside. For example, a potential witness against the Colombos had fled to Europe, but Persico's men had located him and were planning to kill him. Because of the info Lloyd supplied, the hit was thwarted. Three other planned hits—another prosecutor, Bruce Baird, and two FBI agents, Damon Taylor and Denis Maduro—were also prevented. Carmine's crew must've figured out that there was a rat—but they had no idea how close to the top it was.

Lloyd remained a trusted confidant through 1990 when both Carmine and Cowboy Mike were transferred from Marion to the penitentiary in Lompoc, California, fifty miles north of Santa Barbara, a move that in theory would make it harder for Carmine to remotely run Colombo business.

But living conditions in California were a marked improvement. These were the days before Martin Scorsese movies gave us a glimpse of wiseguy life behind bars. Back then, people tended to underestimate the comforts of home that Persico and his good-fellow pals enjoyed. The prison in Lompoc was converted from a minimum-security facility, where crooked accountants and politicians were allowed to play tennis. Those outside the country-club set found ways to make the place their own. Carmine carefully snipped away at his own rose garden on the prison grounds.

He put together a little gang of guys. This crew he called the Italian-American Cultural Club. As was true of most cliques, membership had its criteria. Most were button guys, all but one Italian. They were photographed as a group and used the image on their Christmas cards. There were always parties going on, birthdays, Italy wins a game in World Cup *calcio*, whatever—it looked like they had a caterer. The ICC had an unofficial clubhouse, meetings held at the Group Activity Center, in a room above the family-and-friends visitation center. The facility always made sure there was no alcohol, but good food was tolerated (and shared).

Tolerated was the key word. The prison wanted to make sure no one thought the ICC was a prison-sanctioned body. Lompoc, rowing a p.r. boat against the current, discouraged the notion that it was a "country club."

That said, there was always stuff going on at Lompoc that seemed by any standard to be fun. Prisoners all had jobs, it was true, but their free time was relaxed. The prison had its own band of musical inmates that played on holidays.

We know because Carmine and his band of brothers posed with the instruments on a bandstand—Junior on drums—for a photo. All they needed were wigs and they could've been the Not-So-Young Rascals.

A barnstorming rodeo came to the pen for a show, largely

thanks to Cowboy Mike's connections, with a few real bulls and bucking broncos. There was a mechanical bull. Thanks to his close friendship with Mike, Carmine had an opportunity to ride it, at least straddle the thing long enough for a memorable photo op.

Lloyd's regular letters to the feds continued to stifle Colombo activities, and the crew couldn't figure out where the leak was. Drug deals went bad, jailbreaks were foiled. Cops and judges and lawyers and prison guards who were on the take were outed. Businesses and unions under Colombo control faced scrutiny.

Looking at the situation from Carmine's point of view, he knew that he would never see freedom again, but he wanted to retain power. After all, he had already been boss for sixteen years and was *still* one of the youngest commission members.

Even without Cowboy Mike's clandestine interference, running the family business by remote control got off to a shaky start. Carmine's alleged initial orders from prison were garbled and botched. Carmine was said to have ordered a hit on a lawyer named William Aronwald, who in 1971 joined the Justice Department's Joint Strike Force Against Organized Crime in Manhattan. He'd been in private practice since 1978, but had reportedly pissed off the mob. Aronwald had earned a reputation as a prosecutor that had it in for mobsters. He twice convicted Aniello Dellacroce. But the thing that got him in trouble in 1987 came when, because of his part in an earlier investigation, he was called as a prosecution witness in the racketeering trial of John Gotti. Aronwald's testimony revealed some very sensitive subjects including the absolute "Code of Silence" that Gotti shared with his Gambinos.

Carmine Persico allegedly passed down the Aronwald hit to underboss Joel "Joe Waverly" Cacace, who sent out a two-man team on March 20, 1987. But the guys fucked up royally and that afternoon shot down the target's father instead, a seventy-eight-year-old city parking aide, just as he entered Young's Chinese

Laundry to pick up his shirts. The laundry was across the street from the elderly victim's co-op home in the Long Island City section of Queens. This was only the second time the victim had ever been in that laundry, the first time to drop off his shirts.

The elder Aronwald was being helped at the counter by a woman in her sixties when a man appeared at the door. The woman buzzed him in and he entered firing a .38 revolver. He shot Aronwald five times, twice in the head and three times to the body. The old man spun around a full three-sixty before collapsing to the floor. The shooter was described as a man in his early twenties, fair-skinned, about five-eight, one-ninety, wearing a gray waist-length jacket and faded blue jeans. The gunman never spoke, but ran out of the store and climbed into the passenger side of a double-parked Chevy Monte Carlo, which promptly zoomed off.

The younger Aronwald, the actual target, was in a Florida courthouse taking a legal deposition and was informed of his father's death when a secretary slipped him a note.

How did they botch it so badly? How could they mistake that old man for a guy in his forties? It was a nightmare. Idiots. As is usually true when there's collateral damage, this pissed off the whole crime community. These knuckleheads were giving the rackets a bad name, and so Cacace put out a hit on the shooters in the first hit. None of it made much sense, and there were rumblings that having a leader in the fed pen might present communication difficulties.

Years later (2004), Cacace pleaded guilty to Aronwald's murder, saying "in March 1987 I passed along a message to someone knowing that by passing the message a person would be killed"—although he was best known for ordering a hit on his ex-wife's new husband, who happened to be an NYPD officer.

Prosecutors said that, as part of their case against Cacace, the hit on Aronwald was ordered by Carmine Persico. This despite

the fact that Cacace had not said that in his statement, which remained vague and implicated no one other than Cacace himself.
Carmine ordered the hit, U.S. attorney Patricia E. Notopoulis
said, because "of the manner in which [Aronwald] engaged in
certain prosecutions."

The target, the son of the victim, said he couldn't think of anything he'd done in a courtroom that might piss off Mr. Persico.
Perhaps, just like the lunacy in the Long Island City laundry, the
whole thing was just one massive mistake.

Dominick "Donnie Shacks" Montemarano, who had been with
Carmine since his days on President Street hanging out with the
Gallos, went to prison in 1984, got out in the 1990s, and moved
to California where he became too close for police comfort with
college athletes upon whom he may have been placing bets. He
hung with celebs, no doubt about that, was seen having dinner
with actress Elizabeth Hurley (he was sixty-seven, she thirty-
five), hanging out with movie producers, partying with NFL
quarterbacks, and acting as pallbearer at Sonny Bono's funeral.
He did more prison time in 2003 when a domestic-abuse beef violated his parole.

During the first half of the 1990s, the FBI's codename for
Cowboy Mike Lloyd was "Snake Charmer." When Mike had
earned his deal, the feds tried to set him free but ran into an unexpected obstacle. In order for Mike to enjoy freedom, the State
of Pennsylvania had to forget about his state rap and release him
for extra special good behavior. They didn't want to.

As a result of this wrangling between the state and federal
powers, word leaked that Mike was a rat, and suddenly his time
at Lompoc became more difficult. He instantly plummeted on the
social scale from being an honorary member of the Italian-American
Cultural Club to being a cyst on the ass of the prison.

In 2001, the Pennsylvania Board of Pardons reviewed Mike's case again and unanimously recommended he be released. After all, his work as an informant had resulted in the prevention of the assassination of two federal officers and had resulted in criminal charges being filed against dozens of hoods.

But again there was an unexpected obstacle. Pennsylvania Governor Tom Ridge refused to commute Michael Lloyd's sentence. Ridge said that Cowboy Mike blew the deal when he picked up a knife and held it to a correctional officer's throat. He remained in prison in solitary confinement with a false identity until at least 2005 despite federal efforts to reward him for a job well done.

Part of Carmine's remote-control problem was the increasing physical and familial distance between himself and the guys on the outside who were supposed to be following his orders. Both his brother Alphonse and son Alphonse were having troubles staying healthy and free.

Carmine saw his eldest son, Alphonse T. Persico, as the heir apparent to the Colombo family. With dad absent much of the time, Little Allie Boy had lived the life of a prince, growing up in Carroll Gardens and Bensonhurst, where his name was revered. He was taller and better looking than his dad, and he was the first Persico since Grandpa Carmine the stenographer, to get a decent education. In fact, Little Allie Boy was extremely well-educated by organized-crime standards. Carmine had long regretted not becoming a lawyer and urged Allie Boy to follow that path. But, Allie Boy never came close to the bar exam. He got in two years of pre-law at St. John's University in Queens, New York, before going to work for his father. He was never a soldier, beginning his time in the life as capo, college functioning similarly to officer-training school in the service.

According to Aaron Marcu, Little Allie Boy emerged from his

college experience as "a swaggering classic wannabe." Marcu went on and on about his lousy character, saying Allie Boy was resentful that he didn't command as much respect as his old man. It was hard. Dad was considered a god by the people of Bensonhurst, while Allie Boy was considered just a man. Nonetheless, Marcu said, Alphonse was "taken by the life," and enjoyed nothing more than "bossing people around." (Marcu himself switched sides after his prosecution of the Persicos, and has had a lucrative career defending men of the country-club set accused of white-collar crimes.)

Little Allie Boy's first arrest came in 1983 at age twenty-nine; the charge, trafficking heroin. Colombo lawyers flocked to his aid and, upon closer examination, the charges were dismissed. As we've seen, he was convicted in the 1986 Colombo trial. This turned out to be a key to the tumultuous future of the Colombo family. If Little Allie Boy had remained free, Carmine most likely would have made him acting boss after Big Allie Boy went to prison, and the copious bloodshed that followed might have been avoided.

Carmine's brother Alphonse missed much of his youth because he was in prison for the murder of Stephen Bove and didn't become a prominent gangster until the 1970s in the Colombo family. When Carmine went away, brother Alphonse became acting head of the Colombos. Convicted of extortion in a federal court in June 1980, Big Allie Boy disappeared before he could be sentenced before Judge Jack B. Weinstein of Federal District Court. Wanted by the U.S. Marshals Service fugitive squad, he went on the lam, became a transient, changing his name with each location. Because he had a good business relationship with Connecticut boss William Grasso, Allie Boy hid out for a long time in West Hartford, under Grasso's protection. Persico wasn't the only wanted man that Grasso took care of. When Salvatore "Mickey" Caruana was busted for distributing $173 million worth of weed, he was put up in a Middletown apartment that Grasso arranged for. Grasso was known as a go-to guy for hoods on the lam. He had a DMV insider making fake I.D. cards.

The arrangement for Allie Boy worked well until marshals caught up with him in an apartment in West Hartford on November 9, 1987. The raiding marshals later said that Allie Boy never saw it coming and was startled as he was making sauce when the officers barged in. (Grasso himself came to a bad end in 1989 when a warring crew bumped him off and dumped him in a patch of poison ivy next to the Connecticut River.) Allie Boy's flight had merely delayed the inevitable.

Two days after his arrest he was denied bail, and ordered returned to New York to attend the extortion sentencing he'd lammed on seven years before. At that hearing, he was sentenced to twenty-five years by Judge Thomas C. Platt of Federal District Court, beginning his sentence in "Camp Fed," the Lompoc Federal Penitentiary. He died in a Springfield, Missouri, prison hospital of cancer of the larynx on September 12, 1989, at the age of sixty-one, survived by wife Dora and daughter Suzanne Farese, and two brothers, Carmine and Theodore.

When neither of the Alphonses was around to run the family for Carmine, he appointed a three-man "Ruling Committee" to pilot the ship. It consisted of his cousin, and capo of Little Allie Boy's crew, Vittorio Giovanni "Little Vic" Orena, another cousin Joseph Russo, and Benedetto Aloi.

Orena, as he always did when given the opportunity, took charge. Carmine made it clear that Orena's position was temporary. As soon as Little Allie Boy was free, the top spot would go to him.

Blood, after all, was thicker than water.

As it turned out, putting the sad-eyed Orena that close to power was a massive mistake. Cousin Vic, Carmine learned too late, hungered for control.

* * *

In 1989, the State of New Jersey Commission of Investigation's annual report, included an essay called "The Colombo/Persico/Orena Family," which gave a supposedly thorough and understandably Jersey-centric analysis of the gang.

The family included, it said, 120 made men, plus 450 associates. They were in the business of gambling, loansharking, arson, extortion, labor racketeering, cigarette smuggling, pornography, bankruptcy and mail fraud, tax evasion, counterfeiting, and narcotics.

New Jersey believed Carmine's crew was still heavily into hijackings, in particular the series of recent hijacks near JFK airport. The borgata also dabbled in coin-operated machines, restaurants, and deciding who does and who doesn't get a liquor license. They'd even been experimenting with investing in motion pictures. Although the youngest of the five families started out as a Brooklyn thing, the report said, the members had spread out over the generations, and now lived on Long Island, and in Florida, Nevada, and California.

The State investigation revealed that the Colombo family had been on a steady downslide dating back to the moment Joe was vegetabled. Timing, the report said, had a lot to do with it. The Colombo family's disarray coincided with John Gotti's rise to power in the Gambino clan, and the Gambinos took over a lot of the rackets that had formerly been Colombo. Things improved for the Colombos when acting boss Thomas DiBella retired and Carmine moved into the acting boss spot (Joe Colombo remaining technically the boss until the day he died). Persico got a grip on business and the drain of revenue loss to the Gambinos stopped. The commission report stated that it was when Colombo died that Carmine became boss. The Colombo family's surge in power lasted, however, only until Persico went away. Twenty-six members of the Colombo family also were incarcerated, and that left the ranks depleted. The Jersey analysis saw Salvatore Pro-

faci, son of the pre-Colombo boss, as the greatest threat to Carmine's power. Despite the top guys all going away, the Colombos
continued to operate and profit. The report concluded, "It has
been theorized that the group has to some extent become self-
sufficient, and that the presence of leadership has only been necessary to make command decisions and settle disputes. This
internal strength can be attributed to the organization's ability to
amass large profits from selected activities."

On May 30, 1990, Colombo underboss Benedetto "Benny"
Aloi was among those named in a sixty-nine-count indictment.
Carmine's three-man ruling committee was down to two.

As it turned out, the Jersey commission had been wrong about
one very important thing: Sal Profaci was not Carmine's worst
nightmare. That distinction went to cousin Vic.

CHAPTER FOURTEEN
The Last War

*Little Vic wanted to be boss—so determined that, during the
early 1990s, the blood of hoodlums again stained Brooklyn
streets. Out of this bulb of carnage, paranoia bloomed. You
couldn't tell friends from enemies, and an aria of canaries
sang their cowardly betrayal.*

VITTORIO ORENA, the round little man who would square off
against Carmine in what would be called "The Last War," was
born on August 4, 1934, and rose up from the bottom. Raised by
a single mom, the hoods were his father figures, his source of
guidance and wisdom. They were the big shots in his neighborhood, the only ones with money, and he wanted to grow up to be
just like them. School devolved into Reform School, then to no
school at all—but he learned the labor racket just fine, and used
his expertise to transform himself into a fellow who dressed in
finely tailored suits and projected himself as a legitimate businessman.

Despite his soft appearance, Little Vic had intense green eyes
that could go cold and scare the shit out of a guy. He skimmed
millions off the pensions of unions under Colombo control and
lent that money to degenerate gamblers.

His expertise was washing money. He could've called his end
of the business Dummy Corp. The feds later learned that Orena's
laundry consisted of eleven companies and more than 150 bank
accounts—a system allegedly set up with the help of Orena's
lawyer, Dennis Pappas. Feds knew that loan-sharking money and
other family assets were ending up in the paychecks of mobster's

family members, no-show jobs at ghost companies that didn't seem to do anything other than exist. Authorities could only estimate the millions of dollars that were being laundered because they could never completely determine how the money-go-round worked. It was like deciphering a Rube Goldberg drawing. Pappas's alleged work was so complicated, such an intricate juggling act, that he was known as the Colombos' "finance consigliere." When one of Pappas's accountants smelled something fishy in the numbers he was given, he received a package: a dead fish wrapped in newspaper, a crystal-clear message.

Despite his gangster status, Orena had a very short criminal record: gambling, perjury, loansharking. The man was in his fifties, and he'd served a total of four months in jail—a weekend vacation compared to the Persicos.

Carmine considered his cousin Vic Orena to be obedient and profitable. Only one of those attributes turned out to be true.

Orena had friends outside the family, influential friends—John Gotti, some guys near the top in the Lucchese family. He grew into an extraordinary earner, shaking down labor for their union dues over broad swaths of lucrative turf in New York and Jersey.

Carmine was not quick to figure out Orena's intentions. In fact, during his tenure as acting boss, Orena had several times asked for executive privileges that normally would have been reserved for the boss himself. Each time Carmine said okay. He trusted Vic's judgment. So Orena had the power to recruit new membership and order hits. And he used his power.

In November 1989, Orena ordered a hit on Thomas Ocera, a Colombo guy. It was a shame, too, because Ocera at one time had been useful. He was on the Board of Directors at a plush catering establishment on Long Island called Massapequa Manor, where the clientele was there to be seen—sort of a Russian Tea Room for hoods. But Ocera, who lived in Merrick on Long Island, had sticky fingers, and he'd gotten caught. He was not only skimming the tribute money, but his skimming was so sloppy that it led to the police seizure of loan-sharking records. He was alleged to have been the trigger for a hit on one of Gotti's crew. He'd fucked up twice and needed executing.

Orena gave the word and Gregory Scarpa murdered Ocera with a piece of piano wire.

From the day Orena was made acting boss, Carmine bombarded him with a steady stream of orders. For two years Orena put up with it, but he knew it wasn't working. Carmine was trying to run a business from afar, and it was impossible. The world was changing. The way you went about operating a business was changing. Stuck in prison, Carmine—Orena felt—had lost touch.

Then, the last straw: A TV network approached Carmine and asked if he was interested in making a biography of himself. Carmine liked the idea. Orena was appalled. The boss was thinking about TV instead of business. Besides, there was nothing like the power of TV to bring the heat—and there was enough federal scrutiny on Colombo activities as there was.

By the spring of 1991, Orena was sick of it. He didn't like being an acting boss let alone being a lame-duck acting boss, destined to be replaced by Little Allie Boy as soon as he became available.

Orena had a talk with John Gotti and they dealt. If Vic pulled a *coup d'etat*, Gotti had his back.

It was spring 1991 when Orena decided he was fed up. He tried to do it in a civilized way. He took his plight to the commission and asked that they remove Carmine Persico as boss of the Colombo family and install himself in that position instead.

The commission said no fucking way. There was tradition involved. They would do it the way their fathers and grandfathers had done it. They would poll the capos as to who they wanted as their leader.

Orena instructed consigliere Carmine Sessa to poll Colombo capos with the question: Who should be boss? Orena thought he would easily carry the vote. True, there were some die-hard Persico boys among the capos, e.g., Carmine's brother Theodore. What Orena didn't see coming was that the vote would never happen.

Just asking for a vote was an act of treachery. Without the Persicos, Orena wouldn't be the rich man he was today. One of Orena's jobs was to make sure the Persico family continued to get their cut of the take, even though the men were behind bars. And now Orena was trying to supplant Carmine.

Sessa knew he wasn't going to get through this without at least one powerful man pissed off at him. He decided that his loyalty was with Carmine. It was Junior who'd made Sessa an officer in the family. So, instead of polling the capos as Orena had ordered, he ran to Carmine, telling him the acting boss was attempting a takeover.

Carmine was level-headed about the situation. He calmly weighed pros and cons. On one hand, Vic was a relative, a man in whom Carmine had placed absolute trust. On the other, he was insubordinate, treasonous—and action needed to be swift and final.

Carmine ordered Sessa to put together a team to take care of Orena. This, Sessa did—a five-man team led by Sessa himself. On June 20, 1991, the team parked itself across the street from Orena's Cedarhurst, Long Island, home and waited for their opportunity. They were too obvious, however. As Orena drove home, he spotted them and fled urgently.

As he drove away, wheels squealing, heart pounding, Orena did some quick computing in his head. That was a hit team, he was the target, and the only person with the juice to order a hit on a man of his stature was Carmine Persico, who was thousands of miles away.

After that, there were ninety days of peace talks. Nobody did a head count, but usually at those meetings there were about three times as many crew members loyal to Orena as there were supporters of Carmine. Again, it went to the commission. Was Persico the boss of the Colombo family or not? The Commission refused to take sides, and that meant war.

Cousin Vic sent a message to the Persicos. No way he was stepping down when Allie Boy was released. No way was he sharing the profits from his rackets with the Persicos. Those loyal to the Persicos would be shuffled off the goddamned mortal coil.

One of Orena's key assets was capo Salvatore "Jersey Sal" Profaci, son of Joe, who ran Colombo business west of the Hudson. An FBI bug in a Jersey lawyer's office caught Profaci discussing the reason for his loyalty. He said that Orena was capable, qualified, and a "beautiful person." Carmine, on the other hand, was nuts, and wanted to do stupid things like talking to the press.

"He wants to be on *60 Minutes* with Barbara Walters," Jersey Sal said.

Just as some of the street gangs of Carmine's youth had had two leaders, one for thinking and one for fighting, Carmine knew that, in order to win the upcoming internecine war, he was going to need a fighting leader, a general to lead the troops in a winning war effort. He chose the "Grim Reaper" Gregory Scarpa.

The first salvo, not counting Sessa's aborted attempt to kill Orena himself, came on November 18, 1991, when Orena capo William "Billy Fingers" Cutolo sent a team, including Michael "Mikey Spats" Spataro and Joseph Campanella, to kill Scarpa. Take out Carmine's top gun, the thinking went, and his army lost its *generalissimo*.

After three days of being watched and followed, Scarpa was ambushed in his car, with his daughter and granddaughter in a car directly behind him, but despite a hail of bullets, everyone was okay. According to daughter Linda Scarpa, twenty-two years old at the time, she followed her father's car out of the driveway and noticed a van speeding down the block.

"When I backed out," she said, "I cut the van off. It almost slammed into me and started driving again."

At the end of the street she saw a truck blocking the intersection. She pulled up close to her father and waited for the obstruction to clear, looked down to check on her eight-month-old son and heard popping noises, which she at first thought were firecrackers. She looked up and saw men in black, including black ski masks, carrying long guns with silencers. They surrounded both hers and her father's cars and fired. Thip, thip, thip, thip. She saw her father duck down. She couldn't tell if he was hit. Joe "Fish" Marra, a friend of her dad's, jumped out of his car and began to return fire in a decidedly non-silenced way. Her dad's car looked like swiss cheese. As Linda grabbed the baby and ran back into the house, Greg's car started to move. There was just enough room between a stop sign and the blocking truck for her dad's car to fit through, and somehow he managed to get out of the intersection. There was more shooting. She hysterically told her mom, "Big Linda," that Scarpa had been shot to death, a bit of an exaggeration as Scarpa himself soon walked through the door.

He looked at his daughter and said, "You saved my life. You realize that, right? Don't worry. Everything's OK. I'm going to take care of this. They are all fucking dead. They're going to fucking die, starting tonight."

He was referring of course, to the Orena faction of the Colombo family.

On November 24, Persico-loyalist Henry "Hank the Bank" Smurra was shot in the head and killed as he sat in his car outside a donut shop in the Sheepshead Bay section of Brooklyn. He'd been one of the guys back in June who waited at Orena's house. Joseph Campanella quipped, "Hank wanted a donut, but all he got was a hole."

On November 29, Larry Sessa, nephew of Carmine Sessa, was exiting a barbershop when he was chased down 86th Street, the main drag in Bensonhurst, by a group of gunmen, reportedly including Campanella. Sessa escaped by jumping into a car driven by an acquaintance. When the gunmen opened fire, the driver of the car was wounded in the shoulder and hand. The bleeding acquaintance managed to drive to safety despite his wounds, but not without hitting and injuring three pedestrians, including a four-year-old girl.

On Tuesday, December 3, Scarpa sent a hit squad to whack thirty-eight-year-old Joseph Tolino, nephew of Orena capo Nicholas Grancio. The shooting took place outside a social club in the Gravesend section of Brooklyn. Tolino was wounded in the foot, but his companion at the time, a retired Genovese soldier, seventy-eight-year-old Gaetano "Thomas" Amato, was shot dead.

In a memorable example of perfect mob etiquette, Carmine sent the shooters to offer an apology to the Genovese family for their regrettable fuck-up. Amato, it was agreed, had the misfortune of being in the wrong place at the wrong time.

The cops were trying hard to follow the plotline, but as they used to say at Ebbets Field, you can't tell the players without a scorecard. But they did figure out that Tolino was the target.

At 1:00 A.M. on December 5, 1991, seventy-eight-year-old Rosario "Black Sam" Nastasa was shot and killed as he played cards in the Belvedere Social Athletic Association clubhouse on 63rd Street in Bensonhurst. Nastasa was the second septuagenarian victim in three days. He was Genovese but known for his loyalty to Carmine, so police immediately suspected Orena guns. There was minor collateral damage as Nastasa's forty-seven-

year-old girlfriend didn't quite get her tits out of the way and suffered a graze wound to the right breast.

Throughout the war, Scarpa always found time to keep his FBI
handlers up to date on who hit who and why. For his efforts, he
was paid $158,000 by the Federal Government—our tax money
at work.

On December 6, at 3:55 P.M., thirty-year-old Persico soldier
Vincent "Fat Vinny" Fusaro was hanging a Christmas garland on
the door of his Bath Beach home when he was shot once in the
back of the head and killed. He lived there with his mother and
grandmother. (Reportedly, Greg Scarpa committed this murder
with a rifle.) Bath Beach was a southern suburb of Bensonhurst,
a strip along the ocean between Dyker Park and Coney Island.
Reporters knocked on doors seeking eye- or ear-witnesses to the
shooting, but induced only grim silence. "In this neighborhood,
mum's the word," one neighbor said to the guy from the *Times*.

Fusaro was the night manager of the Venus Diner on Fourth
Avenue in Bay Ridge, Brooklyn (no longer there), a twenty-four-
hour eating establishment known for its mobby clientele, especially during the graveyard shift.

They'd never admit it, but the authorities looked at the war as
a boon to the taxpayers, bullets saving them years of complex
prosecutions. Historians noted that the Persico-Orena war was
the bloodiest in Brooklyn since the first nine months of 1947
when eleven wise guys were rubbed out in Bath Beach and Bensonhurst, almost all in rat-tat-tat-tat drive-by fashion by men in
speeding black sedans.

Then, in one horrible day, the mood of the war changed.

December 8 was the day that things got really stupid. Early
that morning, twenty-one-year-old James Malpiso was shot and
wounded. Malpiso had never been arrested, but investigators

quickly learned that his father was Louis "Bobo" Malpiso, a reputed Orena soldier.

James Malpiso was dropped off at Coney Island Hospital with a hole in his chest at 9:00 A.M., and retaliation was almost instantaneous. Twenty-two minutes later, bullets were flying in Bay Ridge. Gunmen shot up a bagel shop on Third Avenue owned by two reputed members of the Persico faction. The store was in a three-story brick building on a block of small specialty shops. Shot dead in the ambush was an innocent eighteen-year-old boy named Matteo Speranza, who lived with his parents in Bensonhurst, and was making bagels. Speranza was standing behind the counter when the gunmen entered. He was shot first in the head, and there was a pause as the killers watched him slide down the wall, leaving a trail of gore. They shot Speranza twice more, once in the back, and once in the chest, before calmly walking out of the shop.

Speranza had been working at the bagel shop for two months while studying for his GED. He hadn't even been slated to work the day of the shooting, but subbed for a friend, who'd called him the night before saying he wouldn't be able to open up. Speranza had only been in Brooklyn for two years, having grown up in Florida, the son of a Burger King manager. He got the job at Wanna Bagel because his mother was a friend of the mother of one of the owners, Anthony Ferrara. Police records showed that Ferrara had five previous arrests for grand larceny and robbery. Ferrara's partner, Frank Guerra, a friend of the Persicos, had been arrested for grand larceny auto just weeks earlier.

Orena proclaimed his innocence. He said the bagel shop hit wasn't his call, and apparently he was telling the truth. The smell of blood was so strong in the streets of Brooklyn, that careless guys, amateur wannabes, looking to make their bones were carrying out unauthorized hits. Anthony Libertore, a Colombo guy of not much reputation, and his father, wanted to take action like big men but were shocked to learn that it didn't work that way. The sadness of Matteo Speranza's death made the entire underworld feel a collective shame.

And it forced law enforcement's hand. Brooklyn District Attorney's office slapped subpoenas on as many members of the Colombos as they could find. They made sure they recruited guys from both sides. Persico supporters, Orena supporters, everyone in the courtroom. Ninety subpoenas were issued. Forty-one of them were served. Twenty-eight hoods showed up at the courthouse.

Kings County D.A. Charles Hynes told the press, "They've turned this into a B-movie. We're not going to allow this county to become a massive shooting gallery where innocent people are being gunned down."

Outside the grand jury room of the State Supreme Court in Brooklyn, the mobsters kept their shoulders around their ears. Some of them wore sunglasses. They all kept their heads down just in case someone was taking a photo. Judging from this scene, not much had changed since 1952 when the numbers runners of Frankie Shots' crew were rounded up and brought in. Robert D. McFadden was a spectator in the courtroom and said that a lot of the boys looked like "underworld extras" in Hollywood.

There were twenty-eight hoods and almost as many lawyers, the mouthpieces all looking identical with their crisp manner, brief cases, and good posture. One by one the boys were called into the grand jury room, slouching a bit more as they passed a cluster of press armed with pencils and cameras.

The hearings lasted for three hours, less than six minutes per guy. The D.A. offered each of them immunity from prosecution if they'd just tell them something that might help stop the war. To this most of the witnesses made rude suggestions.

Afterward, Dennis R. Hawkins, a St. John's University Law

School graduate and chief of the organized crime control bureau in the District Attorney's office, said that there had been some progress. Not all of the hoods had turned down the immunity offer. Hawkins wasn't specific but did say there would be guys coming back to testify for the grand jury. Of course, he might have been just messing with the boys, promoting discord by making them wonder whose tonsils had loosened.

After a spell of daily death, the war cooled. A week passed without bullets flying, and the D.A.'s office was certain the subpoenas were the reason. On the streets there was a different theory: Matteo Speranza. The pause allowed both sides to consider ways of better controlling their guns. A third theory said it was a holiday ceasefire, like they had in the trenches of World War I. Sure enough, only a week into the New Year, gunfire resumed.

On January 7, 1992, sixty-two-year-old Colombo captain and Orena loyalist Nicholas P. "Nicky Black" Grancio was found shot in the head in his car parked under the elevated train on McDonald Avenue at Avenue U. Wounded in the attack was twenty-six-year-old Anthony Bianco, who had a graze wound to the head. Grancio was the uncle of Joseph Tolino, wounded in a shooting a month earlier. Nicky was whacked by Larry Mazza, a guy who told his secrets from the other side of the witness-protection program. As a seventeen-year-old grocery-store delivery boy, he had been invited in for lemonade by a thirty-something woman wearing a sexy black jumpsuit that had a zipper conveniently running down the length of the front. Her name was Linda Schiro and she was the libidinous *goomada* of Carmine's top gun, Greg Scarpa. (Yes, Scarpa had a wife, daughter, and mistress all named Linda.) When Scarpa caught Mazza with Linda, Mazza thought he was dead meat. But, as it turned out, Scarpa didn't want to kill him, he wanted to use him. Mazza didn't die, but owed Scarpa a long series of favors, all involving blowing somebody's brains out.

"I killed four people for him and I still owed him a favor," Mazza recalled.

Because of Scarpa's still unbelievable relationship with the FBI, it was a busy scene during the last minutes of Nicky Black's life underneath the elevated train at Avenues U and McDonald. Two surveillance teams had their eyes on Nicky. One was a task force of feds and NYPD detectives, and the other was Scarpa's crew, with Mazza sitting in the backseat holding a shotgun.

Law enforcement was tailing Grancio because they knew he was involved in the Persico-Orena war. The Scarpa crew picked up Grancio at Lady Moody Triangle on Avenue U and Village Road in Gravesend. They tailed him to the location under the el, and spotted the car full of cops and waited.

At some point the cops got a call, the surveillance was off, time to move on to other things. Some of the guys thought it was odd to be pulled off a job in the middle of a tail, but they did as they were told. As soon as the cops left, the Scarpa crew went to work.

It appeared that the feds, given the choice between cooperating with the NYPD or with Scarpa, chose Scarpa. But that couldn't be the case, could it? This was Bizarro world. And real. Many years later, the guy that called off law enforcement was prosecuted.

According to Mazza, Scarpa himself was in the car as they pulled up alongside Grancio's car. Mazza rolled his window down and thrust his entire upper torso outside the car through the window.

Scarpa shouted, "This one's for Carmine!"

Mazza put the shotgun to Grancio's head and pulled the trigger. He later recalled, "I actually saw his facial features splatter on the windshield. It was surreal."

* * *

The same crew that knocked off Grancio was back for more on
May 22, 1992, to erase long-time Colombo soldier Lorenzo "Larry"
Lampasi. Using intelligence reportedly gathered by the FBI and
given to Scarpa, Mazza shot Lampasi from a car as Lampasi
pulled out of his driveway in his 1988 Cadillac in the Kensington
section of Brooklyn. Lampasi got out of his Caddy to close and
lock his gate when the crew pulled up. Mazza hit Lampasi with
his first shot, but the target managed to convulse his way onto the
sidewalk where he writhed in agony. The Scarpa car began to
pull away but stopped. The entire crew piled out, surrounded
Lampasi on the sidewalk, and pulled their weapons. Lampasi
managed to spit out, "What did I do?" The answer to that question was twofold—Lampasi had sided with the wrong team, plus
he owed Scarpa money—but went unspoken. They answered by
shooting him as one until he was still and quiet.

Not all of Scarpa's hits involved the Persico-Orena war. Even
before the Colombo Civil War broke out, Scarpa was avenging
wrongs with death dished out in brutal fashion, often based on
info acquired during federal surveillance operations. Scarpa had
his son Joey's eighteen-year-old buddy Patrick Porco whacked
during the 1990 Memorial Day weekend because, the FBI told
Scarpa, he was about to implicate Joey in a murder committed on
Halloween 1989.

On March 25, 1992, John Minerva and Michael Imbergamo
were shot and killed as they sat in a champagne-colored Cadillac
parked outside the Broadway Café, a coffee shop in North Massapequa, Long Island. Imbergamo had no mob connections. Minerva, the target, was a wiseguy who'd recently switched
allegiance from Persico to Orena. (Years later, in 2013, Anthony
Colandra was convicted of lying to investigators about this double homicide. Colandra refused to admit that he was one of the
gunmen in North Massapequa, but did say the double hit was
sanctioned by Colombo street boss, Thomas "Tommy Shots"
Giolli. Colandra, it is said, left the Mafia, became an informant

for the Drug Enforcement Administration, and today lives in relative normality with a job at a church and coaching Little League baseball.

The ramped up Persico-Orena war brought a fresh offensive from the feds. Before they were done, the U.S. Government had indicted sixty-eight mobsters. They convicted fifty-eight, while the remaining ten cooperated.

The war had paused but not stopped following the accidental death of Matteo Speranza. The victim's dad, retired maintenance man Umberto Speranza, was outspoken about his anger: "They say the Mafia doesn't makes mistakes. They say that when they hit, they hit the right people. That's baloney. They kill innocent people."

Who pulled the trigger on young Speranza was a mystery until Christopher Liberatore was given a great deal, considering his crimes, and a spot in the Witness Protection Program, at which time he said, okay, it was me that shot the kid on Third Avenue. He told a Brooklyn Federal Court in 1995 that the hit on the bagel shop had been ordered only minutes earlier, by Colombo captain Louis "Bobo" Malpeso, whose son James had just been shot. There would be no moment for planning strategy or tactics, vengeance was to be immediate. Wanna Bagel was chosen because it was owned by members of Persico's faction.

As Liberatore testified, Umberto Speranza seethed with fury. Liberatore had cut a deal and was going to have a life, unlike his Matteo. Sure, Liberatore was facing life in prison. But that wasn't going to happen, he feared. He was going to walk free. "They should hang him, put him in the electric chair," Speranza said, imagining a rich vengeance in which his enemy would die twice.

For four days Liberatore testified. Speranza said, "So filthy, so bad. How can they be snaking around in the community? They belong nine feet under the ground."

As it turned out, Liberatore was convicted of almost all of the charges against him. The jury, however, for reasons unknown, found him not guilty of the murder of Matteo Speranza. The government kept its word. Liberatore was not sentenced to life in prison. Instead, he got seventy-five years. The joke was on him, and Umberto Speranza slept a little better.

With bullets flying, cousin Vic Orena thought of little other than personal safety. He had fashioned an apartment for himself in the basement of his girlfriend's new suburban house, still under construction, which made it a great hiding spot. Nobody shot at him, but when the police wanted him, somehow they knew just where to look. Cops took him from his underground bunker in Valley Stream, Long Island. During the arrest, police seized four shotguns, enough ammo for a pitched battle, and a bulletproof vest. Orena had planned to shoot it out, but ended up giving up without a fight. He was charged with, among other things, ordering the 1989 murder of Thomas Ocera, the Long Island caterer who'd been caught skimming from Colombo rackets and had been garroted by Greg Scarpa with a piano wire.

Through the hard work of fed prosecutor George Stamboulidis, Orena went down on December 22, 1992, another RICO victim, convicted of racketeering and the Ocera murder, and sentenced to three life sentences plus eighty-five years in the fed pen.

Orena's permanent incarceration put the Colombo family more firmly than ever under the control of factions loyal to Carmine Persico. By the time Allie Boy got out, Orena was in jail, and the coast was clear.

Violence and arrests continued, however, and the split Colombo family was in deep trouble. Persicos and Orenas had been prosecuted without prejudice. Orena's sons, Vic Jr. and John, went down. The Orenas had a zillionaire friend Tom Petrizzo who made his fortune skimming off of major construction projects. He went down, too. Carmine lost three close allies in the prosecutions: brother Teddy, cousin Mush, and Hugh McIntosh.

McIntosh's experiences pointed how difficult it was for parolees in the life to avoid parole violations. When your blood family, friends, and entire social life are all jam-packed with "known criminals," it can be impossible to avoid consorting with them. McIntosh had been paroled in 1992 after serving ten years for racketeering but was again arrested on September 12, 1992, for parole violation—i.e., he'd been seen speaking for twenty-five minutes to Carmine's nephew Daniel on May 23, 1992, at an outdoor table in front of a Brooklyn bar near his home. (McIntosh returned to prison in Springfield, Missouri. In 1997, his daughter filed a lawsuit that he was being mistreated in prison. He died several months later in a Springfield hospital at age seventy.)

The feds didn't believe in giving a break to guys who'd just served a stretch. They were relentless. Six months after Orena was convicted, Carmine's son Allie Boy, only recently out of jail, was one of eleven Colombos and associates indicted in crimes committed during the Persico-Orena war. The indictments were made public on May 14, 1993 in the Federal District Court in Brooklyn. Allie Boy was charged with involvement in five of the murders committed during the war: the murders of Vincent Fusaro, Nicky Black, John Minerva, Michael Imbergamo, and Lorenzo Lampasi.

In March 1993, Ralphie Scopo died in prison, less than a decade into his 100-year sentence. Seven months later, on Wednesday night, October 20, Ralphie's son, forty-seven-year-old Joseph Scopo was returning home following dinner with two men in their twenties, his nephew Dominic Logazzo and future son-in-law Angelo Barrone. It was about 11:00 P.M. and Scopo, a Colombo officer, was in the passenger seat of a tan and gold

1993 Nissan Altima. Barrone drove, Logazzo was in the back-seat. They'd just pulled up in front of Scopo's home in Ozone Park, Queens, a gray two-story rowhouse. Several hooded gun-men approached the car and fired with at least one .380 automatic pistol and one Mac-10 automatic pistol. Twenty-three shells were recovered at the scene, but crime-scene investigators later theo-rized that more than thirty shots were fired. Scopo got out of the car and tried to make a run for it.

He ran too slow and was shot twice in the abdomen and once in the chest. He fell on his face in the leaf-covered street a few doors down from his own home. His nephew was shot once in the shoulder and once in the elbow. The future son-in-law was un-harmed.

Neighbor Bob Tobasko, a UPS driver, told reporters he'd heard four or five shots, so rapid-fire that he thought an Uzi or machine gun of some kind was being used. He ran outside and saw a "guy lying on the ground . . . I was holding his hand, trying to comfort him a little," the neighbor said. "When his son came out, he snapped out of it. He snapped out of it as soon as he saw his son's face." We're not sure what he snapped out of or into, but Scopo was taken by ambulance to Jamaica Hospital where he died two hours later.

In the aftermath of the shooting, eyewitnesses could not agree on how many gunmen there were. Some said two, others three. The getaway car, it was agreed, was a four-door, brown 1984 Buick LeSabre. The car was found to have been stolen from Brooklyn and was recovered only a few blocks from the Queens shooting scene.

Did the Scopo hit indicate a resumption of inter-Colombo hos-tilities? Scopo had been a strong part of the Orena faction, so po-lice looked to the Persico camp for suspects. Joseph Scopo was the former vice president of Local 6A of Cement and Concrete Workers in New York City. He and his brother Ralph Jr. were forced to give up their posts (as VP and President) of Local 6A, as well as officers of the District Council of Cement and Concrete Workers, after the U.S. Government proclaimed those unions to be "tools of organized crime" during the commission trial. With the Scopos out, a court-appointed trustee was placed in charge of the unions. The brothers were barred permanently from the unions. Now one was dead.

A law enforcement official speaking anonymously to *The New York Times* said that the hit hurt the Orena team severely. The cop went on to say that Scopo was a big, burly, powerful man and, along with being with Orena, also had "close ties" to the Gambinos and their boss John Gotti.

Twenty-one years would pass before it would be revealed in court that Carmine's nephew, Teddy Boy Persico, ordered the hit in 1993 while on a prison furlough to attend his grandmother's wake at Scarpaci Funeral Home in the Dyker Heights section of Brooklyn. He allegedly ordered the hit out of the earshot of corrections officers who had accompanied him to the wake, but within earshot of future rat Big Anthony Russo—no relation to Mush.

According to Big Anthony, Teddy Boy said, "You have to go after Joey. To end this war, we got to get Joey. Joey is the target." Russo said that forty-five-year-old Big Frank Guerra, his supposed best friend, whose day job was drug dealing, was in on the hit. Guerra, part owner of the Wanna Bagel shop in Bay Ridge where Matteo Speranza was killed, was a friend of Little Allie Boy and Teddy Boy Persico. Guerra's name had previously come up in reference to Scopo's murder in the 1999 trial of John Pappa, who is serving life for the Scopo hit. For a dozen years Guerra had been a suspect, but prosecutors felt they hadn't enough evidence to convict. According to Big Anthony's statements, Guerra was manning a crash car, his job was to obstruct pursuers of the getaway car. Those who knew Big Anthony thought it odd that he would cooperate with authorities, as he'd never been shy about his hatred for turncoats. It wasn't until he was being held without bail that his lip unzipped. Big Anthony confessed that he was in a car involved in the Scopo hit, and that Frank Guerra was with him. Big Anthony claimed that he got out of the car while the shooting was going on and that his hat was shot right off his head. "I jumped out of the car. I was like a fucking mad hatter. I didn't know what to do," he said. Anthony said Big Frank was in the backseat of the car "laughing hysterical" at the murder. "What the fuck? Are you crazy?" Anthony quoted Frank as saying. At the time of Anthony's initial cooperation, Big Frank was enjoying his freedom. He'd served more than six years on drug charges but had been out since 2006. Big Anthony once was recorded having a shit fit over rats, saying he wanted to chop the heads off of rats. Then he ratted himself. He was facing life. The power of RICO.

During the 1990s, leadership of the Colombos passed back and forth between Allie Boy and Mush, depending on who was in and out of jail. At one point, Mush did four and a half years for jury tampering.

By this time, the Persicos had so much money that they didn't need the rackets anymore. Had they chosen, they could have worked the stock market. They could have invested in real estate. That was the route some of their business partners over the years had taken. But the life was in the Persicos' blood.

In 1994, the *Village Voice* ran a story called "The Mob's Big Wheels" in which they discussed a guy named John Staluppi and his connections with the Colombos. Staluppi bought up a great deal of Palm Beach County in Florida. When controversy followed him, Staluppi denied he was ever crooked. He once co-owned a few buildings with the Persicos. What's the big deal? So what?

You could be legit and work with the Persicos, but in the legit world you had to understand, you were going to have to live with the taint. Staluppi wanted to start a business helicoptering rich Manhattan degenerates to Atlantic City but was denied a license because, according to the Casino Control Commission, he was "a member" of the Colombo crime family. The CCC had evidence. An undercover agent got himself hired as Staluppi's driver, discovered that he had Teddy Boy Persico's and Vic Orena's phone numbers in his little black book. Again, big fucking deal. He sold cars to Orena. Bought carpets with Teddy Boy. All this "family member" business was stereotyping, because he was Italian. Staluppi had to be protective of his precious reputation, perhaps why a reporter digging up dirt on Staluppi found himself being tailed. Staluppi was a Bensonhurst kid, vocational school dropout, nabbed for stealing many cars and reselling them with altered vehicle I.D. numbers. Ten years later he was making $2.5 million a year and owned twenty-nine used-car dealerships. Everybody told him he looked like Robert DeNiro.

On August 8, 1994, Little Allie Boy, now forty years old, was tried in Federal District Court in Brooklyn for Orena war murders. His defense attorney was young Barry Levin, not to be confused with the late Barry Levin of Southern California who got actor Robert Blake acquitted on murder charges. *This* Barry Levin specialized in white collar and RICO defenses. He was a 1984 grad of the University of Bridgeport Law School and because his specialty was a relatively new one, he immediately stepped into high-profile cases.

The trial was one of thirty-six stemming from the Orena war. The prosecution was complex and confusing. Evidence was presented that seemed to indicate Allie Boy's involvement in the 1985 killing of his brother-in-law Steven Piazza after Piazza was physically abusive to Allie Boy's sister, but since that was in the indictment only as an underlying act for a racketeering count and not one of the charges being tried, there was nothing the jury could do about it. The trial lasted six weeks and the jury quickly acquitted Allie Boy.

After the good news, Allie Boy told a reporter from *The New York Times* that the first thing he wanted to do was go home to Staten Island and see his girls. Allie Boy and Teresa had three daughters. And he may have done that, but before long he was in sunnier climes, doing a lousy job of laying low.

Allie Boy moved by himself to Lighthouse Point, Florida, just north of Pompano Beach, where his new digs were perfect for a middle-aged man who'd had it with northeast winters and hassles—and marriage. The small city on the shore had a population of a little over 10,000 and was named after the beautiful Hillsboro Inlet lighthouse that sat on nearby Hillsboro Beach.

He took to the waterfront lifestyle, bought a speedy yacht and called her "Lookin' Good." He was the captain and enjoyed zipping around, skimming across the waves with a salty spray speckling his shades. Broads were everywhere, sex-drenched symbols of Allie Boy's ribald beneficence.

Trouble was, he liked to drive that boat in a manner that attracted the attention of authorities, and when he did it, he also liked to have a small cache of weapons in the boat just in case he was attacked at sea.

Within a year of moving to Florida, things went bad. Coast Guard officers raided his boat off the Florida Keys and found a Mossberg twelve-gauge shotgun and twenty shells, and a Browning .380 semiautomatic handgun and fourteen rounds of .380 ammunition.

He was promptly released on bail, walking free even as a federal grand jury handed up weapons charges in Fort Lauderdale. Both Law and Order were piling on. The case presented to the grand jury was the result of a joint investigation by the Coast Guard,

FBI, Florida Department of Law Enforcement, and the Key West Police Department.

At about the time Allie Boy was buying a boat and calling it "Lookin Good" he and his beautiful wife Teresa, known as Tori, were on the outs and living separate lives. The life, with its dangers and customs, made marriage complicated for many hoods. In this case, the marriage began to crack during Allie Boy's incarceration. He had been in prison for years. They would divorce in February 1993, but were apart for a few years before that.

Just because Allie Boy was in Florida's salty spray and enjoying bachelorhood didn't mean he wasn't keeping tabs on his wife. He knew that Tori had a young boyfriend, twenty-eight-year-old Michael Devine, who was part owner of the popular Staten Island nightclub Hedges.

The love affair ended when Devine was found, forehead on steering wheel, shot to death during the early morning hours of January 24, 1992, in his idling black Nissan Pathfinder in the garage of his condo apartment in the New Springfield section of Staten Island. The car radio was still on when the body was discovered at 8:30 A.M. Tellingly, the gunman had concentrated on only two parts of Devine's body—head and crotch.

The crime scene report read, "Genital mutilation."

No arrests, but—according to U.S. attorney George Stamboulidis—there existed audiotape of Allie Boy saying he "intended to take action" in regard to Devine. Allie Boy said that one of his friends had the color of Devine's car. Devine, word was, had been warned to stay away from Tori, or else.

Tori Persico took the stand once in the matter, in 2012, acknowledged that she was having an affair with Devine—the nightclub owner had swept her off her feet in August 1991—but denied vehemently that the affair made Allie Boy angry.

"He didn't object," she testified.

* * *

It seemed Allie Boy's problems could get no worse, but the authorities were indefatigable. On October 9, 1999, he happened to be back north when he learned he was again a wanted man. Attorney Barry Levin took his client home with him that night and he and Allie Boy had dinner at Levin's apartment while they discussed strategy. Although Levin didn't say it, Allie Boy was no doubt battling an urge to flee. Levin convinced him it was best if he turned himself in. With Levin, Allie Boy walked into the police station in Long Beach, Long Island. Levin explained to the desk sergeant that the U.S. government was looking for his client. The desk sergeant picked up the phone and FBI agents were there in a jiffy to take over. Allie Boy was held without bail on loan-sharking charges, based on evidence dating back as far as 1993. The police came with two warrants. One to arrest Allie Boy and the other to completely search his homes, both in New York and Florida.

Allie Boy was also being charged with RICO violations, with being the head of the Colombo family, the same organization of which, the indictment read, his father had once been boss. When it was convenient for them, the feds were willing to admit that Carmine was no longer the *actual* boss.

U.S. Magistrate Arlene Lindsay ordered that Allie Boy be transported by U.S. Marshals back down to South Florida to face the weapons charges involving his boat. Allie Boy was convicted on the weapons charges, fined $40,000, and sentenced to eighteen months, and three years of probation.

Levin talked to reporters during an impromptu conference in a courthouse hallway.

"They put away Gotti's son, now they want to put away Persico's son," Levin said.

Prosecutors said that at least some of their case was based on a surprise witness, which Persico and Levin correctly guessed was

Chris Paciello, a Miami nightclub owner who at that time was being held on charges that he murdered a Staten Island housewife in 1993 and was ripe to deal. Paciello had made it to the fringes of show biz society by being business partners with a woman who was a close friend of the singer Madonna.

Allie Boy didn't know how much the government knew. All that had surfaced so far regarding Paciello was that he and Allie Boy ate lunch together in a Miami Beach restaurant. It wasn't very impressive, but interesting in that it warranted a written police report.

"What about Chris Paciello?" a reporter asked, referring to the prosecution's so-called surprise witness.

"He's a playboy who'll say and do anything to keep out of jail," Levin said.

Levin complained that the search warrants the feds had used were unreasonable, that they tore up Allie Boy's family home and found zilch. "They took everything that's not tied down," the lawyer said.

As for "zilch," the authorities begged to differ. What they found, they said, was evidence of a criminal syndicate. Investigators discovered $25,000 in cash hidden in Allie Boy's mattress, under the bed, and in a shoebox. Also found, in his briefcase, were loansharking records, fake I.D.s (Allie Boy's picture but another name), and credit cards in the pseudonym. They also found documents regarding the prosecution of Colombos, and these, the government claimed, proved that Allie Boy was still involved in family business despite his move to Florida. In Allie Boy's Park Slope apartment feds found a shoebox full of loansharking records, and a floppy disk under the stove that contained damning financial information, specifically info regarding the laundering of money that had been extorted from Embassy Terrace, a Gravesend catering hall.

Apparently, the government didn't have the restaurant bugged when Allie Boy and Paciello lunched. They didn't know what was discussed. Barry Levin said the lunch was the only time his client was ever with Chris Paciello, so whatever Paciello had to say about the meeting was pure bullshit.

The indictments, if proven to be true, included a glimpse of Allie Boy's activities during the Persico-Orena war. The feds claimed that Allie Boy's known war budget was $200,000. The money went to "body armor, hotel rooms, and safe houses."

CHAPTER FIFTEEN

Billy Fingers, Missing

*White Death came to William Cutolo, who took a meeting
with Allie Boy Persico in Bay Ridge's Cannonball Park
and was never seen again.*

WHILE ALLIE BOY WAS SERVING his weapons sentence in Florida
and his dad was away for good, the new Colombo underboss was
William "Billy Fingers" Cutolo. Like Vic Orena before him,
Cutolo was ambitious and grew increasingly independent. He
saw himself as a hero in the neighborhood. Hell, he played Santa
at the children's hospital every Christmas. Alternately known as
"Wild Bill," Cutolo was the picture of a 1950s mobster with
duck's ass hair and a tailored suit.

Allie Boy's Florida incarceration gave him time to think about
Billy Fingers, who had been on the Orena side of the war and
now chomped at the bit to rise another wrung on the ladder. We
don't know if Allie Boy actually came north to take care of business. He was out on bail but wasn't supposed to leave Florida.
Here's what we do know:

On May 26, 1999, Mrs. Marguerite Cutolo called police to report her husband missing. He'd gone to John Paul Jones Park at
Fourth Avenue and 101st Street at the southern tip of Bay Ridge,
Brooklyn, known as Cannonball Park to the locals because of the
huge Rodman Gun and stacked cannonballs that provide its *objet
d'art*. Cutolo went to the park for a meeting, he said, with Allie
Boy Persico and did not return home.

According to a 2007 U.S. Attorney's Office press release, Cutolo may have been expecting to meet with Allie Boy in person, but when he got to the park he encountered Colombo guns Thomas Gioeli, Dino Calabro, and Dino Saracino. They abducted him, took him to Saracino's apartment and there murdered him. They drove his body out to Long Island and buried it.

The day after her husband's disappearance, Marguerite received a visit at their home from Allie Boy's underboss and Carmine's brother-in-law Jackie DeRoss, who insisted on rifling through Billy's things, searching for something.

Unaware that Cutolo's son had a tape recorder rolling, right out in the open on the dining-room table, DeRoss told the Cutolo kids that they should let the FBI know that Allie Boy had nothing to do with their dad's death, and if they didn't bad things could happen to them.

Clearly, Cutolo had been the victim of a *lupara bianca* style murder—a "white death" in which the body was not easily, sometimes never, found. That style of murder, of course, was more difficult to execute, as the target had to be snatched before he was killed, rather than just shooting him in a restaurant or barber shop or the street, where the body is left lying there posing inside a chalk line for tabloid photographers.

As Allie Boy's Florida term for guns possession neared an end, the feds went back to work, and on January 24, 2001, the day he was released, picked him up (along with 120 others) and indicted him on loan-sharking charges, and for masterminding a "massive stock fraud scheme." Allie Boy and a team of sketchy stock brokers, including cousin Frank Persico, allegedly invented a financial entity called DMN Capital Investments, Inc., and used it to launder funds. The feds called the operation to bust the scheme *Operation Uptick*. The scheme, feds alleged, was to eventually divert and steal the entire pension fund of the Industrial & Production Workers Local 400. Local 400 was founded by Billy Fingers. The attempted crime didn't come off when union pension fund administrator Kathleen Joseph refused to turn the $50 million fund over to the mobsters. Only days after Cutolo disappeared, her refusal earned her a personal visit from Frank Persico.

Following his stock-fraud indictment, Carmine's son Alphonse would never again be free. The evidence against him consisted of documents that allegedly indicated multiple loan-sharking operations, statements made by a surprise witness, and all pertinent material seized from Allie Boy's Florida and Brooklyn homes. The loan-shark businesses, investigators learned, included one formerly operated by Cutolo, who at that time had been missing for two years.

Allie Boy was transported back north. On January 26, 2001, only two days after his Florida release, he was in Brooklyn Federal Court with Barry Levin at his side attempting to have bail set. Assistant U.S. Attorneys Amy Walsh and John Kroger argued that Allie Boy should be held without bail. Allowing him to be free, they said, was allowing him to resume his duties as the boss of one of New York City's crime families. Judge Reena Raggi ordered Allie Boy held without bail.

Afterward, Levin maintained his public pressure on "surprise-witness" Chris Paciello: "I would bet my law license that Paciello has ratted on Persico to get off the hook from a thirty-three-year prison term he faces." Levin characterized allegations that Allie Boy was boss of the Colombos as "preposterous."

Paciello was indeed the prosecution's ace in the hole, a worst-kept secret since the previous November, when, on the eve of Paciello's sentencing for murder, he disappeared and authorities refused to comment.

"We are going to ask for a quick trial and Alphonse Persico will be acquitted," Levin summed up.

During pre-trial hearings, Levin argued on Allie Boy's behalf that the search of his Park Slope apartment by FBI agents was illegal. The search warrant specified that the search was for one of Allie Boy's phones, the contents of which the feds thought would incriminate him. However, during the search the phone was found almost immediately, but was thought to be the wrong phone. As the search continued, the feds found the cash and documents now being used as evidence. If the feds had recognized that they had found the correct phone, the rest of the search would not have been warranted and the evidence would never have been found.

Judge Raggi ruled that the phone incident had been an "honest mistake" by the FBI agents, and against the defense's arguments.

Cutolo top gun and muscle, Joseph "Campy" Campanella of Dyker Heights, was not a man with vices. He didn't drink or do drugs. He married his high-school sweetheart, was known as a family man—but when he wanted to, he could scare the shit out of a guy. Cutolo once dispatched him to frighten someone who was behind on his payments. Campy broke the guy's arm. They scare better when their arm is breaking, it seemed to him.

On July 16, 2001, Campy exited his gym and noticed a green van following him. Thinking it was the feds, he tried to lose the van, thought he had, and drove to Coney Island for a swim. But there, returning to his car, he saw the green van again. This time he recognized the guys in it. "Hey Joe," said one. Another got out of the van with a towel-wrapped gun in his hand. Vincent "Chickie" DeMartino fired five shots from a .357 Magnum, two of them striking Campanella, once in the upper arm as he tried to protect his face and the other in his sneakered foot as he ran, blowing off a toe.

DeMartino, Giovanni "John the Barber" Floridia, and Michael "Mikey Spats" Spataro were eventually convicted of this shooting. It only went to show that you couldn't tell the players even if you had a scorecard.

During the Persico-Orena war, Campanella, DeMartino, and

Spataro had all been on the same side, Orena's side. However, after the war, with Allie Boy in charge, DeMartino and Spataro were loyal Allie Boy soldiers and Campanella was marked for death as a turncoat. (Campanella survived, but returned to a life in which his crew had been stolen away and his family left destitute. He served three years for extortion, turned snitch, helped convict the guys who shot him, turned down Witness Protection, opted to keep his own name and face, and moved—but not that far.)

It was five days before Christmas 2001, the end of a very bad year in America, and Allie Boy and Barry Levin could read the writing on the wall. The prosecution had the goods. Allie Boy's best bet was to deal, so he pleaded guilty to all the RICO bullshit and was sentenced to thirteen years. As part of the plea deal, Allie Boy had to publicly admit that he'd been the acting boss of the Colombo crime family.

Despite the deal, Allie Boy's legal difficulties continued unabated. In 2004, Allie Boy and Jackie DeRoss were indicted for the Cutolo murder. When news of the new charges got to Allie Boy's dad, Carmine admitted he was worried about his son.

"This is the end for him," Carmine said.

The first trial for the Cutolo murder took place in Brooklyn Federal Court over five weeks during the autumn of 2006, with U.S. District Judge Sterling Johnson presiding. The prosecutor was Assistant U.S. Attorney Thomas Siegal. Allie Boy was defended by the young and beautiful Sarita Kedia, who could not have looked or sounded less like a mob lawyer. Born in India and raised in the deep south, she was experienced, having defended John Gotti Jr. back in 1999 when she was still in her twenties. Her beauty aside, she was well-respected as a courtroom adversary, one prosecutor referring to her as a "straight shooter and a very good lawyer." Her soft-spoken nature was deceptive, as she was a tenacious and extremely confident mouthpiece.

The trial's star witness was Kathleen Joseph, the pension fund administrator who had said no and had lived to tell about it. She testified, "Local 400 President John Gannone and stockbroker Frank Persico wanted some documents. He wanted the names of the trustees of the pension fund, the name of the attorney for the fund, the actuaries, the accountant."

"Did you give the documents to him?" asked Siegal.

"No."

She said she thought Frank Persico was acting strangely, and had been for a while, even before she refused to give him the documents. Frank said that he was not aware that William Cutolo was missing, yet replaced Cutolo as V.P. of the union without bothering to hold an election. It smelled to her like a power grab.

That accomplished, he demanded to become a trustee of the pension fund. There was no opening so Gannone resigned, which allowed Persico to move in. Persico, Joseph testified, subsequently attempted to get rid of the fund manager, Smith Barney, so that he could have the fund managed by his "own cronies."

After five days of deliberation, the jury passed a note to Judge Johnson, saying they were hopelessly deadlocked.

After a mistrial was declared, Kedia said: "I had hoped for an acquittal, but it sure beats the other alternative."

Siegal noted that there was no hurry, both of the defendants were already locked up. "I have a strong case," he said, "and sometime next year I will file a motion for retrial."

A second trial was held, and this time defense attorneys had successfully argued for a change of venue because of the case's intense local notoriety. The new trial was held in a courthouse in Central Islip, Long Island, during November 2007 with John Buretta, Deborah Mayer, and Jeffrey Goldberg as the new fed prosecutors. Once again Allie Boy and Jackie DeRoss were tried as co-defendants.

The star prosecution witness at the second trial was Marguerite Cutolo, Mrs. Billy Fingers, who said goodbye to her husband in

1999 and never saw him again. Her appearance at the trial was a bit of a surprise. She skipped the first trial while in the FBI's Witness Protection Program. This time her testimony was strong: "I've been distressed and depressed for eight years because I don't know where my husband was. My husband would never have run away."

Allie Boy's defense team tried to convince the jury that Cutolo had faked his own death, and that Mrs. Cutolo knew all about it. They tried to turn Marguerite into the villain, said that she had stashed someplace all the money from her husband's loan sharking racket.

This "stashing" accusation was not totally unsubstantiated, as Marguerite admitted that, yes, she did at one time have $1.65 million hidden in an air-conditioning vent in her home. It wasn't there anymore because the central air system broke down and a repairman, who just happened to be defendant DeRoss's nephew, came to make the repairs, so she moved the money.

She admitted during her testimony that when she became part of the Witness Protection Program, she took the money with her. Why? Because those were his instructions.

"My husband always told me that, if anything happened to him, *you give them nothing*."

On cross-examination, DeRoss's lawyer, Robert LaRusso, produced ledgers that said her husband had $2.7 million when he disappeared. Marguerite said those ledgers weren't the real ones.

"My husband kept two sets of books," she explained. "One real one and one to be seen by the Colombo family."

She said that she didn't know why the number in the book differed from the money she'd had hidden in the vent.

"I only know what I counted," she explained. "The government let me have the money. I had to take care of the kids."

She had a theory as to where some of the money went. Her son, William Jr., could spend money like water. Junior was also the family member who was most cooperative with the FBI's investigation after his father's disappearance.

But that was all defense obfuscation. The point was rather simple. Marguerite last saw her husband as he left for a meeting in Bay Ridge.

"I know he was meeting Allie Boy," she testified. At the time she thought it an odd time to have a meeting. A Wednesday? Her husband was a man of habits. His Wednesday schedule was set in stone. Mornings at his union office in Manhattan, haircut, and then dinner with his crew at the Friendly Bocce Club in Brooklyn.

Marguerite wasn't done with the damning testimony. She told the jury that DeRoss visited her Staten Island home the day after William's disappearance.

"Did he seem upset?"

"Let's put it this way. There wasn't a tear in his eye."

"Mrs. Cutolo, do you believe there's a chance your husband is alive, that he ran away?"

"My husband never ran away. I'm appearing here for my husband. For his death."

After Marguerite left the stand, the prosecution called Cutolo's daughter, Barbara Cutolo Cardinale. She said that she had reason to believe Jackie DeRoss in particular was involved in her dad's disappearance. Someone at the top of the Colombo family had been responsible for her dad being gone, and she hadn't been shy about saying it out loud, so much so that she received a visit from DeRoss.

"He warned me to shut my mouth," she said. "What he didn't know was that my brother, who was there with me, was recording him."

"What was it he didn't want you to say?"

"I wasn't to express my belief that *Carmine Persico* ordered the hit on my dad."

And so DeRoss's threats were recorded. He told her that bad

things could happen to the mother, children, husband, and siblings, if she cooperated with investigators.

Defense attorney Sarita Kedia later argued, "There is not a single piece of evidence to prove to you that Billy Cutolo is really dead."

The U.S. attorneys not only assumed Cutolo was murdered, they were willing to put Cutolo's murder in historic context: "The Colombo war never really ended, at least not in the minds of men like Alphonse Persico."

In her closing argument, Deborah Mayer told the jury that in 1999, when he disappeared, Billy Cutolo was a powerful man. His crew was large. He was power-hungry, had what the prosecutor called "boss mentality." She reminded the jury that it had been wartime, the Persicos versus the Orenas, and Cutolo sided with the man on the outside over the man on the inside. When the war was over, Cutolo no doubt was hoping for a little forgiveness. He wanted to be allowed to keep his place in the business, but that was not to be. It was when Allie Boy was sentenced to eighteen months for his Coast Guard bust that action needed to be taken. Cutolo knew how to fill a void, and Allie Boy's imprisonment created one. So, to prevent a coup, Cutolo became a void himself, nothingness where there once stood a man. Mayer said that Cutolo was killed and his body taken to a marina in Lindenhurst, put on a boat and buried at sea (which turned out to be incorrect). She said that one month after Cutolo disappeared, one of the men responsible received $50,000 from Carmine Persico.

On December 28, 2007, Allie Boy was convicted of murder in aid of racketeering. He was subsequently sentenced to life in prison. He began his term in the U.S. penitentiary near Coleman, Florida, but in 2015 was transferred to the Federal Correctional Institute in McKean County, Pennsylvania, near the city of Bradford, a medium-security facility built in 1989, where he currently resides.

The Pennsylvania prison was salmon and gray, the buildings showing a Native American influence, low, modern. The entrance for visitors was air-conditioned and softly carpeted. Tropical plants were part of the décor. In the distance were manicured playing fields. There was a running joke among the staff: How long after a visitor arrived for the first time would he compare McKean to a college campus.

On October 6, 2008, FBI agents acting on a tip dug up a partially decomposed body wearing Italian loafers and wrapped in a tarp in a shallow grave in East Farmingdale, Long Island. The body, like that of William Cutolo, was missing the tip of its right middle finger. It was officially identified as Cutolo's by dental records. Prosecutors were somewhat disappointed to find only one body in the hole. The tip had said there would be three, the other two belonging to Richard Greaves who disappeared in 1995 and Carmine Gargano, a Pace University student who disappeared in 1994. The story was the killers feared Greaves was going to turn rat—so the kill was a preemptive strike. Gargano had been offed, the story went, because he had a cousin in the wrong crew.

The murder of Billy Fingers last came up in a courtroom in 2014, when Colombo soldier Dino Saracino was successfully prosecuted by U.S. Attorney Loretta Lynch in Brooklyn for being part of a decades-long racketeering conspiracy, which included his role in the Persico-Orena war and the 1999 murder of William Cutolo. He got fifty years. He was the seventieth member or associate of the Colombos to be put away by the feds.

CHAPTER SIXTEEN
Famiglia

In everyone's family, rain must fall, and it is no different with
the Persicos. Being a Persico is a blessing—and a curse.

ON FATHER'S DAY, 2000, Mob afficianado Selwyn Raab wrote an article for *The New York Times* in which he compared John Gotti and Carmine Persico, both reputed leaders of crime families, both said to be conducting business from behind bars, and both having sons—John A. Gotti, and Alphonse T. Persico, who were also behind bars largely because they'd inherited the family business when dad went away. Raab pointed out that, by appointing their successors and keeping leadership of their organizations under family control, both Gotti and Persico had broken from Mafia tradition, which held that, although it was perfectly acceptable to recruit close family members into the fold, the choosing of one's successor as boss is not at the sole discretion of the old boss.

No previous bosses had named their son as the new boss before Persico and Gotti, Raab said. They were following the rules of kings rather than bosses. Gotti and Persico crowned their sons, who were paying a dear price for it.

The traditional method of succession was meritocracy. The new boss was the guy who'd paid the most dues, and whose command his soldiers most respected. A former director of a state crime commission and mob intelligence chief said that great dissension built up in the Colombo and Gambino families because of nepotism. Guys simply didn't think the sons deserved it. One of the primary reasons for the Orena war was Carmine's insistence that Orena relinquish control when Little Allie Boy got out of prison. Keeping with the Father's Day theme, Raab made it clear that neither Gotti Jr. nor Little Allie Boy blamed their dads for their predicaments. Both loved their fathers and would have called them to wish them a happy Father's Day if regulations had not prevented them from making telephone calls to inmates in other facilities.

Sure, the sons loved their dads, but former FBI supervisor J. Bruce Mouw said he wondered if the dads loved their sons back in the same way: "What father, if he had any love or compassion for his son, would encourage him to become a mob boss or even a mobster? Who would want his son to be in danger of being killed or of being sent to jail?"

Mouw clearly had not adequately considered the perks.

Carmine's son Lawrence had problems that had nothing to do with his dad's career. He was diagnosed as bi-polar as a kid, and had endured a life-long battle with mental illness, sometimes becoming estranged from the family. Lawrence was indicted in the Colombo labor racketeering case, convicted of holding a no-show job as an operating engineer, and sentenced to twenty-one months in prison. In 2003 racketeering indictments, he'd been one of forty-five men swept up. The case involved the takeover of the International Union of Operating Engineers. Dad Carmine came to Lawrence's aid during Lawrence's trial.

Carmine sat down in his prison cell and composed a letter to Federal Judge Sterling Johnson in Brooklyn, a letter that was later made public at trial. In what was described as a "cramped hand," he wrote, "My name is Carmine Persico. I am the father of Larry Persico who is a defendant before you. Please know that he is not mentally capable of committing the crimes attributed to him. I am sure you are aware of Larry's mental condition. This condition dates back to 1972 when I received fourteen years in prison. Larry took it very hard and his troubles began. My wife, Larry's mother, has been taking care of him ever since. Larry has been hospitalized many times but he has never at any time harmed anyone or been a danger to the community. He is a good, hard-working family man who only wants to work to be able to take care of his family and his home. He does not go out to bars at night. He is in bed by nine o'clock. Sometimes his wife gets angry because he never leaves the house and has no friends. He spends no money on himself. He had to be forced to fix his teeth. My son thought it was a waste of money. In the end, his mother gave him the money for his dental work. He also doesn't buy clothes for himself. He owns one suit and his work clothes only. My son would never be part of a RICO case. He does not associate with any person or persons and is not mentally capable to conspire with anyone. He would resent anyone to suggest to him in any way to commit a crime. This is a good, hardworking decent man, Your Honor. Don't allow the Persico name and an overzealous prosecutor the ability to ruin what my son worked for all his life. Please do not allow Larry to pay for his father's sins! Don't allow this injustice to harm a sick boy's life."

That "sick boy" was forty-eight years old. The charges against him were that he had helped use mob muscle to turn two powerful unions into fronts for racketeering operations. The unions represented 6,000 operators of heavy machines such as cranes, derricks, and hoists. They were involved in construction of an addition to the Museum of Modern Art, as well as new (in 2001) minor league baseball stadiums in Coney Island, Brooklyn, and St. George, Staten Island. Prosecutors alleged that Larry claimed to be working on the renovation of Brooklyn's General Post Office, while at the same time holding down a full-time job elsewhere. They said he had committed fraud, racketeering and extortion because he received $220,000 for a job he wasn't doing. The indictment made sure to point out that Larry Persico was of *the* Persicos, as if this alone were evidence of wrongdoing.

Larry's wife and brother also came to his defense, saying he was a hardworking guy, plagued by mental problems. *The Village Voice* called Larry a kind of "Fredo Corleone without a taste for nightlife."

Kid brother Michael Persico told the *Voice,* "He is a manic-depressive. Sometimes the illness plays games with his mind. He is being persecuted because he is Carmine Persico's son."

Research revealed that, despite his family's assurance that Larry lived a simple life without possessions, Larry owned four Harley-Davidson motorcycles and a 2003 Range Rover, which he kept up on the farm.

One thing was for certain, Larry's legal difficulties were doing nothing to help his mental health. In February 2003 he had what was called a "psychotic episode," and was kept for three weeks in Lenox Hill Hospital.

In August, the court ordered Larry to meet with a psychologist on Court Street in Brooklyn but Larry blew off the appointment. He apologized and was subsequently allowed to travel to Lompoc Penitentiary to visit his letter-writing father.

Upon his return he was remanded to the Metropolitan Detention Center where a psychiatrist examined him and later described him as "childlike." He was released in October but again missed a court-ordered appointment, this one before Thanksgiving with a pre-trial investigator. He again said he was sorry, he forgot, but nonetheless was ordered back to jail.

About this time, he picked up a new lawyer, Dale Lionel Smith of Manhattan, who told the press, "My client is a legitimate union man. He went to work and got paid. If you speak to the dispatchers and everyone else involved, they will tell you he worked for his wages." Smith said that Lawrence had been "down on his luck" since.

On January 6, 2010, Lawrence's forty-seven-year-old wife was arrested and accused of having sticky fingers in a Staten Island Target. This wasn't just an air-freshener-in-the-purse deal either. She was arrested after a camera caught her pushing her full shopping cart around the cashiers instead of through them, allegedly with $597 worth of clothing, cleaning supplies, luggage, and other items. Her lawyer, Salvatore Strazzullo, said it was clearly a misunderstanding. "Are you kidding me? Why would she steal from Target?" he said. The woman was released without bail, and the case went away.

In 2016, it was reported that sixty-year-old Lawrence was delivering pizzas for a Dyker Heights pizza parlor.

The soft-spoken Michael Persico, Carmine's youngest son, was an urbane, smooth operator who wore crushed velvet sports jackets. He was not a made man, and had been known to the public as a legitimate businessman, a guy who operated a limousine company and ran the family's Saugerties farm.

But the feds arrested him in 2010 on racketeering and murder charges. The murder was the 1993 Joey Scopo hit. They said Michael supplied weapons and info regarding Scopo's location for the hit. Michael's defense team fought to the U.S. Court of Appeals to get him released on $5 million bail as he awaited trial.

Two years into his ordeal, Michael made the tabloids in New York for romantic reasons. He was, according to a gossipy news item, dating his lawyer, "legal eagle knockout Sarita Kedia," who'd also defended brother Alphonse. She, the paper emphasized, was going to have to help Michael stay free if she wanted more contact with him than was allowed during conjugal visits. The romance, it said, was no doubt cutting into preparation time for Kedia, who had less than a month to get ready for Michael's upcoming trial. The news of the alleged budding romance was first learned when Assistant U.S. Attorneys Nicole Argentieri and Allon Lifshitz filed a letter under seal to Judge Sandra Townes that claimed the accused and his "comely counsel" were an item.

At a May 11, 2012, court hearing, the transcript of which had been obtained by the newspaper, Judge Townes said this to Michael Persico: "If such a romantic relationship exists between you and your attorney, that relationship could potentially affect her decision-making and her representation in this case. In other words, her professional judgment, the government argues, could be affected by her emotional feelings for you."

Kedia was given an opportunity in court to address the issue and she said, "Your Honor, I can absolutely assure the court that I do not have or have I ever had any relationship with Mr. Persico that would in any way compromise my professional responsibility in representing him in his own best interest." Angry, she added, "The government's actions are unprofessional and reprehensible. Michael Persico is a client and friend. But the government's allegation that I have a personal relationship or concern that would affect my representation is not only false, it's desperate."

Judge Townes asked if he planned to keep Kedia on his defense team, and Michael said he did.

The prosecution spoke with the press following the hearing and pointed out that they didn't need to prove that the defendant and his counsel were romantically inclined. They merely felt it necessary to deal with the issue in court before the trial began so the issue would not become appealable down the road.

The charges against Michael were based on surveillance audiotapes of Michael allegedly speaking candidly with a guy named Steve Marcus, to whom Michael had lent $100,000. Marcus owned a piece of a Staten Island trucking company with brother Teddy Boy. Those tapes were never played in public, but were eventually enough to get Michael to deal. The government dropped the murder charge and Michael pleaded guilty to the rest. His defense attorneys set about to delay Michael's sentencing hearing for as long as possible, so—still free on millions in bail—Michael stayed free for years, and he didn't even have to go on the lam.

In 2014, Teddy Boy took the rap for the Scopo hit, pleading guilty to charges that he ordered it (at his grandmother's funeral).

At ten o'clock on the frigid morning of January 18, 2016, in Brooklyn federal court, Judge Dora Irizarry, found herself sitting on her bench for yet another Michael Persico pre-sentencing hearing, while both the prosecution table and defense tables were empty. The judge promptly issued a bench warrant for Persico's arrest and proclaimed that she would consider sanctions against the prosecutor and Persico's lawyer for "unexcused failure to appear." Turned out, Judge Irizarry was the one who had made the mistake. The conference was actually scheduled for 11:00 A.M., and Her Honor had arrived an hour early. The mistake was chalked up to a clerical error. The judge apologized and blamed the wintery weather for her brain freeze.

In October 2016, Michael's mother, the long-suffering Joyce, wrote to Judge Irizarry, woman to woman, asking that she show her son some compassion. The letter, made public by the court, read, "I am getting older and need my son around. He helps me with everything. I am scared that if he is sent to prison I will never see him again outside of that place. Throughout his life, Michael has been a loving son to me and our family and a doting father to all his children." What she didn't say, what she didn't have to say, was that she'd lost her husband and her boys that way, and she felt like she'd given enough to the goddamned government.

Michael's lawyers, now including top-rated NYC defense attorney Maurice Sercarz, pointed out that the letter spoke volumes about Michael's place in his family and the community, as well as his ability to live within the law. Sercarz attached a sentencing memorandum to the filing in which he explained that Joyce Persico's health really did cause her to depend on her son for quality of life, that she suffered from crippling rheumatoid arthritis and had emphysema.

During a pre-sentencing hearing, Michael's lawyers argued that Michael has long struggled to "overcome the infamy," shed the stigma of his last name. He was sick of people thinking he was a criminal just because he was a Persico, and had "conducted himself in a law-abiding manner."

On Friday, July 21, 2017, Judge Irizarry said she could delay sentencing no longer. It was time that Michael faced the music. She said that Michael had a Jekyll-Hyde type personality, with an upstanding side, and a criminal side that his family couldn't even fathom. She determined his punishment after factoring in the 1993 murder of Joe Scopo during the Orena war. Michael, she noted, had according to "more than a preponderance of the evidence" supplied weapons, and let the hitmen know where Scopo would be.

"That murder was part of protecting your family and your family's role with the Colombo crime family," Judge Irizarry added. She then ordered Michael to serve five years in the fed pen. Mother Joyce's heart broke. In the courtroom gallery, Michael's loved ones cried.

In August, Michael's legal team requested he be allowed to remain free until the end of his appeal process, but Judge Irizarry said no and ordered Michael to report to prison on October 20.

In sharp contrast to the sophisticated Michael, was his cousin Teddy Boy, a.k.a. Skinny Teddy, who was the picture of an old-time hoodlum. In March 2010, the *Village Voice* covered Teddy, a reputed Colombo capo, based on the premise that, out of the contemporary batch of hoods lurking on Brooklyn street corners,

Teddy Boy was the one who best talked the talk. He was a chip off the old block. Teddy had spent twenty of the previous twenty-five years in prison, which may have helped sculpt his artistic usage of the English language, issuing forth with dialogue that would make Hollywood screenwriters swoon.

To one mobster who was wearing a wire, Teddy said, "You're not me. If it was up to me, I'd go get a gun and shoot them, or stab them, or beat them up when I seen 'em. I got nothing. They can't fuck with me because I got nothing to lose and they got everything to lose. You can't fuck with them because you've got everything to lose and nothing to gain by getting physical. I can get physical all day long. I can get crazy. I don't give a fuck. What are you going to do, put me in jail? What am I going to lose? My wife, my kids, my house that I own, my $2 million house that I own, or my car? I don't own nothing. I got no wife, I got no kids. I can act like a fool. I'm telling you what I can do, I know you can't do that, I know you don't want to do that."

Following a March 2010 indictment, Teddy was held without bail on charges that included extorting a demolition trucking company hired at Ground Zero. In addition to ordering the Scopo hit, he was a suspect, along with Big Frank Guerra, in the March 26, 1990 drive-by hit on drug-dealer Vincent "Scoobie" Lafaro, in front of Lafaro's home in Bensonhurst. Teddy Boy, the indictment claimed, ordered the hits from prison. Teddy Boy's beef was that it was Lafaro whose blabbing led to Teddy Boy's 1988 conviction, and twenty-year sentence, for trafficking snowy mountains of cocaine. The fed info also stated that during the time Teddy Boy was in prison (he got out in 2004), Big Frank made sure he received a weekly cut ($500) from the coke biz. The same source also said that Guerra was involved in the April 1998 murder of Frank Hydell in front of a Staten Island strip joint. Guerra allegedly told Allie Boy that Hydell was working with the FBI. Allie Boy reportedly passed a message to reliable gunmen in the Gambino family, and the Gambinos were said to have offed Hydell.

In 2009 the *New York Post* reported that a Long Island debt-collection law firm, Forster & Garbus, was suing Allie Boy Persico for $34,000 in unpaid credit card bills owed to the Bank of America. The irony was thick.

The paper asked, "What are they going to do, bust his kneecaps?"

When their attempts to collect began, the firm had Allie Boy's address as being in Bensonhurst, the address of his brother's car service, and were seemingly unaware that he'd taken up residency many years before in the California federal penitentiary.

Big Allie Boy's daughter, Suzanne, has had a lifetime of excitement and heartache because of her lot in life. In 1995, FBI wiretaps on cell phones, home phones, and three business phones located inside strip joints, picked up Suzanne's voice, as well as that of her husband, reputed Colombo capo Tommy Farese, allegedly discussing a plan to launder a million dollars for South American crack dealers and hiding Tommy's piece of gentlemen's clubs in Broward and Palm Beach County, Florida.

The crack dealers turned out to be undercover agents. Suzanne had the charges against her dropped when Tommy pleaded guilty. In 1998, Suzanne wept as Tommy folded his silk tie, removed his belt, handed her the items, and kissed her good-bye. Tommy's lawyer cried entrapment, arguing that no money laundering took place until after government agents started playing confidence games.

During the autumn of 2016, twenty-two-year-old Charles Pickering was standing outside a Bay Ridge bar/restaurant, perhaps smoking a cigarette, but otherwise minding his own business when he was attacked by a man who police later identified as Carmine's twenty-five-year-old grandson, his namesake Carmine Persico, son of Lawrence. Young Carmine, who had recently undergone eye surgery, apparently mistook Pickering for someone he knew and *really didn't like*.

From his hospital bed, his jaw wired shut, Pickering managed to tell the story. He said that Persico approached him outside the bar while he was having a smoke.

"Can I borrow your lighter?" Persico reportedly asked.

Pickering said sure and handed him his Bic. Persico lit his cigarette and handed the lighter back to Pickering.

Pickering recalled, "He said, 'Oh, you look familiar,' and the next thing I know he just hits me."

A reporter at Pickering's bedside asked him if he was worried about Mafia repercussions.

"It's the twenty-first century," was Pickering's reply.

"When did you learn your attacker had a famous last name?"

"Here in the hospital, I saw it on the internet."

"Persico had friends with him?"

"Yeah, three of them. Once I was down they took turns kicking me."

Pickering was in the hospital for three days.

Carmine and his three friends fled but, in his haste, Carmine dropped his car keys. Cops used the keys to unlock a black 2015 Chrysler 200 that was parked near the bar. They traced the car to young Carmine and arrested him. His friends remained at-large.

Carmine was charged with first-degree assault, second-degree gang assault, and freed on $5,000. His legal-aid lawyer told a judge that further punishment was not necessary here because young Carmine was planning to enlist in the Navy, waiting for the Lasik surgery on his eye to heal completely so he could pass a military physical.

* * *

In the spring of 2016, Carmine's nephew, Daniel, fifty-four years old, died after a six-year battle with colon cancer. Danny was the son of Carmine's brother Theodore, and by all accounts a good guy. Daniel's brother, Teddy Boy, went into the life, but Danny remained, as the *Post* put it, "one of the few members of the Persico family who is not in prison or dead." Friends recalled his good deeds. When his brother got out of Greenhaven, after serving seventeen years, it was Danny who sent the limo to pick him up.

A reporter asked a mourner about the family's criminal reputation.

"There's nobody left," the guy said. No more murders. "The old guys are too old and too tired."

Carmine's brother Theodore, Big Teddy Boy, was the Persico brother who'd drawn the least publicity. His brothers were bosses, but Teddy remained a capo, and once a member of a "ruling committee." He "only" spent twenty-two years in prison, mostly for his participation in the Persico-Orena War. The last six of those years were spent in a medical facility because of his failing health. He was arrested outside St. Patrick's Cathedral in 1993 on Palm Sunday, and was released in 2013. After two months in a Brooklyn halfway house, Teddy Boy returned home to Valley Stream, Long Island, where he had been staying out of trouble. He passed away at age seventy-nine on February 22, 2017, in Brooklyn, leaving Carmine as the sole living member of the Carroll Street Persico brothers. He was interred in the Persico family mausoleum in Green-Wood Cemetery.

On Teddy Boy's internet obituary page, one mourner wrote simply, "He was a good earner."

EPILOGUE
La vita è un sogno

*Carmine John Persico Jr. is now both myth and man. In legend,
he remains the leader of a gang, just what he wanted to be when
he was thirteen and laying his precocious rap on the elders of
the Garfield Boys. In reality, power has faded into nostalgia.*

SINCE 2005, CARMINE has been an inmate at Butner Medium I
Federal Correctional Institute in North Carolina, a medical facility, perhaps even cushier than his California digs. Butner was
known as "Camp Fluffy" because of its comforts. Now in his
eighties, Carmine enjoyed a fenced-in one-acre courtyard with a
rec room. He could shoot pool, lift weights, or play basketball, or
perspire under a towel in the "sweat lodge," although his lungs
were bad from smoking and he was more prone to playing
Pinochle and bocce. Carmine's room had a window without bars
and a cell door that wasn't locked at night. He had access to a
computer and a kitchen where he could cook.

The medical condition that got Carmine transferred was a mystery. Maybe respiratory, but not necessarily. His lawyer Linda
Sheffield would only say it was nothing life-threatening.

At Butner, all of the units were named for colleges that played
in the Atlantic Coast Conference. Carmine lived in the Georgia
Tech Unit, where he was known for his skill at games, but often
appeared lonely, homesick for the old days.

Other inmates, the source said, always showed Carmine the
appropriate respect, and were eager to do him favors and be on
his good side. Carmine could always get extra food or specially
prepared meals. All he had to do was say the word.

Carmine was like a business school professor dishing out the wisdom. He liked to tell a story about something an old-time mobster told him when he was just a kid, still on his way up. The advice was, if you go into a business, take over every aspect of it. If you want to run a carpet-cleaning company, for example, don't just provide the cleaning service, but control the people who sell the carpets, supply the carpets, and determine when the carpets need to be cleaned. You take what might have earned you a decent living, and you turn it into something that can draw $1 million per year and go on for decades.

In 2007 a document was made public in a Brooklyn courtroom that stated that, back in 1987, there'd been a vote by the leaders of the five families on whether to hit Rudolph Giuliani, who at the time was a U.S. Attorney at war with the mob. The memo was written by the former FBI special agent Roy Lindley DeVecchio, and read during his trial on charges that he helped Greg Scarpa Sr. commit four murders in the 1980s and '90s. DeVecchio was also accused of giving Scarpa the heads-up on impending arrests so those sought could take evasive action.

Giuliani as we know came within one vote of being snuffed. The memo read, "On September 17, 1987, source advised that recent information disclosed that approximately a year ago all five New York La Cosa Nostra families discussed the idea of killing U.S. Attorney Giuliani, and John Gotti and Carmine Persico were in favor of the hit. The bosses of the Lucchese and Bonnano and Genovese families rejected the idea, despite strong efforts to convince them otherwise by Gotti and Persico."

The motion to off Giuliani was exceptional for the American mob. Though it was true that the Sicilian Mafia eliminated troublesome cops and "magistrates," here in the U.S. the wisdom said hitting government officials was counterproductive. Obviously politicians were once in a while offed, mostly when they were double-crossing sons of bitches, but modern mobsters thought of their families as businesses first. Violence that was bad for business was frowned upon. Of course, it happened. Dallas was crawling with pissed-off gangsters the day JFK was assassinated, and racket-buster Thomas Dewey was a target when running for governor of New York State.

But not this time.

Is the memo correct? That's another question. Does the tale pass the smell test? I could imagine Carmine wanting to hit Giuliani—and info supplied by Carmine's prison pal Cowboy Mike corroborated this assertion—John Gotti on the other hand was not inclined to agree with anything Persico said, and had no history of violence against authorities.

"One vote I won," Giuliani quipped on a morning radio program. Gotti died in 2002, and Carmine had been away for thirty years, so Giuliani figured he'd had the last laugh.

In 2011, the *New York Post*'s Brad Hamilton wrote an expose revealing the diminished state of the Colombo family, then in its eighty-third year, hardly recognizable as the same operation that once had a reputation as the most bloodthirsty of the families. Cousin Andy Mush Russo was said to have been "acting boss" of the remaining Colombos in 2010. The job at that point was to prevent desertion, and try to get back those who'd recently deserted. He tried a "come back to the fold, or else" command. The word on the street was that stray hoods who failed to return would be placed on a hit list, which would then be distributed to the other four families. On January 20, 2011, Mush was busted again—with consigliere Richard Fusco and underboss Benjamin Castellazzo, charged with murder, narcotics trafficking, and labor racketeering. In 2013, Mush went away again, two and a half years for racketeering.

*   *   *

Although the Colombos were hurting, law enforcement was not letting up and continued using wiretaps and wired informants to chip away. Recently they'd used two small-time hoods to gather info, brothers-in-law, Tommy McLaughlin and Peter Tagliavia, survivors of the Persico-Orena war who'd done time and kept their mouths shut. But now they wore a wire to record the conversations of their bosses.

Frankie "Blue Eyes" Sparaco ratted on the "upper echelon." Sparaco's info brought down street boss Thomas "Tommy Shots" Gioeli in 2010 for murder and racketeering.

On January 20, 2011, the feds launched the largest one-day arrest of gangsters in history. While McLaughlin and Tagliavia began new lives as new people, thirty-four members of the Colombo family were arrested, including underboss Benjamin "The Claw" Castellazzo and consigliere Richard "Ritchie Nerves" Fusco. Also arrested that year were Carmine's nephew Carmine, for extortion. While awaiting trial, he was under house arrest, wearing an ankle bracelet, and needed a special order from a judge to go to his girlfriend's house for Thanksgiving dinner.

Carmine must've felt a little lost. When they took Mush, they further lengthened the already vast distance between Junior and the gang he was supposed to be leading. The old traditions were gone. The boys no longer controlled the judges, the politicians. They no longer dirtied themselves with murder before they were made. You had button guys, all they did was earn. They wouldn't hurt a fly.

The feds, those bastards, had the nerve to say that their unknown sources were two made guys. Not just soldiers either. Caporegimes. Hothead hoods were left to guess who they might be.

The FBI predicted there would be multiple killings. "I've heard that people are looking to retaliate," an anonymous fed said, the bloodthirsty bastard. "That Colombo leadership is a dangerous bunch. They are reckless killers. Sometimes it doesn't take much for them to decide someone has to go. With Mush gone, they're rudderless. No one knows who will take over. There's no one left."

At a bail hearing for Mush Russo, actor James Caan, Mush's goombah since pre-production for *The Godfather*, wrote the judge a letter of support. The letter, made public at trial, pointed out that Mush was seventy-six. No spring chicken. Caan wrote that he and Mush went back thirty-five years, and "I've known him only as an unbelievable father, grandfather, great-grandfather, and as good a friend as anyone could be to me and my family. Our two families are intertwined. My son Scott is his godson. He has always been the first to call when any member of my family has been ill or troubled, and always looked after me like a brother. I'd be willing to put up anything of personal value that the court would accept. I would not hesitate a moment to fly in and be present if the court should so request. In short, there's nothing I wouldn't do to see this man where he belongs and where he is needed the most—with his family."

Also supporting Mush was actor Federico Castelluccio who played a hit man on *The Sopranos*. He said he was a painter and Mush a sculptor. Their friendship was based on their common love of art. For the hearing, the gallery behind Mush was packed, standing room only, largely with a group of hearing-impaired people. One member of that group explained that Mush, still the hater of bullies that my mom remembered from seventy years earlier, had come to the defense of a group of deaf children who were being picked on in her neighborhood. Despite the support, Judge Cheryl Pollak denied bail.

In September 2011, after fifty years in the life without taking a bullet, Mush was shot five times in the back by rubber bullets fired by a guard at the Brooklyn House of Detention for Men on Atlantic Avenue. Officials said it was an accident. Mush was apparently on the phone when the same earthquake that cracked the Washington Monument rumbled the jail, jolting one guard into a trigger-happy anti-riot mode. Mush was the only one hit.

Despite the decimated nature of the organization—Colombo active members were cut by more than half in five years—some remained stubbornly convinced that Carmine still called the shots. But who was left on the outside? To whom did he give his orders? His family members were either in prison or out of the life. As few as forty Colombos remained free, it was estimated. The family was in danger of extinction. The Colombos were now smaller and less powerful than the DeCavalcantes of New Jersey (made famous by the TV show *The Sopranos*). One law enforcement source said the clan had done it to itself.

Carmine's family was the family of great civil wars, Profaci-Gallo, Colombo-Gallo, Persico-Orena. The last war had done the most damage. Regarding the after-effects of the Orena war, Brooklyn D.A. Michael Vecchione, who often prosecuted cases against the Colombos, said that they never recovered.

Vecchione explained, "There have been factions in other families, but nothing to this extent. The number of murders and the mayhem was unprecedented." Now there was talk of divvying up what was left of the Colombos and splitting it between the four remaining families. The Colombos still had assets. They had influence in several unions. It was alleged that there was also considerable loan-sharking going on, valuable captains were still active.

By 2016, Carmine's health was failing. He'd served more than thirty years, the only defendant from the commission trial still behind bars. In a motion presented to the court in 2016, Carmine's legal team gave details regarding the old man's slumping health. He needed a wheelchair to get around now because of his emphysema. He was almost blind, had only limited use of his arms. How dangerous could he be? He had spent the great bulk of his years behind bars, how could you punish him any more than you had already?

The same memo to the court addressed the issue of long-concealed FBI files recovered by Carmine's lawyers through a Freedom of Information Act request. According to Persico attorney Anthony DiPietro, those files revealed that Carmine Persico was convicted of a crime he did not commit. Persico's one-hundred-year sentence was based on what DiPietro could demonstrate were false allegations. The memo asked Manhattan Federal Court Judge Kevin Duffy for a status conference.

The FBI files acquired through a 2015 request bolstered a case for sentence relief, the lawyer said, a case already hefty with the exposure of "troubling issues" regarding Carmine's commission trial conviction.

DiPietro's argument was that Carmine Persico was not yet a boss in 1979 and thus could not have conspired with the other mob bosses to commit murder as the government alleged.

Another weak point in the feds' case, a case for which Carmine had spent three decades away, was the fact that they had "illegal and unethical contracts" with the rats who testified against Carmine.

Two memos in particular demonstrated this point, one indicating that "Junior" had been among those voting on whether or not to hit Galante, and another that said Carmine became boss of the Colombos immediately following the mortal wounding of Joe Colombo. Carmine categorically denied both allegations.

DiPietro asked for a "just and timely review," reiterating that Carmine's health problems gave his request urgency. It wouldn't be the first time the court had pity on an old, sick mobster. In 2014, Lucchese consigliere Christopher "Christy Tick" Furnari was released after serving twenty-eight years of his century-long sentence in the commission case. On June 23, 2017, Colombo underboss John "Sonny" Franzese was released from Federal prison at age one hundred. He had been the oldest federal prisoner, and left the Federal Medical Center in Devens, Massachusetts, in a wheelchair. Franzese is expected to quietly live out his remaining days in his Greenpoint, Brooklyn, home with his loving family. Interestingly, Franzese had only been in the pen for eight years, as he was convicted at age ninety-two of shaking down a couple of Manhattan strip joints.

Carmine's battles in recent years have been modest. He recently fought for and won the best seat in the prison dining room, a corner chair with a window that overlooked the prison complex. There he schmoozes with the world's number-one white-collar criminal, Bernie Madoff, pats his round belly, and says, *"Il dolce far niente."*

Details of Carmine and Madoff's relationship came from journalist Steve Fishman, a longtime hoofer of the Bernie Madoff beat. Carmine served as the welcoming committee when Madoff arrived at the penitentiary to begin his 150-year sentence. Carmine gifted history's worst white-collar criminal with shower shoes and taught him the ropes. The two, Fishman said, became fast friends. They were about the same age, Madoff three years younger, and Carmine knew from experience that Madoff's notoriety as "$65 Billion Ponzi Supernova," fleecer of NASDAQ, would make assimilation into prison society complicated—challenging. (Madoff offered to "keep the prison books," but was turned down.)

Sure enough, Madoff committed several prison *faux pas* during his early days in Butner. He wanted to watch a news feature about himself on CBS and broke the prison rules by changing the channel in the TV room. It also ticked off one prisoner who was watching another show. A childish argument ensued, there was a "scuffle," and Madoff was slapped hard across the face. It was Carmine to the rescue. Not in person. He sent over a couple of guys. The inmate who slapped Madoff was "spoken to" and received a "stern warning." Hands off Madoff.

Since then, Fishman said, Bernie calls his fellow inmates "colleagues" and watches any channel he wants in the TV room. To Fishman, Madoff described Carmine as a "very sweet man" and a "good buddy." He admitted to being jealous of Carmine, who received many visits from family members, including his grandkids with whom he was always so loving and gentle. Madoff seldom received visitors. He was on the outs with his family. One of his sons committed suicide in the teeth of the financial scandal Bernie caused.

Madoff, it was said, was not cliquish despite his friendship with Carmine. He didn't hang around with just mobsters. He moved from social group to social group, probably for business reasons, as he has concentrated on money-making angles in prison. That's what he does. Madoff at one point bought the prison's entire supply of hot chocolate and sold it for a profit.

Estimating the net worth of a mobster can be difficult, maybe impossible to do with any precision. Yet those who do that sort of thing have said Carmine's estate may have broken the $1 billion mark—a remarkable achievement for a high school dropout from Park Slope, regardless of how the fortune was accrued. One website listed Carmine as the fourth richest mobster of all time, surpassed only by the wealth of Carmine Galante, Santo Trafficante Jr., and Al Capone.

Not that he has much to spend money on. The aged Carmine Persico sitting in his cell like Buddha reminds me of what Joe Valachi said about him many years ago. The man who introduced the phrase *La Cosa Nostra* to the American people, said that Carmine was a street guy, at his best on the street, at his best outside. Those words have become a sad irony for a man who has spent the last half of his life indoors.

Carmine Persico remained the spiritual boss, the indisputable leader of the gang—even if that gang was just a ragtag assemblage of federal inmates. He was born into a world of options and chose to be Top Cat, alpha male, leader of the pack, a position he still holds in his Federal prison dining room.

When this book was still in the discussion stage, co-author Michael Benson wrote letters to Carmine and Allie Boy in prison. Allie Boy, now sixty-two, lived in the United States Penitentiary near Coleman, Florida. Benson also wrote to their attorney Matthew J. Mari, informing them that a book was in the works and asking if anyone had any concerns. Benson also requested that any family members who might be willing to help with the telling of Carmine's story make their availability known.

On March 9, 2017, Mari called Benson. He did have a concern. Mari said that Carmine Persico was a "level-headed eighty-three-year-old man. He understood the public interest in the story of his life" but there were concerns nonetheless. This was a sensitive time and there were legal battles brewing. Carmine wanted to make it clear, he was no longer head of the family and hadn't been for many years. People thought he ran the family from behind bars but it wasn't true. A figurehead, maybe. A symbol. A man who commanded much respect because of his past, yes. But an actual boss calling shots? No.

Because of flaws in the prosecution's case against Carmine in the old commission case, Mari was seeking to have his client's sentence changed to time served. Thirty-two years. By just about anyone's standards, it was plenty.

The commission case prosecution, Mari said, had told the jury that they had five informants upon whose reports they were basing their claims that Carmine was the head of the Colombo family, ruling from behind bars, when in reality they only had one source, which was revealed by FBI documents to be Greg Scarpa. It had been kept secret until now. They exaggerated their own case, one that attempted to demonstrate that Carmine was the "official boss."

Carmine, the lawyer said, was concerned that a book coming out at that time might raise his personal profile with the public just when he wanted to keep his name quiet. Benson told the lawyer that the book wasn't coming out for a year and a half, at least, and that made Mari happy.

Mari said that Carmine, for the record, denied having anything to do with organized crime in the last thirty-two years that he'd been in prison.

All that is left for Carmine are memories of a mythic life, a life that has left a massive footprint on the world it stomped, a sprawling epic poem of violence. Some scenes from his life have appeared in works of high art, others were his and his alone: running clear the fuck across Brooklyn after the shots in the park, the Blue Beetle's head almost hitting the roof, the sound of brothers in their camaraderie, the smell of smoke-filled rooms, the sound of ice cracking in a glass of whiskey, wandering around the precinct in a zoot suit, Crazy Joey's lion in Mondo's basement, wafting Brilliantine and Wildroot and gunpowder in Grasso's barber shop, how beautiful his wife looked on their wedding night, running across Utica Avenue outside the Sahara Lounge; busting ankles in the daytime, watching Lenny Montana grapple for a tag team belt at night, broads, broads, and more broads, show girls, dancers, future movie stars, the time he asked for an ear but got a finger, the rural life, a farmhouse in beautiful country so far from the Gowanus, DeChristopher, a rat, Cowboy

Mike, a rat, tough lessons, Andy Mush, Lang, Scappi, Apples, guys you *want* to go to war with, and did from the time they were kids, true blue—and Greg Scarpa informing to the FBI during the day, and icing guys at night—for thirty-five years! What a bunch of characters. It was true. *La vita è un sogno.* Life is a fucking dream.

BIBLIOGRAPHY

BOOKS

Benson, Michael. *Inside Secret Societies*. New York: Citadel Press, 2005.

Bernstein, Lee. *Greatest Menace: Organized Crime in Cold War America*. Amherst: University of Massachusetts Press, 2009.

Carpenter, Teresa. *Mob Girl*. New York: Zebra, 1993.

DeStefano, Anthony M. *The Big Heist: The Real Story of the Lufthansa Heist, the Mafia, and Murder*. New York: Citadel Press, 2017.

DiMatteo, Frank. *The President Street Boys: Growing Up Mafia*. New York: Kensington True Crime, 2016.

Glasser, Abraham. "Persico (Carmine) v. U.S., Transcript of Record with Supporting Pleadings." *U.S. Supreme Court Records and Briefs*, 1832-1978, MOML Print Edition, 2017.

McShane, Larry. *Chin*. New York: Pinnacle Books, 2016.

Manbeck, John B., ed. *The Neighborhoods of Brooklyn*. New Haven: Yale University Press, 2004.

Mazza, Larry. *The Life: A True Story About a Brooklyn Boy Seduced into the Dark World of the Mafia*. Amazon Digital Services, 2016.

Polisi, Sal, and Steve Dougherty. *The Sinatra Club*. New York: Pocket Books, 2012.

Raab, Selwyn. *Five Families*. New York: Thomas Dunne Books, 2005.

Red Hook: A Plan for Community Regeneration. Brooklyn: Community Board 6, 1994.

Riccio, Vincent, and Bill Slocum. *All the Way Down: The Violent Underworld of Street Gangs*. New York: Simon and Schuster, 1962.

Robinson, Paul H., and Michael T. Cahill. *Law Without Justice: Why Criminal Law Doesn't Give People What They Deserve*. London: Oxford University Press, 2005.

Sanchez, Tony. *Red Hook Neighborhood Profile*. Brooklyn: Brooklyn in Touch Information Center, Inc., 1986.

Weld, Ralph Foster. *Brooklyn in America*. New York: AMS Press, 1967.

Whalen, Bernard J., Philip Messing, and Robert Mladinich. *Undisclosed Files of the Police: Cases from the Archives of the NYPD from 1831 to the present*. New York: Black Dog and Levanthal Publishers, 2016.

NEWSPAPERS AND PERIODICALS

Brooklyn Daily Eagle

Brooklyn World-Telegram

Chicago Tribune

Cincinnati Enquirer

Cortland Standard

Eau Claire Leader

Elmira Star-Gazette

Fort Myers News Press

Hartford Courant

Lansing State Journal

Long Island Star-Journal

Los Angeles Times

Newsday

New York magazine

New York Daily News

New York Post

New York Sun

The New York Times

New York World-Telegram

Orlando Sentinel

Palm Beach Post

Philadelphia Daily News

Philadelphia Inquirer

Pittsburgh Post-Gazette

Pittsburgh Press

Poughkeepsie Journal

Rochester Democrat and Chronicle

St. Louis Star and Times   *Time*
Santa Cruz Sentinel   *Troy Times Record*
South Florida Sun Sentinel *Village Voice*
Syracuse Post-Standard

WEBSITES

www.cosanostranews.com
www.beatsboxingmayhem.com
www.fbi.gov
www.gangstersinc.org
www.huffingtonpost.com
www.silive.com